PATCHWORK

devotional

365 Snippets
of Inspiration, Joy,
and Hope

THOMAS NELSON
Since 1798

NASHVILLE   DALLAS   MEXICO CITY   RIO DE JANEIRO

Published in Nashville, Tennessee, by Thomas Nelson. Thomas Nelson is a registered trademark of Thomas Nelson, Inc.

Thomas Nelson, Inc., titles may be purchased in bulk for educational, business, fund-raising, or sales promotional use. For information, please e-mail SpecialMarkets@ThomasNelson.com.

Interior Design: Lori Lynch

Some of the contents in this book were published in *A Grand New Day*, compiled and prepared by Snapdragon Group, Tulsa, Oklahoma, USA.

Material reprinted from previously published volumes may have been edited slightly from the original.

Unless otherwise noted, Scripture quotations are taken from the THE NEW KING JAMES VERSION. © 1982 by Thomas Nelson, Inc. used by permission. All rights reserved.

Other Scripture quotations are from the following sources: HOLY BIBLE: NEW INTERNATIONAL VERSION®. © 1973, 1978, 1984 by International Bible Society. Used by permission of Zondervan Publishing House. All rights reserved. NEW CENTURY VERSION®. © 2005 by Thomas Nelson, Inc. Used by permission. All rights reserved. THE HOLY BIBLE: NEW INTERNATIONAL READER'S VERSION © 1994, 1996 by International Bible Society. Used by permission of Zondervan Publishing. All rights reserved. HOLY BIBLE, NEW LIVING TRANSLATION. © 1996. Used by permission of Tyndale House Publishers, Inc., Wheaton, Illinois 60189. All rights reserved. THE LIVING BIBLE. © 1971. Used by permission of Tyndale House Publishers, Inc., Wheaton, Illinois 60189. All rights reserved. NEW AMERICAN STANDARD BIBLE®. ©The Lockman Foundation 1960, 1962, 1963, 1968, 1971, 1972, 1973, 1975, 1977. Used by permission. THE MESSAGE by Eugene H. Peterson. © 1993, 1994, 1995, 1996, 2000. Used by permission of NavPress Publishing Group. All rights reserved. KING JAMES VERSION. NEW REVISED STANDARD VERSION of the Bible. © 1989 by the Division of Christian Education of the National Council of the Churches of Christ in the U.S.A. All rights reserved. THE CONTEMPORARY ENGLISH VERSION. © 1991 by the American Bible Society. Used by permission. THE ENGLISH STANDARD VERSION. © 2001 by Crossway Bibles, a division of Good News Publishers. THE AMPLIFIED BIBLE: Old Testament. © 1962, 1964 by Zondervan (used by permission) and from THE AMPLIFIED BIBLE: New Testament. ©1958 by the Lockman Foundation (used by permission).

Library of Congress Control Number: 2010931782

Printed in the United States of America

10 11 12 13 QG 6 5 4 3 2 1

A FORMULA FOR LAUGHTER

When my anxious thoughts multiply within me,
your consolations delight my soul.

—Psalm 94:19 NASB

I don't usually respond to formulas for this and that; they feel a bit too tidy. But I have developed one for cheerful thinking I'd like to toss your way for your consideration. To begin with, I love to laugh. I believe a giggle is always loitering about even in the most devastating of circumstances.

This isn't denial. I need to feel and express my pain. But I also need to find the light side—and there is *always* a light side! I've noticed that when I laugh about some minor part of a problem or controversy or worry, the whole situation suddenly seems much less negative to me. After a good laugh, I can then rethink my circumstances. As a result, that which was threatening may now seem less threatening.

Paradoxically, after I've found the giggle, I am more ready to get serious (it's a more balanced seriousness) and consider the degree and the extent of my negative thinking. This is when negative thoughts have to be deleted and replaced with those that are realistically positive.

A transformed and renewed mind enables us to manifest an attitude of good cheer. Believe it, think it, and go for it! Don't let life get in your way.

—MARILYN MEBERG (*I'd Rather Be Laughing*)

THE COUNSEL WITHIN

Knowing what is right is like deep water in the heart;
a wise person draws from the well within.
—Proverbs 20:5 MSG

God has put the counsel we need to hear and know within our own hearts. When he made us, he enabled us to store that wise counsel in a very deep, private place he created. It's like a deep river, running through our hearts in a place that's completely quiet and unique to each individual. When we get in touch with that, we find his counsel with a still heart and a waiting, open soul . . . without passion, desire, judgment, or opinions. It's pure and clean and from God. But how do we get in touch with that?

I believe that's where the listening heart comes into play. When a person listens, God-given counsel is drawn out of the heart of the one speaking. A person with a listening heart may ask a few pertinent questions, but for the most part he just waits and listens. He doesn't argue; he listens. He doesn't judge; he listens. He doesn't run ahead; he simply listens.

Therefore, if you want to be wise, listen with your heart—to others, to sounds, to words, to life itself. And in so doing, your heart will grow bigger, enabling you to be of more help to others in their needs.

—LUCI SWINDOLL (*Life! Celebrate It*)

OUR BIG GOD

I will meditate about your glory, splendor, majesty, and miracles.
—Psalm 145:5 *TLB*

Some of us are slowly unfolding miracles, yet miracles nonetheless. In God's timing and for his purposes, he has accomplished his work in me. And I'm grateful he continues the work. He knew I'd falter and question.

Someone once said, "Courage is fear that has said its prayer." That resonates within me. I do many things today not because I feel brave, but because I have prayed and God has answered and met me with his strength in my utter weakness.

I don't know what sends shudders down your spine, what threatens your security, what gnaws at your work, but my prayer is that my encouragement will bring you hope, even if it's just the size of a breadcrumb—enough for you to take the next liberating step. I've learned that life is exceedingly difficult and that God is amazingly big. He will reign over our greatest losses, rectify our worst failures, and remedy our deepest insecurities.

I don't understand all the ways of the Lord, but then I'm not supposed to. Faith carries us through life's unknowns and God's mysteries. But one day, one absolutely glorious day, I will "get it," and more importantly I'll see Jesus face to face. That irrepressible hope keeps me breathing deeply, walking faithfully, and singing triumphantly.

—PATSY CLAIRMONT (*I Grew Up Little*)

3

FALLING FORWARD

The LORD upholds all who are falling.
—Psalm 145:14 NRSV

When I was a little girl, my father was just about the best daddy any daughter could have. He gave me a great picture of the heart of God by always coming the moment I called (or at least that's how I remember it). Therefore, I had a deep trust that my daddy always had my best interest at heart. One day, however, he tested this trust. I was up on a low roof and my dad was on the ground when he asked me to jump into his arms. I stood with my toes at the edge of the roof and could feel myself swaying. I was terrified. Then Daddy said, "Sandi, you're gonna fall either way. If you fall backwards, I can't help you. But if you fall forward, I'm going to be able to catch you."

That is exactly the picture I want you to hold in your mind if you are struggling in any area of your life. If you are wounded by circumstance or the betrayal of others, if you are in despair about your marriage or your children or your future, if you are being swayed by temptation, you probably feel like you are falling. Go ahead and fall, but fall into the arms of the one who can save you.

—SANDI PATTY (*Falling Forward*)

YIELDING TO THE WIND

Jesus answered, "The wind blows wherever it pleases. You hear its sound, but you cannot tell where it comes from or where it is going. So it is with everyone born of the Spirit."
—John 3:8 NIV

Our ability to control often serves us well—in the ordering of our days, in our multitasking, in our dinner parties. On those occasions, we're not sailing. We just step into a motorboat and get it done. We openly take charge of things and happily run our little worlds. But when you are trusting God, you are sailing. Your hair is blown about but not your confidence. Your course is set, not by your own agenda, but by the wind of the Spirit. You have thrown the paddle of control overboard and in faith you have raised the sail to let God take you wherever he wants you to go.

Faith makes us certain of realities that we cannot see. I can't see the sun right now, but I can see the light. I can't see the wind, but I can feel it's there. I take one look up at the sail and there is no doubt. The storms will still come, the fear will still try to over-take me, but faith will sustain me. Faith—at first a gracious gift from God, it then becomes the muscle by which we can keep on trusting. No matter what happens, it is going to be okay.

—NICOLE JOHNSON (*Raising the Sail*)

BECOMING MATURE

> *Anyone who lives on milk, being still an infant, is not acquainted with the teaching about righteousness. But solid food is for the mature, who by constant use have trained themselves to distinguish good from evil.*
>
> —Hebrews 5:13–14 NIV

Why do so many of us stop short of the fullness God intends for each of us? I believe we get comfortable in our immaturity.

I watch birds out my office window all day while I work. I've noticed that when the weather gets rough and strong winds begin to blow, birds seek refuge. They don't protect themselves based on how they feel, whether they want to, or on what all the other birds are doing. Their "get out of danger" instinct tells them what to do, and they do it. But when the storm passes by, it doesn't take long for them to come out again—unscathed, undaunted, and grateful to be out foraging for food once more.

We humans, on the other hand, often foolishly decide to party in the middle of storms. We refuse to take shelter because we think we are smarter than those who say, "There is a storm coming." This lack of wisdom is the mark of immaturity. Remember, what the birds know to do by instinct, we know to do by wisdom. But wisdom by its very nature resides only in the hearts of the mature; that is, those who are in the process of finding their full potential.

—JAN SILVIOUS (*Big Girls Don't Whine*)

CROOKED ARROWS

If we are faithless, He remains faithful; He cannot deny Himself.

—2 Timothy 2:13

"Life is tough but God is faithful" has become my motto. The Bible is full of stories of men and women who in the midst of personal failure and disappointment, even sin, discovered the faithfulness of God.

The psalmist David loved God, but he committed adultery and was responsible for sending a man to certain death. The apostle Peter was privileged to walk side by side with Jesus day after day. He saw the miracles, but when confronted, he claimed he'd never met Jesus.

Human history is an ongoing story of stumbling men and women and the constant grace and mercy of God. God hits straight shots with crooked arrows. It's all about him, never about us, never about the quality of the arrow. But we forget this.

These men left a light on for you and me. David's brokenness lit a candle in the dark. Peter's bruises gave me courage to walk on. This is the purpose of our lives. To learn to love God and to love one another. To let the light of Christ shine through the dark moments as well as in the glory days when everything is wonderful. He is faithful, even when we are not.

—SHEILA WALSH (*Life Is Tough But God Is Faithful*)

DOUBLE OR NOTHING

*Give, and it will be given to you. A good measure, pressed down,
shaken together and running over, will be poured into your lap.
For with the measure you use, it will be measured to you.*

—Luke 6:38 NIV

When my son lost two teeth at once, he stuck them in a Ziploc bag
under his pillow with a sticky note attached that read, "Mom—
More Money!"

As grown-ups, we may be too big to believe in the tooth fairy,
but we still act like children occasionally when it comes to money.
We want more. Martin Luther even struggled with greed: "Many
things I have tried to grasp and have lost. That which I have placed
in God's hands I still have." That quote reminds me of an illustration
I used in *Creative Correction*. I instruct moms to give their children
each a quarter and have them close their hands around it. Then,
take a jar of change and empty it over the children's clenched fists.
How much money do they have now? Still a quarter. Next, I
instruct moms to ask their children to hold the coin in their hands
but keep their hands open, palm up, while a jar of change is poured
over them. Now how much do they have? A lot more!

God loves to give good gifts to his children. The irony is that
we must live open-handedly if we are to experience God's abundance. If we're always thinking about what we can get, how to keep
it, and how to acquire even more, we limit God's ability to bless us
more lavishly than we could ever imagine.

—LISA WHELCHEL (*Speaking Mom-ese*)

ALL GOOD THINGS TAKE TIME

Water wears away stones.

—Job 14:19 NIV

Where would you like to be in six months or a year? And how will you get there? Just as the ant picks up one grain of sand and moves it, then the next one, then the next one—and because of its long obedience in the same direction builds a city—one year from now, we will all be different. We don't get to stay the same, but we do get a choice in how we will have changed, whether it's for the better or not.

In your spiritual lives, too, as you "play the movie forward," where do you want to be in a year's time? If you want to be growing in your faith, closer to God and bold in your prayers, then day by day follow the example of the little ant and set your face in that direction by spending time in God's Word and in worship and prayer every day.

Everything that has value is worth intentional, daily commitment and obedience. I know that it's not easy, but just take the first step, then the next and the next, and before you know it you'll be much farther down the road. Understand it can take time. All good things do. But that's okay, because the journey is worth it.

—SHEILA WALSH (*Get Off Your Knees and Pray*)

A SEATBELT FOR MOM

A happy heart is like good medicine, but a broken spirit drains your strength.
—*Proverbs 17:22 NCV*

The ability to laugh over experiences that threaten to get the best of us enables us to change our perspective. Even in our pain, the ability to enjoy some humor can give relief and restore our balance.

For two years I watched the body of my mother painfully gnarl up on her left side. Believe me, I did more crying than laughing during that time. When she died, I was devastated. Mom had asked that her body be cremated. On the day I picked up my mother's ashes, my husband waited for me in the car. As I opened the door and placed the box on the seat, there was an awkward moment of silence. I broke that silence with a quiet, "Mom, would you like a seat belt?" My husband looked startled and I laughed. It felt good. My mom would have understood—in fact, she would have joined me. It was a painful moment relieved by a quiet laugh.

You may feel there are times in life that simply will not yield even an ounce of humor. I suggest that during those interminable times of pain you search out that spirit-lifting smile or laugh that helps you regain control.

—MARILYN MEBERG (*Choosing the Amusing*)

IT IS ENOUGH

Those who wait on the LORD shall renew their strength; they shall mount up with wings like eagles, they shall run and not be weary, they shall walk and not faint.

—Isaiah 40:31

Eventually, we all have to live in circumstances that are different than we expected. That is the time we must understand that we have choices—the kind of choices we all need to make when our carefully developed life plan takes a U-turn or comes to a sudden halt. We must discover fresh hope and renewed courage when we would rather give up. We must willfully choose to make the future better. We must choose not to waste the sorrow. We must give hope to others in the middle of our brokenness and tears.

Because it is all we have to give, it is enough.

Perhaps you're feeling like folding up your cards. Making hope-filled choices may be the furthest thing from your mind right now. But I challenge you, as I have been challenged, to consider your life from some different angles. Are you willing to take the chance that your "new normal" might offer benefits you never expected? Perhaps even joy?

I can't promise easy answers. In fact, you might wind up with more questions than before. There will be frustration, hurt, and more bumps in the road. But your movement can be purposeful—in the direction of hope.

Take the risk. It is all we have. And it is enough.

—CAROL KENT (*A New Kind of Normal*)

WE WERE BORN FOR THIS!

*Your love, O LORD, reaches to the heavens, your faithfulness to
the skies. . . . How priceless is your unfailing love!*
—Psalm 36:5, 7 NIV

Since the beginning of time, humankind has puzzled over and
considered the questions, *Why was I born? Why am I here? What
is the purpose of life?* It's not unusual to hear those who are in the
middle of emotional depression, personal heartache, financial
calamity, or social disaster pondering whether their lives are
meaningless and futile. Hardship can make us question whether
our lives are actually serving a purpose.

The Scriptures tell us that God loved us before he flung the
stars into place. He loved us even before he created us. In fact, he
chose to create us so that he might make us the recipients of his
never-ending, unfathomable love. We are it! God's best and his
most loved! We don't even have to go to the playoffs. We've
already won. We were born for this!

God did not create us to help around the earth. He did not
create us to do what he can already do. He created us so that he
might love us and have a relationship with us. Then, based on his
love, we return that love, thus establishing a reciprocal relationship. We don't have to do anything to earn this relationship. God
ordained it "even before he made the world."

—MARILYN MEBERG (*Love Me Never Leave Me*)

SEARCHING FOR ANSWERS

The entrance of Your words gives light; It gives understanding to the simple.
—Psalm 119:130

Several years ago, a dear friend gave me a thin, colorful little book called *The Atlas of Experience* by Louise van Swaaji and Jean Klare. It's based on the theory that human beings have always been haunted by fundamental questions and searching for answers. This book opens before the reader a sea of possibilities on which we all travel. By means of its evocative maps and routes, one can follow many passageways that lead to shorelines where our imagination, ideas, feelings, experience, and faith are enlarged.

That's the way life works. It's uncertain and has myriad ups and downs. If we cannot or do not learn from these uncertainties, we'll repeat patterns that keep us treading water. And if we get stuck there, how will we find our sea legs? How will we become adults?

As long as we are in the human condition, we'll have questions. You can count on it! A few of our questions will have easy answers. Others will be difficult, taking time to work out. Some will demand processing with counselors, friends, and God before an answer will come. And some will never be solved this side of heaven. We are not meant to know what to do. We simply have to trust the one who is the keeper of our hearts.

—LUCI SWINDOLL (*Life! Celebrate It*)

13

MESSY LOVE

*If we walk in the light as He is in the light, we have fellowship with
one another, and the blood of Jesus Christ His Son cleanses us from
all sin. If we say that we have no sin, we deceive ourselves, and the
truth is not in us. If we confess our sins, He is faithful and just to
forgive us our sins and to cleanse us from all unrighteousness.*

—1 John 1:7–9

Walking in the light means we are cleansed by the blood of
Christ and able to have fellowship with other believers. We will
be constantly cleansed, wrote John, if we confess our sins as they
surface. When we hide our sins and cover our weaknesses, when
we pretend to be Christian supermen, we live in denial—"the
truth is not in us." We then become isolated from one another
and from God. I think one of the greatest cancers of our day is
loneliness, the way we hide our imperfections and doubts from
one another. I think it's time to tell the truth.

My son loves cupcakes—I frost them with a dark chocolate
frosting. One day I was going out and had on a white cotton
blouse and jeans. He saw me come into the kitchen, and he yelled
"Mom!" and threw his arms around my neck and rubbed his
chocolatey little face in my hair.

I thought, *This is how God invites us to come to him. Not to
clean ourselves up, but to come and bury our face in the mane of the
Lion of Judah. Come as we really are.*

Won't you come to your heavenly Father—just as you are!

—SHEILA WALSH (*Life Is Tough But God Is Faithful*)

MERCY AND GRACE

The eternal God is your refuge, and underneath are the everlasting arms.
—Deuteronomy 33:27

God is everywhere, but I sometimes think he is especially near to the floor of our lives, when we mutter the most profound and heartfelt prayer that's ever been prayed by humans who are overwhelmed by brokenness or sorrow: "Please, help."

One of the most beautiful aspects of the story of the prodigal son in the Bible is that upon his return home, the son was given both mercy *and* grace. Well, you might be asking, what is the difference?

Mercy is not being punished as we deserve. It is being forgiven. The father met the son out on the road and did not chide or scold or dole out his punishment.

Grace is when you are given gift on top of gift that you don't deserve. Grace is the ring and the robe. Grace is the feast and the dancing and the party.

Grace is the Father's wholehearted embrace. Because the Father loves all his children without partiality, he equally offers mercy and grace to both the prodigal and also to his older brother, whose heart was filled with resentment over his brother's actions.

If you find yourself in need of help today, I have a boatload of comfort for you. Both God's mercy and his grace are yours for the asking.

—SANDI PATTY (*Falling Forward*)

CHOOSING FAITH OVER FEAR

"Do not be afraid . . . for I myself will help you," declares the
Lord, your Redeemer, the Holy One of Israel.
—*Isaiah 41:14 NIV*

The nature of love is trust, even when it is betrayed. Trust is what brings us close. Fear, on the other hand, drives a wedge between us.

Fear is in the very fabric of life, because there is so much that we can't control. Maybe that's why "Do not fear!" is repeated in the Bible more than one hundred times. God is constantly telling us not to be afraid, because he knows we almost always are. And for good reasons. But it isn't fear that's the problem; it's what fear makes us do that concerns him.

One thing I've learned is that I'm not the person I want to be when I sit trembling in the dark. I'm not the person I want to be when I'm swirling out of control in a cyclone of fear. What is going to happen now? What if . . . what if . . . what if . . . what if . . .

I don't want to live that way.

When I kneel by my bed and ask God to look after my loved ones and trust that he is doing so, I'm choosing faith over fear.

—NICOLE JOHNSON (*Raising the Sail*)

IT IS DONE

Jesus said, "All that the Father gives me will come to me, and whoever comes to me I will never drive away."
—John 6:37 NIV

When Jesus Christ, God in human form, willingly hung on the cross to pay for every sin you and I ever committed or ever will commit, he made a bridge for us to get back to God. We are all sinners, separated from God (see Romans 3:23). So he did for us what we can never do for ourselves. We can never be religious enough or go to church enough or pray enough or give enough to perfectly keep God's law and therefore reach God. It is impossible.

Think about a speed limit. If the law says go twenty-five miles an hour and you go twenty-six miles an hour, even if you *meant* to go twenty-five miles an hour, you are guilty of breaking the law. No flexibility. That is the way the law operates. A mature woman knows she can't keep God's law perfectly, so she recognizes her need for a Savior and accepts the free gift of eternal life that comes through Jesus Christ. Once it is done, it is done. She stands firm no matter what wind blows. Once you have come to the Father, your life in him is a done deal. You can stand firm!

—JAN SILVIOUS (*Big Girls Don't Whine*)

JESUS IS ENOUGH

I am persuaded that neither death nor life, nor angels nor principalities, nor things present nor things to come, nor height nor depth, nor any other created thing, shall be able to separate us from the love of God.

—Romans 8:38–39

No matter what kind of problem may land on our backs, all we finally have is Jesus, and he is worth it because he loves us.

Yes, we still have questions. Should we hesitate to ask them because we're supposed to have all the answers? Satan loves it when we are silent, afraid to ask the questions that can lead us to understanding.

Some of the greatest words Paul ever wrote start with questions: Can anything separate us from the love Christ has for us? Can troubles or problems or sufferings? If we have no food or clothes, if we are in danger, or even if death comes, can any of these things separate us from Christ's love?

Paul's answer is that nothing—*absolutely nothing*—in this entire world can separate us from the love of God that is in Christ Jesus our Lord.

Here is where we must start. Even in the darkest night, the most blinding pain, the most maddening frustration—when nothing makes sense anymore—we keep going because he alone is worth it all. Holding on is hard—it can seem impossible—but it is worth it because Jesus is worth it. No matter what happens, Jesus is enough.

—SHEILA WALSH (*Life Is Tough But God Is Faithful*)

RECHARGING

"Whoever abides in me and I in him, he it is that bears much fruit... These things I have spoken to you, that my joy may be in you, and that your joy may be full."
—John 15:5,11 ESV

I recently reread the following paragraph in my journal from when my children were smaller:

> I'm very sleepy, I'm tired of taking care of sick kids, and my son seems out of control. All rules have disintegrated because he's sick. The doctor's office is closed. I have no idea when Steve will be home. There are 4 hours 15 minutes before I can put the first one to bed. I feel fat and unmotivated. And there's nothing good to eat in this house.

At the time, I thought the answer was doing less for me and more for them. I ended up unhealthy, stinky, and out of touch with the world beyond my little house. But when I did take time for myself, I came home more in love with my family than when I left.

No matter what stage in life you're living, take time to recharge. First, plug into the Power Source and jump-start your day with Jesus. He is the genesis of joy. It makes him happy to see us happy. He doesn't want us running on empty; he wants our joy to be full.

Then, figure out what fills you up. A bubble bath? A dinner date? A good book? Prayer? Do it. Receive it! Then return refueled and ready to give to your family out of the overflow.

—LISA WHELCHEL (*Taking Care of the Me in Mommy*)

MY REAL FRIEND

Jesus said, "I have called you friends."
—John 15:15

I can't begin to tell you how freeing it was when I first embraced Jesus Christ as my real Friend. For so long, he was simply a gigantic *idea* to me. Although I believed them to be true, the unfathomable images of Savior, Redeemer, and the ultimate sacrifice for mankind made God so big in my mind that what I knew of him didn't translate to what was going on in my everyday life. I had always been told of God's great love, and somewhere inside I believed it. But what completely melted my heart, what completely liberated me from choking insecurity, wasn't just the truth that Jesus loved me—but that Jesus *liked* me. He LIKED me! Exactly as I was.

Jesus had long been my Redeemer, but when I accepted him as my real Friend and began living like he was my Friend, my true healing began. I was ready to discover the truth of who I am without the masks, without the pretense, without the charade. Knowing and understanding Jesus as my Friend helped me see myself in a new light: the security I found in my relationship with him helped me open the door of possibility and see a glimpse of the person I could be.

—NATALIE GRANT (*The Real Me*)

CERTAIN OF GOD'S STRENGTH

*Even when you are old, I will be the same. Even when your
hair has turned gray, I will take care of you. I made you and
will take care of you. I will carry you and save you.*
—Isaiah 46:4 NCV

I have loved candlelight since Jack jumped over the candlestick.
A Chinese saying suggests, "It is better to light a candle than to
curse the darkness." That truth caught my attention because I'm
given to highlighting the negative before I discover the positive.
I've gone through some crushing blows, more than I thought I
could bear, only to discover in my weakness new levels of Christ's
strength.

The candelabra-truth that God rises up mighty in our weakness blazes throughout Scripture. Moses, when confronted by
God's voice in a burning bush, was told he would lead his people
out of captivity. What was Moses' response? He suggested God
send someone else. But the story goes on, and so does Moses, for
he may have knelt down stammering, but he rose up a robust
leader who blazed paths to the promised land. Moses is just one
of the throngs in the Bible who was tempted to be more certain
of his weaknesses than he was of God's strength.

Add my name to that list. What about you?

—PATSY CLAIRMONT (*Catching Fireflies*)

‖ ‖‖ ‖ ‖ ‖ ‖

A NEW KIND OF NORMAL

My soul melts away for sorrow; strengthen me
according to your word.
—Psalm 119:28 NRSV

At some point, most of us will encounter a challenging situation that permanently alters the rest of our lives. It might be a knock at the door, a middle-of-the-night phone call, or a diagnosis from the doctor that changes the future as you envisioned it. It could be that your married child gets a divorce and you will no longer have opportunities to spend time with your grandchildren because they will have moved away with the other spouse. It may be that all of your friends are having babies and you've been told you will never be able to carry a child.

What you once thought of as "normal" will be adjusted to a new kind of normal. The question is: how will you respond? Will you close the blinds on communication with other people, focusing only on your personal pain and deep grief, or will you choose to live a meaningful and vibrant life, even it it's different from the life you always wanted? Will you make choices based on unshakable truth that will not only enhance the quality of your own life but also bring renewed hope and fresh courage to people in your sphere of influence?

Whatever you do, choose life. It's the first step in getting a foothold in your own new kind of normal.

—CAROL KENT (*A New Kind of Normal*)

THE RIGHT STUFF

When the kindness and love of God our Savior appeared, he saved us, not because of righteous things we had done, but because of his mercy. He saved us through the washing of rebirth and renewal by the Holy Spirit.

—*Titus 3:4–5* NIV

If there is any one thing I want to impress on you, it is for you to know the amazing freedom—inside and out—that comes with Christ's loving gift of salvation. My hope is that you know who you really are, as God knows you. And that you understand his unconditional love that continues no matter what you find when you delve into your innermost thoughts and feelings. In acknowledging and valuing his constant, unwavering love, you can find freedom from the hard and hurtful experiences of life, and you can get beyond even those old, painful wounds that refuse to heal.

God created you, and he has a plan for you, a plan that leads to your divine destiny. He has put within you the "right stuff" that can, if you choose to utilize it, enable you to defy defeat and accomplish that destiny. He has equipped you to choose victory when adversity strikes. Knowing you have what it takes, you're freed from living in fear that bad "somethings" might happen to you in the future. Something bad probably will happen, that's just the way it is in life, but you'll get through it, and God will be there to help you get through it.

—MARILYN MEBERG & LUCI SWINDOLL (*Free Inside and Out*)

LISTEN UP!

Love the LORD your God, listen to his voice, and hold fast to him. For the LORD is your life.

—Deuteronomy 30:20 NIV

There are two types of listening—listening with your head and listening with your heart. While I realize that people often listen and make decisions with both heart and head, in many ways it's impossible to separate them. I want to discuss them separately, however, because I so strongly feel unless we learn how to separate the two, we won't be able to make some decisions at all. Our evaluations will be too muddled.

When I was younger, that was often my dilemma. I simply couldn't decide between what my heart felt and what my mind thought, so I did nothing. I know a lot of people like that now. They operate out of involuntary inertia, unable to differentiate between knowledge and feelings. When we live between those two poles, it's very hard to make sound decisions.

Our primary goal as mature Christians, of course, is to find a happy medium between what our hearts tell us and what our heads tell us without compromising obedience. Nobody totally achieves that perfect balance, but the Holy Spirit can help us with our efforts. He comes alongside us and enables us to reach a conclusion we can live with.

—LUCI SWINDOLL (*Life! Celebrate It*)

NEVER THIRST AGAIN

Jesus answered her, "If you knew the gift of God and who it is that asks you for a drink, you would have asked him and he would have given you living water."
—John 4:10 NIV

In the Bible we read about a woman drawing water from a well. But instead of simply filling her water vessel and heading back home as she had a thousand times before, she encountered a man sitting near the well who forever changed her life.

The man asked her for a drink. Sounds simple enough, right? But then he said that God could give her living water, and she would never thirst again. Now that statement gained her attention.

Never thirst again. Who wouldn't want that kind of water? Who wouldn't want the burden of daily responsibility lifted off her head . . . much less have the ache of her thirst relieved?

The Samaritan woman was searching for something that would quench her longing and perhaps fill her loneliness. No wonder Jesus' offer of living water captured her attention—and the empty cistern of her heart.

Jesus' offer to give us living water is as clear and pure now as it was that day at Jacob's well. He doesn't withhold his offer because we are empty, broken, or contaminated. In fact, he understands our condition, and he comes with the cleansing water of forgiveness, inviting us to drink and be forever refreshed.

Are you thirsty?

—PATSY CLAIRMONT (*All Cracked Up*)

POP-UP PAIN

As far as the east is from the west, so far has He removed our transgressions from us.

—Psalm 103:12

Let's face it: there are some wrongs that we cannot make right. Once the feathers are out of the pillow, there is no way to get all those feathers back in. We simply have to grieve and accept the all-encompassing mercy and grace of our Father. Then we must ask for the forgiveness of others after we express our sorrow.

Though God forgives us right away, it may take many of the hurting, wounded human beings around us a lot longer to heal. They are all too human, as are we. Sometimes we still struggle with forgiving ourselves. We experience what I call "pop-up" pain—at times our hearts ache with the heaviness of what we did and the fallout that lingers.

When "pop-up" pain happens and I feel frozen in my failure, I just try to imagine my Father running down the road to meet me. I look in his eyes—brimming with acceptance—and remember that it isn't about my failures, it is about his love. It is about being God's beloved daughter, who is always welcome home. Then I dry my tears, lift my eyes toward heaven, and sing with all the gratitude my heart can hold the song he gave back to me.

—SANDI PATTY (*Falling Forward*)

WHERE'S THE GOODNESS IN THAT?

Jesus said, "I have come that they may have life, and that they may have it more abundantly."
—John 10:10

I gave up. I surrendered. I let go. I stopped being in charge of my spiritual goodness, because I didn't have any spiritual goodness. I had worked for God and yet withheld my heart from him. I'd sought to please him, like a father who is hard to please, and missed that he was pleased with me. I tried to do so many things *for* God that I missed being *with* God. Where was the goodness in that? I discovered that the Christian life is not about trying harder. It is not about keeping it all together. It is about trusting in the one who can keep it all together. If we just roll up our sleeves and try harder, we are not walking with Jesus. If we can do it all ourselves, what do we need him for?

When I gave up, I felt a gentle stirring in my soul. He whispered to me, "Jesus came to give you life. Peace—real peace on the inside, from all of this climbing, striving, and worrying. Joy—unabashed delight in life, regardless of the circumstances. Love—foundational, unconditional, never-ending love." I didn't have to work for these things, I just had to surrender to them. I had to stop long enough to let them overtake me. Again and again.

—NICOLE JOHNSON (*Fresh-Brewed Life*)

FAINTING GOATS

My heart is glad, and my glory rejoices; my flesh also will rest in hope.

—Psalm 16:9

I have a sister-in-law who raises fainting goats. What a contrast they are to the little leaping lambs! These goats are slightly nasty and not very pretty. They meander about foraging for food until they are startled by life in the goat yard and then they just up and faint! They can't stand to be startled, so they don't take time to rejoice. They just faint to get away from reality. They are programmed to avoid dealing with it!

Humanly speaking, they are like women who refuse to face the truth. They don't recognize that God is in control and in the situation that startled them. They just faint and go to La-la Land until the distress passes by. Of course, when they come to, the circumstances are still there. What good did their little escape do? The answer is none. Mature women know that no matter how much they might want to be like Scarlett O'Hara and deal with life's realities *tomorrow,* that is no way to live.

No matter your circumstances, rejoice and rejoice again, because God is the author and finisher of life. He is in the middle of everything you face, no matter what. That's worth knowing and holding on to.

—JAN SILVIOUS (*Big Girls Don't Whine*)

LEANING ON HIS STAFF

Even though I walk through the darkest valley, I fear no evil; for you are with me; your rod and your staff—they comfort me.
—Psalm 23:4 NRSV

As I look back down the path of my life, I see the care God took every step of the way to draw me to his side. He spoke softly to me through all the years, "I love you. I will walk beside you. You can count on me."

When I think about the story of Job in the Bible, I would never choose his life. I can't imagine the pain of losing all your children, your home, your health, and yet there is something about pain that repaints the picture of life. Of who we are, of who God is. I've said it myself. I look at my life. I think of the things I've suffered, but even though I would not have chosen this path, I would not change a single day, a single step.

Why? Because I am now a different woman. It's one thing to say that the Lord is my shepherd; it's quite something else to be unable to walk one more step by yourself, to lean on that staff, and to be held up.

I've heard the same thing expressed by so many of you who share devastating losses but wouldn't go back because what you have tasted of the love and grace of God in the midst of pain is breathtaking. It's true!

—SHEILA WALSH (*Life Is Tough But God Is Faithful*)

FULL OF POTENTIAL

*"And I tell you that you are Peter, and on this rock I will build
my church, and the gates of Hades will not overcome it."*
—Matthew 16:18 NIV

My middle child was having a particularly stinky attitude. She was
fighting her father and me about everything. It was one of her
"if-you-say-it's-black, I'll-say-it's-white" days. In the midst of this
negativity, our family saw the movie *Seabiscuit*. The title character
is a horse that initially seems impossible to train. Seabiscuit is
challenging, feisty—and yet, full of incredible potential.

I saw much of my daughter in that underdog-turned-champion
horse. Her strong will, fierce competitiveness, passion, and indi-
viduality allow her to look life straight in the eye and say, "Bring
it on. Show me what you've got. Because I've got Jesus!" Those
characteristics may make her more challenging to parent at
times, but they will always put her in the winner's circle.

I like to read biographies, and in my reading, I've realized
that very few famous people were compliant children. Most of
them were strong-willed, had ADHD, or exhibited learning dis-
abilities that we as a culture are always trying to "cure." Remember
that Jesus chose disciples who were, by all accounts, as determined as they were faithful. I'd like to think that God, who has
given all of us different gifts, different opportunities, and different personalities, celebrates his children just as they are. There is
no limit to what he can do with our lives if we are willing.

—LISA WHELCHEL (*Speaking Mom-ese*)

THE REAL ME

Those who look to him are radiant.

—Psalm 34:5 NIV

I tried for so long to be perfect. I wanted so badly to look like those girls in my magazines that I harmed my health trying to find validation. But finally I found that the greatest sense of self came from finding my worth in God.

I'm not saying I no longer care how I look. I still love fashion. I find great satisfaction in adapting the latest trends to my personal style and wearing them modestly. I am always trying to find a new way to motivate myself to exercise, and I remind myself that taking care of my health is respecting the body God gave me. I love lip gloss, and I'm always looking for a new method to achieve that rosy complexion, so far be it from me to tell anyone not to wear makeup! But I've learned that if I want to have a true glow, I have to fix my focus on God, not on my makeup case.

As I looked to God, I found the key to my self-worth. As I uncovered the truth that Jesus really loves and accepts me, I was finally able to begin accepting myself. I discovered my sense of being. In short, when I found the real Jesus, I finally discovered the real me.

—NATALIE GRANT (*The Real Me*)

LAYERS

Yes, I am sure that neither death, nor life, nor angels, nor ruling spirits, nothing now, nothing in the future, no powers, nothing above us, nothing below us, nor anything else in the whole world will ever be able to separate us from the love of God that is in Christ Jesus our Lord.

—Romans 8:38–39 NCV

When we were kids, layers may have been protective sports gear or a playtime costume we cast aside when we stepped out of our extracurricular roles. As children, we could be ourselves, knowing we are loved and protected by our families, no matter what. We didn't have to pretend to be something we were not.

But inevitably, something happens that changes our blissfully vulnerable and honest existence. Something hurts us—something we may not even remember fully as adults—and gradually we begin to build up layers of protection to keep from getting hurt again.

Meanwhile, there sits the God of the universe, who created us to be his beloved children, longing to pull us into his loving embrace, rub us on the head, pat us on the back, and tell us how wonderful we are. Whatever layers are weighing you down, my prayer is that God will deal with you the same way he's dealing with me. Tenderly, graciously, loving, God is helping me peel those layers away to find and celebrate the original me he created.

—SANDI PATTY (*Layers*)

PLEASE AND THANK YOU

*Everything is for your sake, so that grace, as it extends to more
and more people, may increase thanksgiving, to the glory of
God.*

—2 Corinthians 4:15 NRSV

Many of us grew up in homes where we were taught to say please
and thank you. During those years, we were learning to be polite.
However, as life weaves its tapestry of good times and bad times,
we face new decisions. The words *thank you* can be difficult to
internalize when life seems unfair and it appears that God is not
answering our prayers for a desired outcome. Sometimes it's easier
to choose withdrawal and denial over active participation in life.

When it seems as though everyone around us is experiencing
the abundance of God's blessings while our situation continues
to spiral downward, expressions of thanksgiving and praise can
disappear from our vocabulary. Sometimes, while deep in our
own pain, it's hard to express joy to others who are experiencing
God's blessing and abundance. We try to be happy for them, but
inside we wonder why our lives and family situations haven't
turned out better?

Think about your own new kind of normal. Make a list of ten
things you have to be thankful for in the middle of an unexpected
or an unwanted change in your life. Practice praying through that
list, verbalizing your thanks to God for any benefit, however
small, of your unforeseen circumstances.

—CAROL KENT (*A New Kind of Normal*)

HIS SPECIAL TREASURE

GOD, your God, chose you out of all the people on Earth for himself as a cherished, personal treasure.

—Deuteronomy 7:6 MSG

No one wants to be overlooked, ignored, or discounted in any way, but I don't believe there is anyone on earth who has not felt the sting of rejection. If rejections happen to us often enough, the inevitable assumption is that we aren't good enough, lovable enough, or smart enough to be included.

We generally assume our value is determined by what we *do*. If I do my job well, I may be promoted. If I do it poorly, I may be replaced or demoted. The same mentality is true with human relationships. If I'm pleasant, people will probably want to be around me. When I snarl and hiss, I'll undoubtedly find myself without lunch partners. The earthly system is easily understood by all of us. Our performance is crucial to success as well as social acceptability.

The mind-blowing truth about the God of the universe is that he does not use the performance system. In the mind of Creator God, there is no questioning your value. You are chosen by him, and if that truth alone does not melt your socks, consider this: You are also viewed as his special treasure. You don't work toward it, earn it, or struggle to become good enough. Quite simply . . . you have been chosen.

—MARILYN MEBERG (*The Decision of a Lifetime*)

LISTEN WITH YOUR HEART

My dear friends, you should be quick to listen and slow to speak.
—James 1:19 CEV

How can someone learn the fine art of listening with the heart? Let me suggest some ways.

First of all, make it a practice to listen to other people without your own agenda in mind. No matter what they say, pay attention to their words and keep your eyes on them as you drink in their sentences.

Second, don't interrupt—no matter how absurd their words, ideas, or stories may sound to you or how much you want to say something you think is vital.

Third, don't be afraid you'll forget your comment if you don't say it right now. Chances are, you won't. And if you do, your comment probably wasn't that important anyway.

And finally, don't offer an immediate solution. Many times, the key to listening with one's heart is the ability to simply hear what other people have to say without trying to help them solve anything.

People tend to share only when they feel accepted. The minute somebody judges us or tries to set us straight, we clam up because we want to be received, just as we are. The truth is most of us know down deep inside what to do in trying situations. It may take us awhile to get to it, but it's there . . . in our hearts.

—LUCI SWINDOLL (*Life! Celebrate It*)

TURN THE LIGHT ON

The LORD is my light and my salvation; whom shall I fear?
—Psalm 27:1

"Fear has friends," I warn women when I address the topic of being afraid. When you emotionally surrender to one fear, you open the door to a myriad of others. I learned that the hard way, through my own experience. And I paid with years of my life. I'd like to offer you a shortcut.

When you are afraid, don't give in to fear—turn on the light!

> + *Turn on the light of God's Word.* "For God has not given us a spirit of fear, but of power and of love and of a sound mind" (2 Timothy 1:7).
> + *Turn on the light of faith.* And risk taking the next step out of your self-imposed limitations. What do you have to lose? Fear? Go for it.
> + *Turn on the light of your mind.* Believe what you can't see, which is that God holds you safely in his care no matter where you are and that he is unfolding his plan for your life. You can't travel outside his presence.
> + *Turn on the light of friendship.* Let others know when you are uneasy and then allow them to stand with you. It will comfort you, strengthen you, and keep you humble. We weren't meant to go this life alone.

—PATSY CLAIRMONT (*I Second That Emotion*)

SURVIVING A CRISIS OF THE SOUL

*[The LORD] heals the brokenhearted, and binds up their
wounds.*

—Psalm 147:3 NRSV

I have found that there are three things broken people need in
order to survive a crisis of the soul.

First, you need people who will be "Jesus with skin on." A few
"unshockable" saints who don't try to *see through you* but instead
show up in work clothes with their spiritual sleeves rolled up to
try to help *see you through*. They are the good Samaritans among
us who don't lean back in an above-it-all posture, clicking their
tongues, analyzing why you are lying facedown in the dirt. They
simply bring bandages and try to get you where help can be
found. They are the "safe people." And for a while, perhaps a long
while, you'll need to put barriers up to protect yourself from
"unsafe people."

Second, you need a "safe place," a physical space apart from
the maddening crowd where you can have the space and time
and nurturing environment that will help you to find your life's
balance, your sanity, and your faith again.

Third, you need a "safe God." Not, mind you, a tame God.
Not a watered-down version of God. But a great and powerful
God who is as tender as a Shepherd is with his littlest lost lamb.

—SANDI PATTY (*Falling Forward*)

BEYOND ALL TIME

Jesus said, "Live out your God-created identity."
—Matthew 5:48 MSG

Who am I? Have you ever lain awake at night asking that question? I take that back. Most women work too hard to miss sleep by lying awake at night, much less asking questions! So the questions probably come at other times. *Who am I?* Do you ever feel that you're faking your life? That you're living someone else's life, and you're not sure whose? You wonder how you got to this place of disguise. You want to give yourself to God, but what self are you going to give?

There is only one who can tell you this: the Lord himself. And he wants to tell you, he wants you to know your reason for being and to be led by it. But it is a secret he will entrust to you only when you ask, and then in his own way and his own time. He will whisper it to you not in the mad rush of your striving and your fierce determination to be someone, but rather when you are content to rest in him, to put yourself into his keeping, into his hands. Most delightfully of all, it is a secret he will tell you slowly and sweetly, when you are willing to spend time with him: time with him who is beyond all time.

—NICOLE JOHNSON (*Fresh-Brewed Life*)

YOUR FAVORITE BAD FEELING

Finally ... whatever is true, whatever is noble, whatever
is right, whatever is pure, whatever is lovely, whatever is
admirable—if anything is excellent or praiseworthy—think
about such things.

—*Philippians 4:8* NIV

If we can't control anything else in our lives, we can control what we think about. But when we have been buffeted by a situation that throws us, it is easy to abdicate our control and go to our "favorite bad feeling." That's the feeling we went to as a child because we learned that it helped us get what we wanted. Once you are an adult, you will find that it is the first place your mind rushes when there is something troubling on your mental radar screen.

Some of us cry, some pout, some sleep, some eat chocolate, some go shopping, some withdraw, and some slam doors, some clean house, some sit and stare. You could probably fill in your own favorite bad feeling. But you don't have to respond that way, you can choose not to go there. Circumstances rarely change, but how you feel about the circumstances can change dramatically. How you feel is up to you, not to anyone else in your life.

Peace is the result of choosing to focus your mind on what is true and honorable and right. When you choose to do that, it is amazing how much peace will overtake your mind and heart.

—JAN SILVIOUS (*Big Girls Don't Whine*)

HIDDEN PLACES

*God has reconciled you by Christ's physical body through
death to present you holy in his sight, without blemish and free
from accusation.*
—Colossians 1:22 NIV

When guilt occupies the secret places in our lives, we can let it
cripple us, or we can allow God to set us free.

I didn't understand it at the time, but my mind and emotions
were really running on two different tracks when I was a teenager.
Part of me was a fervent teen who wanted to serve God, and the
other part was a frightened little girl who felt guilty.

I can see that part of my motivation was really wanting to
serve God, but also driving me was the fact that I wanted to push
myself harder than anybody else to prove to God that I was worthy of his love. My hidden places controlled my life, but I didn't
realize it. I knew God, but I still needed a freeing touch from him.
In many ways, I was like the searching people Jesus met as he
walked the dusty roads of Palestine, individuals whose hidden
places kept them trapped in lives they longed to change.

We all have a choice. When guilt occupies the secret places
in our lives, we can let it cripple us or we can allow the painful,
healing light of God's love to set us free.

—SHEILA WALSH (*Life Is Tough But God Is Faithful*)

THE WISDOM OF SMART GIRLS

Tune your ears to wisdom, and concentrate on understanding
... Search for them as you would for silver ... you will gain
knowledge of God.
—*Proverbs 2:2–5* NLT

A rich, multifaceted Hebrew word encompasses the essence of what it takes to become a Smart Girl: *châkam*. The original word, for which we have no English equivalent, embodies *wisdom, knowledge, experience, insight,* and *judgment*—everything we most need to make good choices. Its meaning could be summarized as "an intelligent attitude toward the experiences of life."

The book of Proverbs is full of references to *châkam*. Those who have this quality can walk through life with confidence in each choice they make. Making good choices isn't natural in our fallen human condition, but each of us can develop this skill by learning and mastering the how-tos of decision making.

Sometime in early childhood, most of us learned a vital life principle: Stop, Look, and Listen before you cross the street. When we were learning to drive, another step was added: Stop, Look, Listen, and *Look Again.* And, Smart Girls have added this essential element of defensive driving to their toolbox of practical life skills when it comes to making any choices.

If you want to be a Smart Girl who lives in the power of God's *châkam*, consider, with your heart open to God's input, how you can put it into practice.

—JAN SILVIOUS (*Smart Girls Think Twice*)

41

THE HANDIWORK OF GOD

My frame was not hidden from You, when I was made in
secret, and skillfully wrought in the lowest parts of the earth.
Your eyes saw my substance, being yet unformed.
—Psalm 139:15–16

Your self-image is not this ethereal, theoretical thing that is hard to get your hands around. It is who and what you picture yourself to be. How you feel about you. Do you base how you feel about yourself on the expectations of others? Who do you think you are?

True self-worth is not based on what you feel about yourself or even on what others think about you. True self-esteem can only be based on how God sees you. You are only who God says you are.

And what exactly does he see when he looks at you?

God's definition of beauty is vastly different from the world's standard, so it may be easier to answer that question by first saying what he doesn't see. He doesn't see your flaws and failures. Remember, he doesn't make mistakes. He sees you as beautiful, and if you then view yourself as anything less, it's like you're saying to God, "Hey, maybe you need to get your eyes checked."

You are not a flawed creature, an accident in God's otherwise-perfect design. You are the beautiful handiwork of God, and he has a plan and a purpose for your life.

—NATALIE GRANT (*The Real Me*)

LOVED BEYOND BELIEF

You made my whole being; you formed me in my mother's body.

—Psalm 139:13 NCV

God loves us beyond knowing. Several years ago, I went with my pregnant daughter-in-law to get a 3D baby scan. She had been through the usual sonograms, but none showed us the baby's face. This time we hoped for a clearer view of her firstborn. The room was dark and the monitor hazy as the technician rolled the scanning bar across her belly. Then we saw it: Baby Rachel's face appeared on the screen. Her eyes, her nose, her little chubby cheeks, and even her hair standing straight up! How amazed we were.

When Rachel was born, I was thrilled to finally know this amazing baby, whom I had seen even before she had come into the light of day. That early glimpse took my breath away and only made me love her more when I first held her. Later, I thought, *If I can feel that surge of incredible joy over the birth of one of my granddaughters, how much greater is the Father-heart of God toward his girls?*

Just imagine how heaven grew silent and his heart swelled with joy when you arrived on earth! From the moment of your conception, he hovered over every week of your growth in the womb. God is crazy about you!

—JAN SILVIOUS (*Big Girls Don't Whine*)

FRESH-BAKED GRACE

But grow in the grace and knowledge of our Lord and Savior Jesus Christ.

—2 Peter 3:18 NCV

When my dad was a boy, he and his buddies would play football in the street. Invariably, someone would miss a catch and the football would land in Old Lady Russell's yard, and Old Lady Russell would rant and rave if she caught the boys sneaking into her yard. On one day, she snatched up the football and disappeared into her house. The youngsters headed home, miserable.

My grandmother watched my dad walk in dejectedly, and asked, "What happened?" After Dad told his mom what happened, Grandma handed a fresh-baked cherry pie to Dad and said, "I made this cherry pie for Old Lady Russell. Will you take it over to her house?"

With great fear and trepidation, Dad carried the cherry pie down the street. When Old Lady Russell came to the door, he said, "This is a cherry pie from me and my mom. We thought you might like it."

Old Lady Russell melted. She invited Dad in, they had a visit, and she gave him the football back. From that day forward, the kids never had a problem with Old Lady Russell. In fact, she would sit on her porch and watch the boys play.

What a lesson Dad learned that day. It's a lesson about the power of grace.

—SANDI PATTY (*Layers*)

FELLOW STRUGGLERS

> *In God, whose word I praise, in the* LORD, *whose word I*
> *praise—in God I trust; I will not be afraid. What can man do*
> *to me?*
>
> —Psalm 56:10–11 NIV

The "wounds" of being vulnerable mean some people will turn their backs on us, judge us, and criticize us in front of others. The cost can be high. However, the "healing" of being vulnerable means we no longer live in fear of having our secrets revealed. I am not advocating starting every conversation with our worst struggles. There are times and places when God leads us to speak up, but we need to be aware of when it is appropriate and whom it will impact. In the process of responding to the divine nudge of his voice, we discover amazing freedom and contagious joy.

Our openness, when fitting, makes us a magnet for the people around us who are longing for just one person in their lives to be "real," to listen to their story without raising an eyebrow, to let them weep without providing advice. Instead of being competitors who are trying to impress each other with how perfect we are, we become fellow strugglers who are attempting to live out our faith in an authentic way. Our carefully constructed facade melts away and is replaced with the genuine version of ourselves. Fear taunts, people will reject you. Faith says, allow God to use the broken places of your past to give hope to someone else.

—CAROL KENT (*A New Kind of Normal*)

WE ARE THE CHOSEN

I have chosen you and have not rejected you.

—Isaiah 41:9 NIV

Few of us have any comprehension that we have value far greater than any masterpiece to be sold at a Sotheby's art auction. Most of us assume we're closer to being garage sale material—ordinary and not especially appealing. Why do you suppose it's so difficult to accept that divine opinion of ourselves? Why don't we just settle down and allow God to be what he wishes to be—our daily companion?

We've all probably experienced some sense of being thrown away—by divorce, by the rebellion of one of our kids, by a boss's disapproval, by a friend's rejection, by criticism from a parent . . . the list goes on.

We desperately want to hear the words "I love you." Those words are like drops of water on our parched and love-starved souls.

What's the answer to this common soul devastation? God! All of the Bible tells us we have been chosen, we are loved, and . . . we will never be thrown away by him.

What are we chosen for? We've been chosen for a relationship with him.

Why? Because we are his treasured masterpieces. A heavenly treasure is never thrown away; neither is it sold at a garage sale.

—MARILYN MEBERG (*The Decision of a Lifetime*)

PICKY, PICKY, PICKY

Don't be nitpickers; use your head—and heart!—to discern
what is right, to test what is authentically right.
—John 7:24 MSG

Criticism is one of the hardest things to take and one of the easiest things to give. Unless we listen with our hearts we can find a hundred reasons to criticize other people—how they dress; what they drive; where they shop, travel, or go to church; their values, political beliefs, sexual or philosophical lifestyle; their thoughts on any given issue; their home, family life, husband, wife, children . . . right down to how they part their hair.

Jesus has a lot to say about being critical or judgmental. He is adamant about anyone passing judgment on another human being.

Jesus tells us not to be "picky, picky, picky." But we all are to some degree. Nitpickers find fault and criticism with everything they encounter, and they're a curse in the household of faith. They're maddening to the human race and *especially* to the body of Christ. Jesus is the only one qualified to judge, because he's the only one who sees our hearts and listens with his. Our judgment of another is no better than the information we have (or think we have), but Jesus knows us better than we know ourselves. He has the total picture.

—LUCI SWINDOLL (*Life! Celebrate It*)

47

ROSE OF SHARON

I am the rose of Sharon, and the lily of the valleys.
—Song of Solomon 2:1

I'm impressed with the rose because of its fruitful existence. It begins as a bud, which has a beauty all its own; gracefully unfolds into velvet overlays; and then, with its last breath, when crushed, it leaves a heady fragrance and drips precious oil. Okay, there is the thorn issue, but in the overall scope of flower life, the rose is the reigning queen.

As we consider the beauty and grace of the rose, we're not surprised to discover that Jesus is called the Rose of Sharon. He was born a bud of a babe in a manger; his beauty unfolded before others with each humble step he took; and in his last breaths on earth, with thorns pressed into his head, after being crushed by our sins, he shed precious drops of his blood and released a forever fragrance of love. In the overall scope of our life, Christ is our coming King.

That sacrifice, Christ's broken body, now calls us to receive the crushing blows of life as a way for his fragrance to be released through us. Our crushed and drooping lives become a holy potpourri. Take a shattered heart, mix with a crushed spirit, intermingle with Christ's oil of mercy, stir with his healing touch, and season with divine love. What a magnificent fragrance.

—PATSY CLAIRMONT (*All Cracked Up*)

THE ARMS OF GOD

*Cast your cares on the LORD and he will sustain you; he will
never let the righteous fall.*
—Psalm 55:22 NIV

Even though you may have been taught as a child that God is
good and God is love, you may have a hard time grasping the
truth of this when it comes to yourself personally. If your view of
God is a condemning one (or even partially this way), I recommend that you immerse yourself in everything the Scriptures say
about the love, mercy, grace, and forgiveness of God. Spend as
long as it takes dwelling on these Scriptures until you recognize
that you are God's beloved daughter and there is nothing you
could do that could make him love you any more than he does
right now. There is nothing you could do that would cause him to
love you any less.

Once you have given yourself this triage of hope—soaking
up the truth of God's love and revising your view of God—you
will be well on your way to trusting him. You cannot possibly fall
into the arms of a God you don't trust. If you hesitate to fall into
the arms of God, there's a good chance you don't yet know the
depth, the height, or the breadth of his deep, deep love for you.
Fall in love with the one who waits to catch you up in his strong,
gentle arms.

—SANDI PATTY (*Falling Forward*)

49

NO OTHER LOVE

There is no fear in love, for perfect love casts our fear.
—1 John 4:18 NLT

We are loved passionately by God. And I don't know why. It is a mystery, and it must remain a mystery. To understand it is to dismiss it as we are prone to dismiss every other love in our lives. If we discovered that God loved us because we were smart, then we would try to do everything we could to be smarter so he would love us more. If we met someone smarter than we are, we would fall into despair. So I don't think God will ever let us know the reason that he loves us as passionately as he does. I don't have a clue why God loves me. But I believe in the core of my being that he does. So I surrender to it. I stop fighting it. I cease trying to figure it out. I collapse on it.

Nothing can take his love from us. I can say that of no other love. God pursues us, courts us, and woos us to remind us. His love changes every day; it either intensifies or my understanding of it grows. His love is all we have ever dreamed of. And his kiss, the most passionate we will ever know.

This love is why we were made.

—NICOLE JOHNSON (*Fresh-Brewed Life*)

THE SIGNS OF A MATURE WOMAN

He who has begun a good work in you will complete it until the day of Jesus Christ.

—*Philippians 1:6*

When a woman asks God to work in her heart and mind and learns to replace the old ways with mature thinking, she will notice an incredible difference in her life. Here are some ways to challenge your thinking as a mature woman in process. (It is always good to have a standard by which to check yourself.) Look for these signs in your life. A mature woman:

- thinks things through to their natural conclusion. She can see not only the present but the future as well.
- thinks about how her actions will affect others.
- can see more than one side to any situation.
- doesn't take things personally.
- understands that life is never "all about me."
- is a good, fair, and reasonable negotiator.
- may like fairy tales, but she likes true stories, too, and she is well aware of the difference.
- may tire, but she won't allow her fatigue to control her general attitude and demeanor.
- knows what is best for her and is disciplined enough to go after it.

—JAN SILVIOUS (*Big Girls Don't Whine*)

51

TRANSFORMING PRAYER

My ears had heard of you before, but now my eyes have seen you.
—Job 42:5 NCV

Does the actual act of prayer, of throwing ourselves on the mercy and grace of God, change us? I think one of the most powerful books in the Bible to support and perhaps to answer that question is Job.

Job says (and this is my paraphrase): "God, I knew about you before, I knew of all the marvelous things you have done. But now that I have been in the ring with you for several rounds, I have a completely different kind of relationship with you and a new understanding of your greatness."

That's one of the many things I find interesting about Job's story. It's not the story of a treacherous man who encountered God and was converted by the experience. It's the story of a godly man who through tragedy and very bitter dialogue with God came to a whole new understanding of who God is. In other words, he wasn't a man who was changed from "bad" to "good." He was a man changed from "good" to "better"!

I long for that for each one of us. More specifically, I thirst for that in my own life—that my prayer life would become so vibrant, intense, and moment-by-moment I cannot help but be changed.

—SHEILA WALSH (*Get Off Your Knees and Pray*)

RIGHT OR RIGHTEOUS

My dear brothers, take note of this: Everyone should be quick to listen, slow to speak and slow to become angry.
—James 1:19 NIV

My ability to form instant opinions and quick answers has been a plus for me in parenting, business, and in my ministry. Over the years, though, God has taught me that I shouldn't always say everything I think. During one particular season, I wrote in my journal, "I'm finally at the place where I'm willing to believe when Scripture says, 'Be slow to anger and slow to speak,' it doesn't mean, 'Except for you, Lisa. I admire your quickness.'"

This desire to be right makes it challenging for me to "turn the other cheek." Most of the time when I disagree with my husband, I would rather let tensions boil between us because I feel he has wronged me and that it's his place to come to me, repent, and resolve the conflict. But when I am tempted to nurse my wounds, I try to remember the verse that says, "But when you are tempted, God will give you a way out so that you can stand up under it" (1 Corinthians 10:13b NIRV). It's true! God always throws me a life preserver: that not-so-subtle nudging that prompts me to set aside my pride, go to my husband, and say, "Let's talk about this."

When I do, my heavenly Father, like most dads, reminds me that life isn't fair and the Christian life certainly isn't about getting what I think I deserve. Ironically, sacrificing my own desires to serve God is the quickest way to find the abundant life God promises.

—LISA WHELCHEL (*Speaking Mom-ese*)

THE GET-ACQUAINTED SESSION

The LORD used to speak to Moses face to face, as one speaks to a friend.
—*Exodus 33:11* NRSV

Sooner or later everyone experiences the reality that sometimes life is hard, pain is tangible, and hurt is genuine. But Jesus, who looks past the shell to the you inside, is interested in the details.

We all know people who constantly look at everything but us while we're talking to them, distracted instead of listening. Not Jesus. In fact, I believe if he were physically sitting in the room with me he would stop to hear my story, and while he listened, he would look me in the eye.

Maybe it makes you a little uncomfortable to picture yourself sitting alone with Jesus in a personal get-acquainted session. If so, you may feel inadequate, illegitimate, inferior, or imperfect, even though you've been told again and again that those aren't the feelings you were created to have. Maybe you know who Jesus is, but you don't know him. You have prayed until you are out of breath, yet you still feel empty and incomplete, so you stopped praying.

Try again. Talk to him. Ask him to become evident to you. And once you've asked him to authenticate himself, you must also be genuine with him. You have to be real.

—NATALIE GRANT (*The Real Me*)

THE FORGOTTEN WOMAN

I say this because I know what I am planning for you," says the Lord. "I have good plans for you, not plans to hurt you. I will give you hope and a good future."
—Jeremiah 29:11 NCV

Hagar was a slave of Abraham and Sarah, and she did as Sarah wished, no matter how outrageous the demands. God had promised Abraham he would have numerous descendents, but as time went on and no children were forthcoming, Sarah told Hagar to sleep with her husband. When Sarah saw Hagar pregnant, the sight tormented her. Out of fear, Hagar ran away. As she struggled, an angel of God appeared to her and told her to return to Sarah. The angel promised Hagar her son would the first in a great nation. Hagar returned and gave birth to Ishmael.

Fourteen years passed before Sarah gave birth to Isaac, and Hagar and Ishmael were sent into the desert again. When they ran out of food, Hagar laid Ishmael under a bush to die. God heard Ishmael cry and sent an angel to Hagar, who told her God's promises aren't derailed by human circumstances. Hagar and Ishmael were saved.

The thing I love most about Hagar's story is the mercy God extended her. God gave her a future. To everyone else Hagar was a nobody, but not to God. If you are a woman who feels forgotten, I hope Hagar's story will help you see God never forgets you. He never takes his eyes off you.

—SHEILA WALSH (*Let Go*)

55

HE CHOSE US

God has said, "I will never leave you nor forsake you."
—Hebrews 13:5

Prior to the cross, Jesus endured hours of agonizing physical and emotional torture. Yet not once did he cry out. It was not until that culminating pain of separation from God that the heart of Jesus broke.

Jesus took upon himself every sin, every pagan inclination, and all that is unholy in creation, and he died for it. For Jesus, the greatest hurt was the momentary abandonment from God, his Father. It happened because God, in his holiness, cannot look upon sin. When Jesus became the embodiment of sin, he was rejected. He was abandoned. He was ditched.

If you can identify with that feeling, you're not alone. But I've got great news for you. Jesus' separation from God—and ours—was bridged immediately the moment that sin-debt was paid. He was instantly restored to full correctedness with his Father. It's absolutely mind-boggling: we, too, are instantly awarded full family membership the moment we confess our sin and receive the forgiveness for which Jesus died.

That means we will never be abandoned by him. We will never be a throwaway from him. We will never be rejected by him. We'll never be ditched by him. We didn't get left by him. He chose us. He loves us and will never leave us.

—MARILYN MEBERG (*Love Me Never Leave Me*)

STUDENTS OF LIFE

Jesus looked up at his disciples and said, "Do not judge, and you will not be judged; do not condemn, and you will not be condemned. Forgive, and you will be forgiven."

—Luke 6:37 NRSV

We're all looking for a place to be totally accepted just as we are, without criticism from others. We all want to be in a church body or group of friends or with a support team that will stand with us when we're facing an earth-shattering issue in our own lives. Especially if it's a private thing—struggling with homosexuality, going through a divorce, having an abortion, being involved in an affair, running from the law—any of those things qualify. And more. We all want somebody in our lives who won't pass judgment.

Nobody has answers to these dilemmas. We're all students of life with its confusing struggles. Let's try to be patient with each other, giving the benefit of the doubt and waiting for the Lord to work in the lives of those we love, while we give our prayerful support.

Remember these words written by George Washington Carver, a slave in the 1800s: "How far you go in life depends on your being tender with the young, compassionate with the aged, sympathetic with the striving, and tolerant of the weak and the strong. Because someday in life you will have been all of these."

—LUCI SWINDOLL (*Life! Celebrate It*)

LET'S LISTEN TO JAMES

Consider it a sheer gift, friends, when tests and challenges come
at you from all sides. You know that under pressure, your faith-
life is forced into the open and shows its true colors.
—James 1:2–3 MSG

One of my favorite books is the book of James. I'm aware that some people aren't fond of James, because he talks a lot about works. But I love that the apostle James brings balance and accountability to the believer—and to me, because I need it! While I know God loves me no matter what I do, I also need to know that disobedience does interfere with my progress and growth. I'm certainly no theologian, but I know I'm often my biggest obstacle along the way.

So . . . come join me. Let's crack open the book and see what James has to say about hardship. He begins by saying, "Consider it a sheer gift, friends." Hardship is a gift? Well, I don't want it under my Christmas tree! It's just natural to bolt and run when life tightens up. I guess that's why James had to tell us to sit tight and be thankful. Even though this is a tall order from James, it's also full of hope. When I understand that pain, loss, and difficulty have a purpose, a work to do within me, I can learn to see meaning in my suffering. I'm grateful James reminds me of it. I don't know how God does it; I'm just grateful he does.

—PATSY CLAIRMONT (*All Cracked Up*)

STEP INTO THE RIVER

> *When the priests got to the Jordan and their feet touched the*
> *water at the edge (the Jordan overflows its banks throughout*
> *the harvest), the flow of water stopped.*
>
> —Joshua 3:15–16 MSG

Sometimes, even when we realize we are beautiful, free, and beloved children of God, we continue to play the victim. I found it was tempting to stay mentally stuck on one sad page of my life and never fall forward into freedom. Don't make that mistake.

I urge you to consider making a choice, right now, today, to get well. Even if all you can pray right now is, "God, help me be willing to be *willing*"—it's a beginning, that important first step.

One of the songs I've sung is called "Step into Joy," and it's about deciding whether you are going to stay on the sidelines and whine, "Why doesn't joy ever come to me?" or step right into it. I love the story in Joshua 3 where God instructed the Israelites to cross the river Jordan. That river was roaring! But God promised he'd make a way. And as soon as the priests who carried the ark reached the Jordan and their feet touched the water's edge, the water from upstream stopped flowing. Did you catch that? They actually had to step into the river *before* God parted the waters. God blesses our baby steps of faith.

—SANDI PATTY (*Falling Forward*)

HOLES IN MY SOUL

He satisfies the longing soul, and fills the hungry soul with goodness.
—Psalm 107:9

Coming face-to-face with the fact that there are empty places in our lives that haven't been filled. Yearnings. Wanting more than we have: more love, more enjoyment, more passion, more hope, more rest. The hope of finding something that will satisfy the rumbling we feel in the stomach of our souls.

Our yearnings, longings, cravings, and hopes are telling us something: there isn't enough love, peace, hope, friendship, and intimacy on this earth to completely satisfy us. We will always want more.

This feels like a no-win situation. Are longings one big cosmic setup for frustration? Perhaps, if we view them as something to be overcome or eradicated. If we spend more time trying to get them "filled up." But if we lean in close, and put our ears to the chest of our soul and listen to our longings—they can teach us to understand God and ourselves in a way that would not happen if we were permitted to have everything we longed for.

The holes in us are actually *supposed* to be there. The holes are the things that make us who we are. The holes are the places God has reserved in us for himself! The longings identify our real hunger. A hunger that drives us to him to be satisfied.

—NICOLE JOHNSON (*Fresh-Brewed Life*)

THE SECRET

I have learned the secret of being content in any and every situation.

—Philippians 4:11 NIV

I know a secret! What secret is that? It's the same secret the apostle Paul spoke about in the book of Philippians. Contentment with the life you have been given is a choice.

Your true value is not about whom you married or didn't marry. It is not about how good you are at what you do. It is really just about one thing: What is your relationship to God? Have you made the decision to allow him to call the shots? Have you decided to listen to him and let him comfort your soul? Have you given up your perceptions of how you think life should be? Have you accepted the fact that your life is in his hands, and that he will enable you to do everything you need to do? Can you face each day with the confidence that you can do all things through Christ?

If so, my friend you are living with joy and contentment the life you have been given. What a difference it makes when you give in and give up! You reach the point of living life with nothing to prove and nothing to lose. You can choose contentment and accept the sweet comfort of Christ's presence and provision for every step of the way.

—JAN SILVIOUS (*Big Girls Don't Whine*)

GOD'S THOUGHTS

> *Your thoughts—how rare, how beautiful! God, I'll never comprehend them! I couldn't even begin to count them—any more than I could count the sand of the sea.*
>
> —Psalm 139:17–18 MSG

Did you know that the God of the universe, the sovereign ruler over all the earth is thinking about you? Our president has the people of the United States of America on his mind on a daily basis. Occasionally, some are granted the privilege of a personal meeting and a few exchanged words; then, it is time to move on. He probably doesn't go to sleep each night thinking of everyone he met that day, never mind the millions he has never met.

But God our Father is thinking about us every day, and his thoughts are one hundred percent accurate. He doesn't think we are smarter or less able than we are. He doesn't think we are as godly as the image we try to present at times or dismiss us as hopeless wretches when that is how we feel. God knows all that is true and loves us totally.

God always sees us as beautiful and amazing; it is we who change as the world around us changes. Our challenge is to keep the image of the woman God sees more prominent than the image of the woman we see with our human eyes. The new hat that God offers for our wardrobe represents putting on his truth every time we look in our human mirror.

—SHEILA WALSH (*I'm Not Wonder Woman*)

GARBAGE IN, GARBAGE OUT

For as he thinks in his heart, so is he.
—*Proverbs 23:7a Amplified*

A few nights ago, I woke up suddenly from a great night's sleep. As I turned over on my pillow to see if my husband was up making coffee yet, I noticed strange music running through my head. "She don't lie, she don't lie, she don't lie—cocaine!"

What?! What had I been dreaming? Then it hit me: my son had played a CD by Eric Clapton for me the night before, and this was a line from one of the songs. I remember hearing that particular line and talking about it, but I don't remember memorizing it so I could sing myself to sleep (or awake) with it later.

It was a good reminder how important it is to be intentionally aware of everything we allow to enter our eyes, ears, and hearts. What are you watching on television and movies? What are you reading? Are you surrounded by friends who fill you up?

It isn't just about you. What you allow inside your heart and mind is what will inevitably be poured out on your family and friends. What you receive is, most likely, what you will give.

So, what should we be receiving? Jesus told his disciples, "Receive the Holy Spirit" (John 20:22 AMPLIFIED). We fill up with the Spirit through praise, Bible study, meditation, prayer, and rest. We learn how to take care of ourselves by taking time to receive from God. So take a moment today to receive—and maybe to think about what's better left unheard.

—LISA WHELCHEL (*Taking Care of the Me in Mommy*)

WHO AM I?

"Before I formed you in the womb I knew you, before you were born I set you apart," says the LORD.

—Jeremiah 1:5 NIV

If all we do is look at our outer shell, we're not all that unique. For example, there are many people who look like me: blonde, medium-length hair, petite, blue eyes. Actually, I think I have really pretty eyes. They are as blue as the Caribbean Sea. The depth of their color reminds me of the true depth that is inside me.

Writing that felt funny, but it also felt good. Why are we so timid to point out the things we like about ourselves? I've always spent my time listing those things about me that I don't like. But it sure feels good to recognize those things about my shell that I do like.

But who I am isn't the color of my eyes. I am the one peering out of them. I am the one who is hiding inside this skin of mine. And who is that, exactly? Well, I'm still figuring that out. I don't know if there is one answer or several. I am not the woman I was five years ago, and hopefully I am not the woman I will be five years from now. I am evolving, changing, becoming. It's not so much who I am but that I am a work in progress, striving to become more like the one who made me.

—NATALIE GRANT (*The Real Me*)

SHINE BRIGHT

*In the same way, you should be a light for other people. Live so
that they will see the good things you do and will praise your
Father in heaven.*
—*Matthew 5:16 NCV*

I've known a plethora of lighthouses . . . walking and talking towers who, at critical moments, have guided me to shore. Several years ago in Minnesota, I met a tall, lit tower by the name of Mary Jo. Mary Jo has Lou Gehrig's disease, and while she can't talk because her vocal chords are paralyzed, she says volumes.

I met Mary Jo at a Women of Faith conference, amid a sea of thousands of women. This woman was critically ill and required many attendants to care for her, yet there she was in a specially designed wheelchair. At first I thought how heroic her friends were to bring her, but I learned it was Lighthouse Mary Jo who had brought them. What's more, I discovered Mary Jo is a busy mom who attends all of her son's sporting events, makes up menus for the family every week, constructs honey-do lists for her husband, and checks in with her children on their homework and grades.

Don't you think she's brave? Don't you think she's bright? Most folks bail on the daily tasks when they are fighting for their lives, but not this lighthouse. Mary Jo's faith sends a clear message—not an SOS, but "This little light of mine, I'm going to let it shine."

—PATSY CLAIRMONT (*Catching Fireflies*)

GOD'S DIVINE MASTER PLAN

The wise mind will know the time and the way.
—*Ecclesiastes 8:5* NRSV

To what degree do facts determine your decisions? Frankly, I tend to be a "fly-by-the-seat-of-the-pants" type of decision maker. I like to know the facts, but sometimes there's simply too much information.

I think it is wise to be a fact gatherer and make well-informed decisions based on those facts. The truth is, though, some experiences come into our lives whether or not we have the facts.

For those times when our knowledge of the facts does not seem to influence the circumstances in which we find ourselves, it is important to remember there is a divine master plan. The master plan that is based upon God's love for his creation provides peace in the midst of turmoil, faith in the midst of uncertainty, and joy in spite of loss.

It is encouraging to know we're not alone as we make our decisions in life. We have the freedom of personal choice, but we also have the promise of God's participation. We are not robots responding to divine directional switches. The way our decisions are made reflects our human uniqueness. But the existence of a divine master plan where our decisions are honored or perhaps even altered reminds us we all have the promise of a divine partnership.

—MARILYN MEBERG (*The Decision of a Lifetime*)

WORDS THAT STING

When you talk, do not say harmful things, but say what people need—words that will help others become stronger.

—*Ephesians 4:29* NCV

When you think about the relationships in your life—friends and acquaintances, family members, co-workers, or fellow students—is there anybody who has hurt you by what they've said? Their words might have been an offhanded comment or a momentary attack. Their words might have been just an aside, but they stung deeply and left you reeling.

I want to suggest six principles that often help me when I'd rather react or attack instead of listening to the one who makes me feel chided. Although the pain may not go away immediately (or maybe ever), the effort to apply helpful actions will see you through and keep you from giving up on that other individual.

1. *Let the person finish talking before you say anything.* Sometimes all the other person wants is to make her point known.
2. *State back to the person what you think she said.* We can easily misunderstand what's been communicated, so try to repeat to the other person.
3. *Own what you believe to be true about her words.*
4. *Thank her for being honest with you.*
5. *Try not to personalize what is not your problem.*
6. *Pray with the person to whom you have been listening.*

—LUCI SWINDOLL (*Life! Celebrate It*)

THE FILTERS OF KINDNESS

Who can find a virtuous woman: for her price is far above
rubies. . . . She openeth her mouth with wisdom; and in her
tongue is the law of kindness.
—*Proverbs 31:10, 26* KJV

What coils your rubber bands into a flaming missile? Tele-marketers? Taxes? Teenagers? Tardiness? Traffic?

I remember a male stranger being infuriated because he thought my friend and I shouldn't have eased into his lane of traffic, even though he wasn't close and we had scads of room. The guy sped up and then went bonkers as he tried repeatedly to force us off the highway. Then he pulled in front of us and slammed on his brakes.

More times than I would like to admit, I've emotionally slammed on the brakes of my frustration in front of a loved one. But I've learned it can take a lifetime to correct that kind of tire-screeching approach. It leaves skid marks on people's spirits, and they become self-protective and look for the nearest exit.

Scripture guides us toward more dignified resolutions, ones that leave all of us intact. When we put our words through the filters of kindness, anger won't have a chance to exact a greater price from everyone involved. If our motive is to reconcile differ-ences and not to offend our offender or to prove her wrong, then we will have a heart resolve that leaves us feeling settled and holds the potential for restoration of the relationship.

—PATSY CLAIRMONT (*I Second That Emotion*)

SURVIVAL TIPS
(*Extra help for the early days following a crisis*)

> *Whatever things were written before were written for our learning, that we through the patience and comfort of the Scriptures might have hope.*
>
> —Romans 15:4

You might feel like you are losing your memory or going crazy. Don't worry—this is normal. Just go with it!

Keep your tasks for each day small and short. Make lists. This will clear your mind just a bit and unburden your overtaxed brain. Write each one down and check them off—even if your list says, "Get up. Get dressed. Cry. Dry tears. Eat. Nap. Cry. Get undressed. Pray for the day to end. Sleep."

Have a good cry if you need to, whenever you can. Tears are a language God understands, and they clear your body of built-up toxins.

Laugh as soon as you possibly can, even if it is dark humor. Laughter releases tension and perks up your whole internal system. You'll know you will live through your crisis the minute you can laugh.

You may feel like you need to be demoted to life's slow class. You probably won't be able to read a lot, and the Bible may seem daunting. Be gentle with yourself. Meditate on one or two comforting Scriptures or quotes. Talk to God as if he were your friend, and tell him everything without fear. He can take it.

—SANDI PATTY (*Falling Forward*)

MORE SURVIVAL TIPS
(Extra help for the early days following a crisis)

> *Pursue righteousness, godliness, faith, love, patience, gentleness.*
> —I Timothy 6:11

Remind yourself that if you've survived thus far, you'll make it around the bend and be stronger than ever before. You are probably already starting to grasp one of the gifts of having been in crisis. You get the gift of perspective—it is very clear now what matters and what doesn't.

Visualize yourself in the arms of Jesus. Let him hold you and remind you that you are his beloved child. Your picture is still on his refrigerator.

Breathe in, breathe out, put one foot in front of the other. Some of these early days are simply about endurance, holding on, and letting time do its work. You will feel better. You will survive.

Hold your loved ones close, especially if they are able to express their love in kind and helpful ways.

If none of the above works for you, you might do what I did—go to a batting cage! I would spend about fifteen minutes trying to hit the stuffing out of a baseball. Every time I would swing, I would really get into it, sometimes even imagining that I was hitting the problems right out of my life. It worked for me!

—SANDI PATTY (*Falling Forward*)

THIRSTY FOR GOD

He satisfies the thirsty soul and fills the hungry soul with good.
—Psalm 107:9 TLB

Saint Augustine said that our souls will never find their rest until they find it in God. *He* is the treasure. Our longings will point the way to him every single time. Each longing in my life that I have discovered, or that has discovered me, drives me to confront a truth that I might not have confronted otherwise: I need God. I am thirsty for God. Desperately thirsty. In every area of my life. I was made by him and for him, and apart from him, I will not be satisfied. My desires for things to fill me and make me whole bear witness to the one who will fill me ultimately. My longing to be known reveals to me the existence of a greater knowing by the one who created me. My hunger for heaven gently sings to me a haunting lullaby that reminds me why we will never feel fully at home here.

It is easy to miss this. Listen closely to your longings.

God is the only one big enough to hold our longings. He created them, and when we bring them to him, we have finally found the right place.

—NICOLE JOHNSON (*Fresh-Brewed Life*)

SHE "GOT IT"!

> *It was Christ who gave some to be apostles, some to be prophets,*
> *some to be evangelists, and some to be pastors and teachers, to*
> *prepare God's people for works of service, so that the body of*
> *Christ may . . . become mature, attaining to the whole measure*
> *of the fullness of Christ.*
>
> —*Ephesians 4:11–13* NIV

Hannah Whitall Smith, author of *The Christian's Secret of a Happy Life,* was a woman of profound influence in her time as well as today. But she didn't become that woman of influence naturally or overnight. She was born into a prosperous family who practiced a barren religion that left her with no answers. When she and her husband, Robert Pearsall Smith, came to Jesus Christ, she found a new source of hope. But even then, everything was not wonderful. She struggled with her longing for some physical evidence that she truly knew Jesus. Life wasn't what Hannah thought it would be.

But at that point, Hannah came to believe, even in her pursuit of certainty, that *faith* was the stabilizing message of Scripture. She chose to take God at his word. She chose to recognize that he was always with her. She chose to believe that he is a loving Father. These choices enabled her to grasp the life for which God had created her.

Hannah Whitall Smith "got it," and as a result, enabled others to "get it" as well. Despite the challenges of her circumstances, she chose to become a mature, fully-committed woman of God.

—JAN SILVIOUS (*Big Girls Don't Whine*)

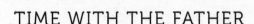

TIME WITH THE FATHER

Draw near to God, and he will draw near to you.

—*James 4:8* NRSV

I truly believe that one of the most important lessons I am learning at the moment is the call to spend some alone time with God in the midst of the rush of my life. Christ knew that his times were in the Father's hands. He knew that he was about to walk through the darkest night a human being would ever experience, and it was in his times of quiet communion with his Father that he received the grace and strength for what was to come. He made a place in his inner closet to sit with his Father and be still.

Think about your life for a moment. Are you anxious about anything? What are the thoughts that typically run through your head as you rush from thing to thing? When was the last time you found a quiet spot to sit and do nothing but enjoy being there (without falling asleep!)? Are you facing a dark and difficult time in your life?

It isn't enough to simply remove activity from your life. You must replace it with something better. You are invited to fill the void with the intentional habits of a strong, peaceful woman. You can live in this world with its constant change and threats, from within and without, and know his perfect peace.

—SHEILA WALSH (*I'm Not Wonder Woman*)

GREAT IS HIS FAITHFULNESS

Because of the LORD's great love we are not consumed, for his compassions never fail. They are new every morning; great is your faithfulness.

—Lamentations 3:22–23 NIV

A dear neighbor was going through an excruciatingly painful season of life. One morning during my devotions, I read Psalm 102 and felt it spoke directly to my friend's situation:

"Hear my prayer, O LORD, and let my cry come to You. Do not hide Your face from me in the day of my trouble; incline Your ear to me; in the day that I call, answer me speedily. For my days are consumed like smoke, and my bones are burned like a hearth . . . My enemies reproach me all day long; those who deride me swear an oath against me . . . But You, O LORD, shall endure forever, and the remembrance of Your name to all generations."

Have you ever felt like my neighbor or like King David, the author of this psalm? Read the last verse again. It holds the key to holding on. Though everything around you may change, God will not. Though everything in your life may fall apart, God will remain a constant presence and support. He is the same Lord now, in the middle of your hopelessness, as he was yesterday in the midst of all your joy. If you are suffering, you may be full of questions. Take them to God; he is the answer. Just as David did so long ago, hold on to the Lord.

—LISA WHELCHEL (*Speaking Mom-ese*)

EAGERLY CHOSEN

*The LORD said: "Before I formed you in the womb I knew you;
before you were born I sanctified you."*
—*Jeremiah 1:5*

We are chosen. We are set apart. We are meant to live big, big lives full of joy—unafraid, loved supremely by the one who created us. And God didn't choose us because he thinks we're always going to win. In fact, he chose us knowing that we may be clumsy, self-conscious, ashamed, too quick to give our opinion, dreadful at listening, full of pride, shy, too smart for our own good, or possessing a host of other characteristics that are deemed by the world as the traits of a loser. God knows us intimately, in all our imperfections, and he loves us beyond measure. That truth—rooted deeply in our hearts, coloring every thought that runs through our minds—is more than enough to see us through the game.

When was the last time you were eagerly chosen, picked out of the crowd, or given recognition? Do you remember what that felt like? Were you surprised, or did you see it coming? How did the people around you react? What would your life look like today if you truly believed what God says about you—that you were chosen, even before you were born? Understanding who you really are will change your life.

—NATALIE GRANT (*The Real Me*)

THE HARDEST PERSON TO FORGIVE

If anyone belongs to Christ, there is a new creation. The old things have gone; everything is made new!
—2 Corinthians 5:17 NCV

A couple of years ago I was invited to speak at a women's prison near Little Rock, Arkansas. I spoke on freedom and forgiveness—that true freedom is not the absence of bars but the very real presence of Christ. As I sang at the end of my message, women stood with their arms stretched out to God, tears pouring down their faces. Two things became very clear that night: (1) forgiveness has the power to heal the most brutal of wounds, and (2) the most difficult person to forgive is the one we see in the mirror every morning.

Most of us find it hard to forgive ourselves for some of the things we do. We beat ourselves up with what-ifs and if-onlys. The only door to true freedom and forgiveness is to face what we did square in the eye and own it to its full extent.

If God forgives us, then we must forgive ourselves. You were bought with a price, dear sister. Every sin is covered by the life-blood of the Lamb. Forgiveness is a powerful weapon that overcomes evil and brings healing to our wounded souls.

—SHEILA WALSH (*Let Go*)

A HOPE AND A FUTURE

"I know the plans I have for you," declares the Lord, *"plans to prosper you and not to harm you, plans to give you hope and a future."*
—Jeremiah 29:11 NIV

In spite of our best-laid plans, we all experience being broadsided by the unexpected and the unwanted. To what degree does the divine master plan figure into our experiences? In fact, what is a divine master plan?

The Bible clearly states that God does, indeed, have a plan for each of us. We are not creatures wandering haphazardly from point A to point B. We are told that his plan is designed to give us a future and a hope. The degree to which we can mess up the divine master plan with poor choices or disobedience is a matter of some debate. But I do know this about the divine master plan: God created the plan to show his love for us, not his judgment of our mistakes. His plan offers forgiveness when we need it, encouragement when we feel weak, and clarity when we don't see clearly.

If you've ever thought you have blown it too badly for God to love you, forgive you, or make anything out of your life, remember: not only are you a divine treasure, you are one for whom God has a plan—a plan that will give you a future and a hope.

—MARILYN MEBERG (*The Decision of a Lifetime*)

STARTING POINTS

Your beginnings will seem humble, so prosperous will your future be.
—Job 8:7 NIV

Do you travel? I do! A lot! And there are certain things I have to take on every trip. I've learned first to work on the knowns—cosmetics, underwear, medications, pajamas, and night-light (I never travel without a night-light). Then I move to clothes, shoes, and accessories, depending on the season, engagement, and destination. It finally comes down to a science. Starting with what I know (in any dilemma) is helpful and will ultimately get the job done.

Starting points of any endeavor can be debilitating. We don't want to start something because it seems too hard, too involved, and too much work. Whether it's writing a term paper, building a house, saving money, losing weight, or packing for a trip, we don't know where to begin—so we don't.

Life's highway is littered with people who had good intentions but never punched the start button. I know a few people like this, and their questions are always the same: "How did you do that?" "How do you always finish projects?" "How did you plan that far-fetched vacation to that out-of-the-way spot?" The answer to each of these is the same—*start*. Nobody has the key to the outcome, but we all have the key to possibility. Open the door and walk through it.

—LUCI SWINDOLL (*Life! Celebrate It*)

WHAT IS HOPE?

Lord, what do I look for? My hope is in you.
—Psalm 39:7 NIV

I wonder if it's possible to fully describe hope or how it feels. I know hope feels bigger than my ability to hold it inside without becoming airborne. It activates fresh shipments of blood, energy, and gratefulness that seem to surge with holy force. Hope seems light like a wisp of down on a soft breeze; it's sparkling clean like a new sky after a spring rain. Hope is a baby's coo, a toddler's first step, a prodigal's return.

Wait . . . oh, now I'm getting it: hope is an infinity pool that has no boundaries. It can't be limited to a word, a phrase, a dissertation, or even a heavily-volumed library. Hope is eternal and, therefore, beyond us to define. Yet sometimes I see hope in a life, and when it's there you can spot it, even if you can't touch it or taste it, because hope is palpable.

Hope is definitely an inside job. While we can't pump it up, we know it when it arrives. It fills the air with honeysuckle and fresh water. Hope shows us a better way, a higher path, a different perspective. Hope reconfigures hearts. Redirects energies. We not only pursue hope as a lifeline, but also hope pursues us. It is the essence of Christ.

—PATSY CLAIRMONT (*I Second That Emotion*)

PARTNERSHIP WITH GOD

Jesus said, "Get up, take your bedroll, start walking." The man was healed on the spot. He picked up his bedroll and walked off.

—John 5:8–9 MSG

If you've ever had a garden of any kind, you know that God is the one who does the miracle in making the seed grow. However, you also know that you had to get out of your bed, plant the seed, water it, and weed it. Growing fruits, veggies, or flowers is a partnership between the gardener and the Creator.

The same is true for recovering from any trauma or crisis in your life. It has to be a partnership between you and God. God will bless, guide, lead, and heal. But you have to seek out the help. You have to dial the number of a recommended counselor. You have to read books that will help retrain your brain. You have to have a "come to Jesus" moment every day. When the man at the pool of Bethesda assured Jesus he wanted to get well, Jesus said, "Get up! Pick up your mat and walk" (John 5:8). He asked the man to *do something* to prove his desire was sincere.

What I have learned is that lasting change means to conscientiously make three joyful choices: the choice *to reveal*, the choice *to heal*, and the choice *to be real*. (And isn't it just too cute how they all rhyme?)

—SANDI PATTY (*Falling Forward*)

HE GIVES US HOPE

We have this hope as an anchor for the soul, firm and secure.
—Hebrews 6:19 NIV

God gives us some powerful promises to live by. We are not without hope. He has given us his word that one day we will live in a better place than here. A place where our longings will be met. First Corinthians 13, verse 9, reminds us that "for now we only know in part. We love in part, we speak truth in part." Everything is in part. Can you remember when you were a child? You loved as a child loves, simple and free. It was good, but it wasn't even close to what it would be. And remember when you grew older? You loved as an adult, passionate and committed. But one day—one glorious day—we will love as God loves.

Right now, it's like looking in one of those mirrors that isn't glass. It's really difficult to see anything. You get an image, but there's no definition. However, one day we will see him face-to-face—his glorious face to our less-than-we-want-it-to-be face. Right now we can only see a dim reflection, but one day we will look into his eyes—the eyes that have seen from the foundation of the world.

—NICOLE JOHNSON (*Fresh-Brewed Life*)

WITH ME IN THE FUTURE

*Continue to reverence the Lord all the time, for surely you have
a wonderful future ahead of you.*
—*Proverbs 23:18 TLB*

As I look back over the seasons of my life, I feel as if I have spent
so many years thinking about what it would be like when . . .
What will life be like when I get married? What will it be like
when I have children? What will life be like when I have an
empty nest? What will it be like when I'm a grandmother? Now I
know the answers to all those questions. What life will be like
then has been revealed, but only in the past few years have I
stopped thinking about the future and what it will be like. I finally
have learned a great truth: when each season comes, it will be
what it will be. There is an appointed time for every event yet to
occur, and God will be with me in the future just as he has been
alongside me all the way, every step, for every event and for
every feeling, good or bad.

We have today, my friend. That's it. We have the joy of yesterday's memories and the delight of future anticipation, but we
have no tangible reality except today. This day is yours. This is
your time to do, to be, to accomplish, to fulfill your reason for
living.

—JAN SILVIOUS (*Smart Girls Think Twice*)

OH, TO BE FREE

The LORD sets prisoners free.
—Psalm 146:7 NIV

The ability to dream and to believe God's dream for our lives requires a liberty of soul and spirit. Although our circumstances may be confining, our spirits do not have to be confined. Internally, we can be free!

I wonder what comes to your mind when you reflect on the word *freedom*. Perhaps your first thoughts are of happy memories, going off to college, or driving your first car. You may think of external freedom, of someone released from prison or hostages liberated. As world events are piped into our homes every day, you may think of images from overseas. I will never forget the pictures of high school girls in Afghanistan who were able to take off their traditional burkas after the liberation of Kabul. Their smiling faces told a story of what it felt like to finally be free to expose their faces to the sunlight.

The freedom that we are looking at here, however, is not simply external freedom. What we are pursuing, by God's grace, is the internal liberty that comes from Christ alone. Freedom is not the absence of bars but the presence of Christ. It is not a changing of our circumstances but a changing of our hearts.

—SHEILA WALSH (*God Has a Dream for Your Life*)

PRAYER SCHOOL

Draw near to God and He will draw near to you.
—James 4:8a NASB

I've always struggled with prayer; I just don't enjoy it. I would rather do something or even talk about doing something than bring up a subject over and over again. My reasoning is, *Lord, I've made my requests known to you. I've left them at your feet, and I trust you to answer me. Why do I need to bring this up again?* Despite these frustrations, I've always wanted to be a prayer warrior. I just haven't been able to pull myself up by my bootstraps enough to pray long and hard.

Then one year, I attended a convention in San Francisco and felt led to repent of my prayerlessness. I believe God understands the different seasons of a mother's life. He knew how hectic things had been for me, and for years he had been gracious about it, but now he wanted me to enter a new season.

I returned home from the conference refreshed and ready to make a change. I made a space in one of our closets where I could sit on the floor and the kids couldn't easily find me, and there, I began to pray out loud (speaking audibly made it more real for me). I also decided not to set my goals too high, committing at first to meet the Lord there for just five minutes a day.

These little steps made a big difference in my prayer life. I still struggle with consistent prayer, but God is teaching me day by day how to communicate more with him.

—LISA WHELCHEL (*Speaking Mom-ese*)

INSIDE AND OUT

Great is our Lord, and mighty in power; His understanding is infinite.
—Psalm 147:5

If God sees me as priceless, as a treasure, as one worthy of sacrificing his only Son for, how can I believe less of myself? To believe myself unlovable, unreachable, or unacceptable is to believe that God made a mistake. And God does not make mistakes. His understanding is infinite.

Anyone capable of mistakes would be finite, not infinite. God is not like me. I make mistakes and misjudgments. I change my mind and say things I don't mean. I have destructive thoughts at times. Not God. His works are wonderful, and he thinks about me a lot (see Psalm 40:5)! In fact, as unimaginable as it might seem, God thinks so much about me, and about you, that his thoughts are too many to number.

I belong.

I am accepted.

I am loved.

I am alive.

To say these words and believe them to be true is absolutely mind-blowing. In the midst of my struggles with self-acceptance, I came to understand that God really knows me—inside and out. He knows when I'm faking, and he knows when I'm being real with him. He desires the real me. And he wants nothing more from me than that.

—NATALIE GRANT (*The Real Me*)

FEELING GOOD ABOUT FEELING GOOD

But the Lord said to Samuel, "Don't look at how handsome Eliab is or how tall he is, because I have not chosen him. God does not see the same way people see. People look at the outside of a person, but the Lord looks at the heart."
—1 Samuel 16:7 NCV

I've been on every diet and weight-loss plan ever invented. In my closet I have sizes 14, 16, 18, and none-of-your-business. I hate being heavy, and I've tried dozens of ways to take off the pounds.

For a long time, the way I'd layered myself in extra weight was a huge downer for me, something I was aware of almost all the time. It's something I still struggle with, but lately, more than I want to be smaller, I want to be *healthy* so I can be an active, involved wife, mother, and friend. So, instead of fretting about my weight, I try hard to focus on feeling good about feeling good.

On my good days, I do my best to eat a healthy, balanced diet, and I simply enjoy being me. I really have come to like and accept *me* from the inside looking out. On my troublesome days, I look in the mirror and groan, unable to see the abundantly blessed person inside my body. Then, a two-word prayer fills my head and heart: *God, help!*

He answers that plea by reminding me to look in the mirror, not with my own eyes but with his.

—SANDI PATTY (*Layers*)

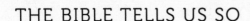

THE BIBLE TELLS US SO

> *All Scripture is God-breathed and is useful for teaching,*
> *rebuking, correcting and training in righteousness.*
> —2 Timothy 3:16 NIV

The Bible tells us who God is and also much of what he thinks. I realize some of you reading this may be skeptics who don't believe the Bible. The reality is, I can't prove the Bible to be true. There are, however, many convincing reasons to believe it to be true. To cite a few, isn't it interesting that this Book has inspired the highest level of moral living known to humankind? And this Book speaks of a Christ who is admired and quoted even by skeptics?

Consider this: the Bible is made up of sixty-six books that evolved over a period of fifteen centuries. It was written in three different languages by forty different human authors ranging from kings to fishermen. All those authors with centuries between their writings are in total agreement as they describe who God is and what his purpose is.

How does one account for that total unity of theme and message? Quite simply, it's because God wrote the Book! He has a message he wants his people to hear, so he stated it over and over through different biblical writers down through the centuries. That message has never changed: God loves his people and wants a personal relationship with them.

—MARILYN MEBERG (*The Decision of a Lifetime*)

TELLING THE TRUTH

He who speaks truth declares righteousness.
—*Proverbs 12:17*

The book *Telling the Truth: The Gospel as Tragedy, Comedy, and Fairy Tale* by Frederick Buechner has a wonderful story about how the role of the pastor—or anyone—is to stand in the pulpit and simply tell the truth. If you don't tell the truth, everyone in the building knows you're lying.

I discovered that in my own life. I spent so many years in ministry trying to be inspirational, trying to show what it would look like if someone sold out to God. Now I know that my apparent perfection left a gulf between me and other people. My open brokenness was the first bridge that allowed people to cross over and come to me.

Admitting our need for help to quit being victims or abusers or addicts or hypocrites can free us and the generations to come. I want to live with real people. And I want to be real too.

Perhaps some of us walk with a limp. Perhaps we will always have scars. The one we follow has carried his scars for a long time, and he longs for us to show him ours so he can heal them. And he longs for us to reach out to one another as servants and fellow travelers on this treacherous journey called life.

—SHEILA WALSH (*Life Is Tough But God Is Faithful*)

START WITH WHAT YOU KNOW

*To him who by the power at work within us is able to
accomplish abundantly far more than all we can ask or
imagine.*
—*Ephesians 3:20* NRSV

I live in the first and only house I have ever built and, I'm sure,
ever will. It's a once-in-a-lifetime project. When I started, I knew
zero about buying a lot and building a house on it. But I punched
start, and my desires began to move down the track. I started
with what I knew—I called a real estate agent, hired a builder,
began making drawings of what I wanted, sent e-mails, asked
questions, and kept going. I started doing what I knew and when
we start there, the unknowns begin to clear up little by little.

We will never get anywhere unless we start. If we begin with
a feeling or an urge to do something we've never done before,
and if we have the confidence and freedom to believe it can be
done, then somehow the difficulties attached to it begin to lose
their scary power of intimidation. By trusting in God and believing all things are possible with him, doors to the unknown begin
to open; and in time, a sense of certainty sets in. Now the house
is finished. I love it, live in it, and have learned from it numerous
lessons about God's keeping his word and giving me abundantly
more than I could have ever asked or thought.

—LUCI SWINDOLL (*Life! Celebrate It*)

STOCKING THE PANTRY

The LORD guides the humble in what is right and teaches them his way.
—Psalm 25:9 NIV

Food, what an emotional magnet! It's a lifetime challenge—well, not for everyone. Some folks actually manage it just fine. Then there's me. Therapists say eating is one of our earliest nurturing memories, and therefore many of us try to comfort ourselves with food. One remedy is to keep our emotional and spiritual pantries stocked with healthy, nutritious items like these:

→ *Dignity*—I have found dignity comes as we embrace our heritage in Christ and as we choose to do what is ours to do.
→ *Discernment*—While this is a gift, it also is worked into our hearts as we learn from our mistakes and seek God's counsel.
→ *Intelligence*—This is showcased as we apply God's Word to our own hearts before we offer it to others and when we think before we speak or react.
→ *Self-control*—This means placing balanced boundaries on our choices and our habits.
→ *Preparedness*—This means having on hand items such as the wine of God's spirit, the humble heart of a lamb, and the fruit of righteousness.
→ *Fortitude*—This involves internal resolve for whatever arises regardless of the difficulty level.

—PATSY CLAIRMONT (*I Second That Emotion*)

REVEALING YOURSELF

The Lord is fair in everything he does, and full of kindness. He is close to all who call on him sincerely.

—*Psalm 145:17–18* TLB

The first thing we have to do in order to reclaim joy is to be willing to be vulnerable—an open book, warts and all, before God and at least one other person (a counselor or trusted friend). There's a story in the Bible about a woman who had some kind of disease that involved bleeding, and for twelve years she had consulted every healer imaginable. No one had been able to help her. When she heard Jesus was coming to town, she must have known he was her last hope. But he was surrounded by crowds, and in the crush of people, she could not get his attention. She barely managed to simply touch the edge of his garment—and she was healed! Not only that, but Jesus stopped in his tracks, having felt some power go out of him, and asked that whoever had touched him would *reveal* herself or himself. The woman was rewarded for her choice to *reveal herself.*

So many women are walking around with tumors of secrets, cancerous emotions, or broken spirits that have mended the wrong way because they weren't tended to in a healthy way. The first step to healing is to reveal your deepest hurts and struggles to God and then to one other safe person.

—SANDI PATTY (*Falling Forward*)

EMBRACING YOUR BEAUTY

God has made everything beautiful in its time.
—Ecclesiastes 3:11 NIV

For some women, beauty has been the enemy. Beauty, or the perceived lack of it, has been the cause of painful rejections, missed promotions, struggles in marriage, or even self-hatred. Given the challenge, let alone the opportunity, to embrace beauty seems about as dumb as trying to spit into the wind. But the more we dismiss beauty as belonging to others, the more we reject opportunities to nurture our spirits.

We must embrace our beauty because beauty is part of who God created us to be. We are mind, body, and soul. Each of these elements possesses beauty in its own right and deserves to be embraced. That embracing transforms us to live our lives in a whole and healthy, honoring-to-God way.

Are we seeking to embrace beauty so that the world will accept us? No. Beauty needs to be redeemed unto the Lord. Do we embrace beauty so we can look as if we have it all together spiritually? No. Beauty is embraced because we don't have it all together, and we are trusting God in a more radical way than ever before to make something beautiful out of our surrendered lives.

—NICOLE JOHNSON (*Fresh-Brewed Life*)

PERFECT TIMING

As for me, I trust in You, O LORD; I say, "You are my God."
My times are in Your hand.

—Psalm 31:14–15

Do you have trouble resting in the fact that God is in control and that he knows the times and seasons in your life? Think twice before you are tempted to worry or force life to move at your pace. God moves according to his sovereignty, not according to our timetable, and peace will come only when you learn to trust his timing in every area of your life.

Resist the urge to constantly ask questions like, "When is Mr. Right going to come along?" or "When will I get the promotion I deserve?" or "What will happen if my biological clock runs out before I get pregnant?" When you grasp the truth that when he moves it will be according to his perfect plan, it makes a huge difference.

God is the God of all times, and to know him is to know faithfulness itself. He has the big picture in mind, and he knows the plans he has for you. Your times are safe in his hand. There is no need to be anxious about when God is going to answer your prayer or move on your behalf. You can relax in the certainty that his ways and his timing are perfect.

—JAN SILVIOUS (*Smart Girls Think Twice*)

THE TRUTH ABOUT DOUBT

Be merciful to those who doubt.

—Jude 22 NIV

Why did you do this, God?

Is this just one more thing that you are asking me to experience so I can better understand others when they suffer? If it is, I quit!

If I had your power, I would never let those I love suffer!

I can't do this, Lord!

I realize these prayers might be disturbing to some who have never believed it appropriate to question God. But I'm not relating my story for sensationalism; at that time in my life, that's where I found myself: at a moment of mistrust in God.

Be truthful—haven't you ever felt the same way? Have you ever been desperate to regain control when your life has taken a drastic and unexpected turn? I imagine so. After all, our world is imperfect.

But God understands and allows our doubt. Why? Because if we use it productively in our relationship with God, it changes us.

Yes, there is something to Satan's allegation that when Job's life was going smoothly, it was relatively easy for him to maintain a grateful attitude toward God. What Satan didn't realize, though, is that when we humans dig deep into our souls and pour out our hearts, even in bitterness, God is there and we come to know him more deeply than ever before.

—SHEILA WALSH (*Get Off Your Knees and Pray*)

PUT YOUR HAND IN HIS

Your ears will hear a word behind you, "This is the way, walk in it," whenever you turn to the right or to the left.
—Isaiah 30:21 NASB

My husband, the kids, and I were vacationing in the Northwest with our friend Bill and his family, and we had all decided to go on a hike. Each destination was more breathtaking—and memorable—than the next.

My favorite part of the whole day, however, was the journey. Hiking the trail behind Bill and his three-year-old daughter, Marissa, I reflected on the father-heart of God. Sometimes Bill carried his little girl; other times he simply held her hand. Occasionally he let her walk alone, but he never let go of her with his eyes. All along the way he provided encouragement, saying "You can do it," or "You're a good little hiker," as if he were noticing for the first time. "Oh, Daddy," Marissa would protest, "you always say that! And you always say I'm smart too."

Our heavenly Father is like that. He cheers us on and tells us we can make it, supporting us when we're tired or scared or want to give up. That's one of the reasons I like to read my Bible every day. I like to hear my Father tell me over and over that I can make it to the end of my journey. And I know that I will because he constantly guides me, reminding me when to hold his hand, when to let him carry me, and when to enjoy being the apple of his eye.

—LISA WHELCHEL (*Speaking Mom-ese*)

LIGHT HOLDERS

Lord, you give light to my lamp. The Lord brightens the
darkness around me.
—2 Samuel 22:29 NCV

The young Texas boy was diagnosed with cancer when he was two years old, but chemotherapy knocked out the disease, and all was well until a couple of years ago, when his dad died of cancer about the same time the young boy's cancer returned. A tumor had wrapped around the ten-year-old's jugular vein, and the surgery to remove it took eighteen hours.

As he recovered, his family wanted to keep him distracted. So he was given a hog to tend to, and when the county fair rolled around, he entered his hog in the competition.

It didn't win a thing.

The hog was, however, selected for the fair's auction. So there the young boy stood in the ring with his hog, and the bidding started. The community, recognizing an opportunity to lift up the courageous boy, kept bidding until the winner walked away with an imperfect hog for $36,000.

Jesus came to redeem us in the midst of darkness that we might be light holders. Here is an example of a community ready to hold up a candle in the midst of a young boy's darkness.

—PATSY CLAIRMONT (*Dancing Bones*)

WHO IS GOD?

The LORD is gracious and compassionate, slow to anger and rich in love.

—Psalm 145:8 NIV

This is just a sample of what the Bible has to say about God:

1. *God was before everything everywhere.* "Before the mountains were created, before you made the earth and the world, you are God, without beginning or end." (Psalm 90:2).
2. *God is the Creator of all things.* "By the word of the LORD were the heavens made, their starry host by the breath of his mouth" (Psalm 33:6 NIV).
3. *God's nature is love.* "The LORD is loving toward all he has made" (Psalm 145:13 NIV). "The LORD is good and his love endures forever." (Psalm 100:5 NIV).

If we choose to believe that God has always been, that he is the Creator of all that is, and that his nature is love, we can stop making up our own versions of God. But we can't stop here in our formulations because there is more we need to know about him. It is astounding to realize that two thousand years ago, in accordance with the divine master plan, God sent his Son Jesus to this earth! This world-altering event changed the assumptions and images of God forever.

—MARILYN MEBERG (*The Decision of a Lifetime*)

DESIRE TO FORGIVE

Be kind to one another, tender-hearted, forgiving each other,
just as God in Christ also has forgiven you.
—*Ephesians 4:32* NASB

About a year ago, I got an e-mail from someone who had attended a Women of Faith conference in Hartford, Connecticut. She confessed when she came that weekend, she'd been very burdened by a relationship that had gone awry many years before, but she couldn't forgive the person who had wronged her.

She wrote something like, "You spoke about being hurt by a friend of yours for twenty-five years because she had told a lie about you. I couldn't believe it! I sat there, stunned. It's like I was hearing you say, "Listen to me. You don't have to live like this any longer. You can find hope if you want to. Start with a desire to forgive, and you can." Amazingly, when I heard you, it was the first time in years I wanted to do something to put an end to my rotten attitude. Thank you."

Forgiveness doesn't come by osmosis. And it's not easy. It begins in our will and moves through our body as we take steps to change things. It's humbling to forgive those who hurt us because there's something in us that wants them to suffer. But those feelings rob us of all the freedom that's possible to enjoy through Christ. And freedom won't come until we *start with forgiveness.*

—LUCI SWINDOLL (*Life! Celebrate It*)

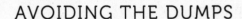

AVOIDING THE DUMPS

Jesus said, "Do not let your hearts be troubled. Trust in God; trust also in me."
—*John 14:1* NIV

Have you noticed individuals with certain temperaments just have an innate spring in their steps, a jiggle to their wiggle, a throttle on their waddle, no matter what befalls them? Still other personality types are given to bouts of melancholy.

Here are some of the ways I've found to help me not take the escalator down into the dumps every time things don't go my way:

→ *Our wills are powerful.* We can choose how we behave. We don't have to be a victim to our emotions, nor should others have to be.
→ *We don't have to wear our sadness like this year's fashion statement.* We can deliberately don kindness and compassion for others.
→ *Enlist a prayer partner.*
→ *Monitor the types of stimuli around you.* Don't work yourself into a mood by what you view or listen to.
→ *Relax—not everything we think needs to be formed into words.* Remember, the Tower of Babel didn't stand. Conserve your energy, preserve your friendships . . . shh.

—PATSY CLAIRMONT (*I Second That Emotion*)

BETTER OR BITTER?

> *Why are you cast down, O my soul? And why are you*
> *disquieted within me? Hope in God; For I shall yet praise*
> *Him, the help of my countenance and my God.*
> —Psalm 43:5

What is the difference between those who become more alive and beautiful and get *better* after crisis or loss and those who grow old, ugly, and *bitter*? I think those who get better have learned the secret of gleaning the lessons from their losses. They do not waste their pain.

Those who grow bitter seem to have an especially hard time openly asking God to teach them something of eternity, particularly after they either have experienced a major loss or have fouled up in some way. They may no longer trust God because he didn't protect them from their pain. They might even be afraid that God will point his finger at them, saying they don't deserve his help, that they are not worthy of healing. So they deflect and reject and play the blame game and never allow God to enter into the most secret part of their hearts and lovingly heal what is wrong and forgive what has been done.

People who get better, on the other hand, allow God into the center of their situations, *expecting* healing. They ask God not only to walk with them through the pain, but to redeem their sorrow so that their future can be better.

—SANDI PATTY (*Falling Forward*)

YOU ARE BEAUTIFUL

Charm is deceptive, and beauty is fleeting; but a woman who fears the LORD is to be praised.

—*Proverbs 31:30 NIV*

There is no beauty in makeup. Expensive clothes will not make you beautiful. The secret lies in being an alive, awake woman with something to offer the world. Namely, yourself. Beauty is less about your face and more about your smile. Less about the shape of your eyebrows, more about the light in your eyes. Less about the length of your legs, more about the bounce in your step. Real beauty is being a viable, vital human being. As you participate in your life with a warm smile and a generous spirit, you are beautiful.

Living your life will bring out the beauty in you because it is uncovering you. It is revealing more of the authentic you that is beautiful. Because life is a living, breathing work of art, you are a painting as you go. Be a masterpiece. Drink in life. Laugh too loud. Compliment others constantly.

Cultivate beauty all around you. Plant a garden. Embrace beauty wherever you find it—in the fall leaves, in the spring flowers. This will help you embrace it in yourself. When you appreciate a sunset or your child's clay candlestick or a beautiful piece of music, you are saying yes to beauty. You are saying yes to God.

—NICOLE JOHNSON (*Fresh-Brewed Life*)

A WAY WITH WORDS

Let everything you say be good and helpful, so that your words
will be an encouragement to those who hear them.
—*Ephesians 4:29* NLT

You and I make an impact on other people by what we say. We can offer them life-infused words or we can throw death darts at them. We can purpose to bless them or curse them simply by our choice of words.

My hairstylist, Rodney, has a gracious way of giving words of affirmation to the women who visit his salon. He speaks kind words of encouragement and offers a listening ear to weary women who sit in his chair. He is a focused listener who truly hears his clients' words, and he often writes cards of kindness, sympathy, and support to those who are going through a difficult time. When you sit in Rodney's chair, you have his undivided attention; he doesn't get distracted by chatting with other people in the shop. His job is to beautify hair, but he draws on the power of words to beautify hearts and uplift spirits as well.

Compliments breathe amazing life into a woman's soul. When someone says that she loves your outfit, comments that your jewelry is beautiful, or asks "What's that great perfume you're wearing?" she has offered you words of life. You hold your head up a little higher because someone has noticed something special about you. When it happens to me, I appreciate it so much.

—JAN SILVIOUS (*Smart Girls Think Twice*)

THE MOVIE OF YOUR LIFE

This then is how we know that we belong to the truth, and how we set our hearts at rest in his presence whenever our hearts condemn us. For God is greater than our hearts, and he knows everything.

—1 John 3:19–20 NIV

One of my dearest friends in this world, author and speaker Ney Bailey, once said to me, "Imagine that a movie was made of your life. Nothing was left out. Everything that you have ever thought or said or done was displayed on the big screen for anyone to see. How would you feel?"

My initial response was that I would be ashamed. It is one thing to take refuge in the absence of what I might consider to be "huge" sins, but to have all my secret thoughts and feelings revealed would be terrifying. The truth is that we all hide part of who we can be when left to our own humanity. Then Ney said, "God has seen your movie, and he loves you anyway." Let's stop for a moment and let that sink deep into our hearts and souls.

The God of the universe, the one who holds the stars and the moon in place, knows everything about us and loves us with unprecedented abandon. He knows the good, the bad, and the ugly. He knows the things we are proud of and the things we hide. He knows it all, and he invites us to come just as we are and live the dream he has for each of us.

—SHEILA WALSH (*God Has a Dream for Your Life*)

A GLIMPSE OF HOPE

O Lord . . . may you be praised forever and ever! Yours,
O Lord, is the greatness, the power, the glory, the victory, and
the majesty. Everything in the heavens and on earth is yours,
O Lord, and this is your kingdom. We adore you as the one
who is over all things
—1 Chronicles 29: 10–11 NLT

I'm naturally, by temperament, an extremely positive person, but during one particular time of my life, I remember feeling hopeless. I simply could not see how the rest of my life was going to be anything but stuck in a bad marriage, with a husband who was unwilling to change and no way of escape.

I was sitting in church when we began to sing a familiar praise song about trust in God. For a few minutes, I caught a glimpse of hope, and I held on for dear life. If I had not fastened my gaze on what I knew was true of the character of God, rather than focusing on the bleak future in front of me, I don't know how I would have survived those desolate times.

I used to think worship and praise was about God. I thought it was something he needed—or at least wanted. I realize now that whenever I sing about the Lord's awesome power, his faithful goodness, and love without measure, I'm not telling him anything new, but I am reminding myself of something I've temporarily forgotten. When we remember his awesomeness, our challenges look smaller in comparison to his greatness.

—LISA WHELCHEL (*Taking Care of the Me in Mommy*)

UNIQUELY, PERFECTLY YOU

God looked at everything he had made, and it was very good.
—*Genesis 1:31 NCV*

When you find yourself with a few quiet moments, do you ever wish you were someone else? Do you long to be different?

Throughout my years of traveling, I have become close to a girl named Sarah. We write to each other at least once a week. From Sarah I am leaning to step beyond what feels comfortable and trust God will meet me there. Sarah is confined to a wheelchair, but she has become very involved in her parish's prayer ministry and weekend retreats and has seen God use her life in many ways. Sarah finds the courage to move beyond physical barriers to live the life she knows she has been called to. She didn't ask to be born with spina bifida, but she refuses to let the limitations of her body define her. Sarah believes she is Sarah for a reason.

Before we were able to take our first gasps of air, God knew every bone in our bodies. He knew the eyes that would never see and the limbs that would not work and the ears that would not hear. He knew us, and he gloried in us. How then could we presume to believe we should be different, no matter the difficulties in our roads?

—SHEILA WALSH (*Let Go*)

PART OF THE FAMILY

You should behave . . . like God's very own children, adopted into his family—calling him "Father, dear Father."

—Romans 8:15 NLT

Do you realize what those words mean? You, dear one, were up for adoption, and God the Father chose you to be in his family. God the Father chose you to be his child. What a sweet truth to realize that you are a chosen, deeply valued treasure to the God of the universe. He wants to adopt you! But unlike most adoptions, you have a choice in deciding whether you want to be adopted.

Let's assume wisdom guides your choice and you decide you want to be adopted. What do you do? What do you say? How do you close the deal? Let me suggest you simply tell the Father, through Jesus, you want to be in the family. Tell him you agree to the terms of adoption: confession of sin and then believing in and receiving Jesus as Savior. Simply pray, "Lord Jesus, I want to be adopted into the family of God. Thank you for choosing me. Thank you, Jesus, for dying for all my sin. I believe in you, and I receive you as my Savior."

If this prayer expresses the desire of your heart and you have agreed to the terms for your adoption, you, dear one, have just made the decision of a lifetime!

—MARILYN MEBERG (*The Decision of a Lifetime*)

A GRATEFUL HEART

Let the word of Christ dwell in you richly as you teach and admonish one another with all wisdom, and as you sing psalms, hymns and spiritual songs with gratitude in your hearts to God.

—Colossians 3:16 NIV

When something doesn't go my way or come down the pike the way I want it to, I tend to gripe. It can be any number of things that irritate me—delayed flights, being put on hold, or having to wait in line. Traffic jams. Interruptions. People who don't keep their word. You name it! (You have your own list, don't you?)

At times like these when I'm tempted to gripe, I have to start talking to myself. And when I come to my senses, this is what I say: "Luci, if you can't be content in this moment of inconvenience, be content that it's not worse. Shut up and count your blessings."

But there are times I can't pull myself out of that morass until I *start with a grateful heart.* Our constant attitude should be gratitude. But it seems to be the rarest of virtues. God has given us thousands of reasons to celebrate life every day, even in the worst of times, if we just open our eyes, live in the moment, take in the beauty, and see the possibilities. It's been said, "The worst moment for the atheist is when he feels grateful and has no one to thank."

—LUCI SWINDOLL (*Life! Celebrate It*)

BREATHING SPACE

*Return to your rest, O my soul, for the Lord has dealt
bountifully with you.*
—Psalm 116:7

We all need breathing space from our routines, relatives, and other relationships. But here's my biggest struggle: how to get away from me. I often get on my own nerves. When I start to gripe at myself, I sometimes head for the beauty parlor, maybe because it's such a girly thing to do. Of course I enjoy the personal attention and usually the results. Besides, it gives me a mini breathing space.

I think every woman should have a lost-in-space place. It needs to be something you do and somewhere you go that not only pleases your senses but also results in satisfaction. What a reprieve for our emotions to have something to look forward to in the midst of the hustle and bustle, even if it's just to take a few moments to flip through the pages of a home magazine or to sink into the wonder of a well-woven tale. After a few pages of walking around in someone else's fiction, our reality seems easier to face. After a good read I seem to breathe easier. Last week to unplug I went for my first professional facial, which had to have been invented by angels on a sabbatical. It was heavenly.

—PATSY CLAIRMONT (*I Second That Emotion*)

SOMETHING TO BE GRATEFUL FOR

He who cherishes understanding prospers.

—*Proverbs 19:8* NIV

The Bible is full of examples of people who gleaned understanding from their pain. The apostle Paul, for example, "caught" the lessons of gratitude, particularly in his letter to the Philippians. He asked God to help him see his bleak circumstances with an attitude of thankfulness, and soon the very chains that held him bound in prison became something to be grateful for.

At this season of Paul's life, he had learned the lessons of a grateful spirit so well that the book of Philippians is overflowing with the word *joy*—despite his circumstances being less than ideal, to say the least. (Most of us would consider being chained to a Roman guard 24/7 to be something of an inconvenience.) Paul shares at the end of the book that he has learned the secret of contentment so that he can live just as happily in riches or in poverty, in prison or free—and in fact, he actually spends a bit of time discussing whether it would be better to live or to die. Now that's a free man! He saw that all circumstances carry with them some lessons that lift us closer to God if we allow the Lord to use them for our good.

—SANDI PATTY (*Falling Forward*)

THE WAY YOU LOOK

GOD judges persons differently than humans do. Men and women look at the face; GOD looks at the heart.

—1 Samuel 16:7 MSG

It is so easy to believe that God is silent on the subject of beauty. Maybe it is because the church is silent, or maybe it's because we have to be so still to hear what God is saying. Either way, so many women simply think God is not saying anything about how they feel about themselves. Here is the simple truth: God loves you passionately and intensely, and that love has nothing to do with the way you look. It isn't affected one ounce by the size of your blue jeans or the way your nose slopes up or how much dental work you've had done. It isn't lessened by wearing the wrong dress to a party or having no skill in applying makeup or by hating exercise. God simply loves you as you are.

But before we just gloss over that and go right on to the next thing, let me ask a hard question. Have you let that truth into your soul? I mean, really let it in? God is the one who has never criticized you or belittled you or made fun of your appearance in any way. He is the one who formed you, and said afterward, "This is good."

—NICOLE JOHNSON (*Fresh-Brewed Life*)

WISE WORDS

The speech of the upright rescues them.
—Proverbs 12:6 NIV

Have you mastered the art of talking to others and to yourself in kind, helpful ways? Our words are what we use to communicate from the inside out. They tell volumes about the health of our thoughts because we only can verbalize what has passed through our brains.

A dear friend of mine told me, "I think I've been whining, and I don't believe I want to keep that up." I listened as she listed all of the bounty in her life, and then she said, "But I think I've gotten in a habit of complaining about what I have to do, and I've realized I wouldn't have it any other way. There are women all over the world who would love to have the life that I live." I smiled at my friend's wise words. She remembered that the words we speak influence the quality of the life we live. She, like you and like me, has been richly blessed, and she doesn't want to lose sight of that.

The ability to speak gives us power in our own lives and in the lives of others. With that power comes great responsibility. What we say is heard not only by others, but also by the God who loves us and who has given us all that we have.

—JAN SILVIOUS (*Smart Girls Think Twice*)

GOD LOVES YOU! YES, YOU!

Blessed be the LORD, for he has wondrously shown his steadfast love to me.

—Psalm 31:21 NRSV

If I had to give you my life's message in one sentence, it would be this: as you are, right now, God loves you; and that will never change.

God loves you not because of who you are or what you have done but because of who he is. Your behavior does not impact the heart and character of God. You might think that on good days, God is proud of you; and in your not-so-attractive moments, he loves you less. But that is applying human logic to the heart of God, and it will always come up short. There is life-changing truth in the message of these three little words:

God loves you.

You!

Not just the woman whose kids learn their Bible verses while yours struggle to remember their names. Not just the woman who has been happily married for many years while you are still waiting for a husband. Not just the woman who is pregnant one more time while you weep with empty arms.

God is crazy about you.

When we grasp this truth, really get it as deep as the marrow in our bones, it changes everything. Now we have a place to build our dreams again.

—SHEILA WALSH (*God Has a Dream for Your Life*)

IT'S A GOD THING

"Can you solve the mysteries of God? Can you discover everything there is to know about the Almighty? Such knowledge is higher than the heavens."

—Job 11:7–8 NLT

I was reminded of God's awesome love for his children at a retreat in Houston. I asked the ladies to introduce themselves. One said, "My name is Cindy, and I have a daughter here on earth and another one in heaven." Another said, "My friend, Laura, here, also lost a daughter."

A few minutes later, Cindy looked at Laura's name tag and noticed her last name was Yankowitz. "Yankowitz?" she mused out loud. "Melissa Rose Yankowitz?"

Laura heard her and was astonished. "How did you know my daughter's name?"

Cindy replied, "Because my little girl is buried two tombstones down from your little girl. For eight years, I've visited my daughter's grave and noticed the dates on your daughter's tombstone. I've often thought of the mother who also lost a child so young."

These two moms came from different areas of Texas and had never met. God sat them down at the very same table on the first night of the retreat. Was this a mere coincidence? Don't believe that for a second!

Just as God had plans for those two women, God also has plans for you and your family. You may not realize it, but God is always at work in the lives of his children!

—LISA WHELCHEL (*Speaking Mom-ese*)

ALL AGLOW

Your word is like a lamp for my feet and a light for my path.
—*Psalm 119:105 NCV*

Do you know a good lamp-ologist? I'm in dire need. Lamps litter my premises, much to my husband's dismay. Les prefers ceiling lights, floodlights, torches, and bonfires. The more glaring the light, the happier he is. I, on the other hand, prefer the homey, warm, and romantic light of a lamp.

If I had to select a lamp to give an award to, it would be the one custom designed just for me. And guess who made it . . . my husband, the old lamp disser himself. I watched Les huddle over a pattern with all those glass fragments, which he patiently placed. When the pieces were strewn around the workbench, it looked like chaos; once they were soldered, the lit brokenness turned to beauty. That lamp carries an enlightening message about the beauty God can make out of brokenness.

I love when a lamp is lit inside of me that has never been turned on before. Sometimes the Lord will do this lamp lighting through his Word, a person, the arts, nature, or circumstances. I would like to be a light that keeps doing what I was created for . . . shine.

—PATSY CLAIRMONT (*Catching Fireflies*)

NEW WAYS OF LIVING

*Do you not know that your body is a temple of the Holy Spirit
within you, which you have from God, and that you are not your
own?*

—*1 Corinthians 6:19* NRSV

Did you know that the Holy Spirit lives in you? The moment you
said yes to Jesus, the Holy Spirit entered your interior world,
which motivates and guides your exterior world. The Holy Spirit
literally lives in you and, in so doing, wants to teach you new ways
of living.

Many people have misconceptions about who the Holy Spirit
is and how he operates. Possibly you, too, have wondered who he is,
how he operates, and what it means to have him living within you.

The answer to the question of who he is, is simple: he is God.
However, while the answer is simple, understanding it is not so
simple. The Holy Spirit is the third part of the Trinity. The Trinity
is composed of three divine entities: God the Father, Jesus the
Son, and the Holy Spirit. All those entities have separate roles, but
all are God.

We must recognize that much of God is a mystery and often
beyond our comprehension. But here's what is clear: the Holy Spirit
of God is your personal power pack. As you continue your Christian
walk, it's fantastic to know that living within you is this Spirit who
means to give you the power to begin new ways of living.

—MARILYN MEBERG (*Assurance for a Lifetime*)

DOING WHAT IS EXPEDIENT

The prudent are crowned with knowledge.
—Proverbs 14:18

Do you have trouble doing those things in life that are practical, prudent, or suitable for the moment? The doing of them may not be long-term, but they have the best immediate end in view. They're the methods we employ along life's way to make life work better and easier for us. These little temporary enterprises are born out of our desire to achieve a particular goal.

When I was in my twenties and thirties, I had four jobs. All but the first job (I worked for Mobil Oil Corporation as a draftsman-artist) were jobs of expediency. They were short-term with an end view in mind. My reason for all those jobs, obviously, was to have more income for personal goals I had set for myself during that time. Now my financial needs have changed, and I don't have the energy to do any more than I'm doing. But they served a very important purpose back then.

I do other things now for expediency's sake. I can think of twenty things I do every day, week, and month that enable me to reach my goals. But five years from now, I may do none of them. They serve their purpose now, and now is where I live and have to get the job done. You get my point!

—LUCI SWINDOLL (*Life! Celebrate It*)

FRESH OXYGEN

Two are better than one, because they have a good reward for
their toil. For if they fall, one will lift up the other.
—*Ecclesiastes 4:9–10* NRSV

Sometimes what I need most is to plug into others. My girlfriends are a lifeline. Yes, they can contribute to some of my emotional knots, but more often than not they resuscitate me.

Here are some of the ways I've received fresh oxygen from my friends:

→ *Friends help us think.* They often bring a different perspective that opens up a new view.
→ *Friends help us hear our inconsistencies and pinpoint blind spots.* I'm not suggesting that's fun, but it's valuable.
→ *Friends help pull us out of small spaces.* Even when they share their struggles, it can give our fears wings as we realize that we're not alone in our emotional complexities.
→ *Friends rally when the winds of hardship bluster across our paths.*
→ *Friends believe in us.* They applaud our gifts, and they celebrate our good fortune.
→ *Friends aren't perfect and may not be forever.* My caution would be not to expect more of a friend than she can give. My expectations have been too high at times, and that only leads to disappointment, ill will, and exhaustion.

—PATSY CLAIRMONT (*I Second That Emotion*)

PETER, PETER!

The Lord said, "Simon, Simon! Indeed, Satan has asked for you, that he may sift you as wheat. But I have prayed for you, that your faith should not fail."
—Luke 22:31–32

In the book of Luke, there's a story about Simon Peter's journey from being a brand-new disciple—full of vigor and self-assurance—through the valley of disappointing himself and the one he loves most. But through this realization of his fallenness and a deeper understanding of the love and mercy of his best friend, Jesus, Peter emerges shabbier but more beautifully real. Before Peter's denial of Christ, right before the crucifixion, Jesus warned him that the enemy "has asked to sift you as wheat." He also assured Peter that he had already been praying for him. What does sifting mean? In biblical days, it meant the wheat was put through a sieve to separate the grain from the chaff.

In Peter's case, what was sifted out of him was overconfidence and pride. Peter went on to become a great leader in the early church. And like other great leaders, he realized that he was totally dependent on God to do his job. He developed the qualities of empathy, integrity, trust, and a realness of heart, and the early Christians came to trust him. Like some other Christ-followers I know, Peter had some of his fur rubbed off. He'd been sifted and humbled and become more compassionate, more genuine and more authentic.

—SANDI PATTY (*Falling Forward*)

NO APOLOGIES

*Don't be concerned about the outward beauty that depends
on fancy hairstyles, expensive jewelry, or beautiful clothes. You
should be known for the beauty that comes from within.*

—*1 Peter 3:3–4* NLT

If you have given up on your outward appearance out of fear or
self-rejection, now is a great time to begin healing. A special fragrance or a new pair of shoes can show your soul an act of
kindness. Clothes don't define you; they reveal you. Makeup isn't
meant to cover anything up; it is intended to help you look as
alive as you feel. Start allowing the living, breathing, feeling you
to encounter the world in an authentic way, with no apologies!

There is freedom from the tyranny of beauty. I am embracing
it. If you could see me, you would laugh out loud. I'm sitting at
my computer with wet hair in two-day-old clothes. Not a pretty
sight. But we live by faith, not by sight. I feel beautiful. Right now.
Because I am alive and awake and participating in my life. I am
loved and cherished, and I love and cherish others. I am embracing my beauty as I am. For years my mother told me I was
beautiful, but I didn't believe her. She told me that beauty wasn't
about what I looked like. Today I am at the best place of my life
to choose to believe her. And paint my toenails.

—NICOLE JOHNSON (*Fresh-Brewed Life*)

DREAMS AND EXPECTATIONS

My soul, wait silently for God alone, for my expectation is from Him.

—Psalm 62:5

Have you noticed? We tend to enter adulthood with great expectations. Young girls do a lot of dreaming about what their lives will be when they grow up: Of course, dreams and reality don't always run on parallel tracks. One of the best lessons I have learned in my journey is this: what might have been does not exist, so don't even go there! It saves so much torment and expended energy when we refuse to ponder the "if onlys" and stick to reality.

Is your life different from how you once dreamed it would be? Perhaps you are making the best of relating to a difficult and defiant child you expected to be cuddly and compliant. Or you may be holding the household together while your husband travels constantly and you both endure the lonely nights. Maybe you're single while your heart longs for a mate, caring for a parent who has forgotten who you are, or dealing with debilitating illness yourself?

Much as we may wish our situations were different, we have what we have, and a wonderful serenity comes in accepting each person and each situation as God's plan for us. Amy Carmichael, missionary to India for fifty years, said it best: "In acceptance lies peace."

—JAN SILVIOUS (*Smart Girls Think Twice*)

LIVES THROWN WIDE OPEN

Love is patient and kind. Love is not jealous, it does not brag, and it is not proud. Love is not rude, is not selfish, and does not get upset with others. Love does not count up wrongs that have been done.

—*1 Corinthians 13:4–5* NCV

I think that very little disturbs our peace and crushes our dreams more than the area of our relationships. We thrive when they are good and healthy, but when they're permeated with conflict and pain, we suffer. We either strike out like a wounded animal or withdraw inside our shells. But God wants us to live lives thrown wide open to his love and abandoned to his care. He calls us to love others with a generous heart.

How on earth is that possible? There is no earthly way to love like this. We are simply not wired to be that selfless. But I have discovered that in Christ there is another path offered to us. On this path, we choose to love simply because we are loved by God. We are not threatened, because God is in control. We are not defensive, because we have nothing to defend. We are not arrogant, for we are teachable. We are not bitter, because we forgive. We are not blown around by the whims of those surrounding us, because we have determined to hold on to what is true no matter what appears to be true. We are not easily offended, because we extend grace. We choose to see beauty in absolutely everyone.

—SHEILA WALSH (*God Has a Dream for Your Life*)

THE STINKY SUIT

"Do not worry about your life, what you will eat or drink; or about your body, what you will wear. Is not life more important than food, and the body more important than clothes?"

—*Matthew 6:25* NIV

My suit smelled as though it had been soaked in mold-water. My suitcase had gotten wet the week before, and even though my luggage had dried out before I packed my clothes, it still retained a mildew smell that had transferred directly to my outfit. Unfortunately, I didn't realize what had happened until it was too late to change, and I was already on my way to meet Dr. James Dobson for the first time! Thankfully, I was being interviewed on his radio show, so the audience couldn't smell me. And Dr. Dobson either had a stuffy nose that day, or he was too polite to mention it.

Sometimes, life throws us curveballs. It's not worth making a big deal out of them. In the bigger scheme of things, most aren't really worth the stress. And often, as in the case with my stinky suit, what is consuming to us isn't even noticed by others.

Worry buys us nothing. So don't get all worked up over life's inevitable bumps in the road. The Bible says there is a time to cry and a time to laugh (see Ecclesiastes 3:4). If you have a choice, laugh about it.

—LISA WHELCHEL (*Speaking Mom-ese*)

THE CROSS MOLECULE

I praise you because you made me in an amazing and wonderful way.
—Psalm 139:14 NCV

I recently listened to a sermon by Louie Giglio on the subject "The Greatness of God." Louie described a protein molecule in the human body called laminin. Laminin is the cell-adhesive protein molecule that literally holds us together. I decided to look it up . . . and it's breathtaking.

If you have access to a computer, it's worth checking out. Search for "laminin," and you will see the shape of this tiny protein molecule that holds our bodies together is that of the cross. Isn't that amazing? This tiny little form is multiplied many thousands of times over inside our bodies. It can't help but remind us that God is ever-present in our lives—in the very marrow of our bones!

There is nothing random about our lives. God has formed every tiny cell in our bodies. It is a great mystery to me that the cross is built into our DNA, and it is an overwhelming comfort. Built into the very fabric of our beings are salvation and healing. My dear friend, I pray that God, by the power of the Holy Spirit, would reveal to you as no else can just how *loved* you are. It is written in your very DNA.

—SHEILA WALSH (*Let Go*)

OVERCOMING THE WORLD

The Holy Spirit helps us in our distress. For we don't even know what we should pray for, nor how we should pray. But the Holy Spirit prays for us with groanings that cannot be expressed in words.

—Romans 8:26 NLT

As believers, we have a wonderful freedom to access the power of the very Spirit who lives within us. When we encounter problems involving marriage, kids, our finances, relatives—anything—the Holy Spirit "helps us in our distress." We are not alone. He knows, he cares, and he is there. Our prayers ignite his power to meet our needs.

You may be wishing your problems were as simple as impatience, health, or decision making. Some of you are anguishing over issues of alcoholism, drug addiction, pornography, or promiscuity. How can the inner presence of the Holy Spirit help you deal with those huge challenges? Let me point you to a fantastically encouraging statement Jesus made; it's recorded in John 16:33: "Here on earth you will have many trials and sorrows. But take heart, because I have overcome the world."

What did he mean? The world is full of many evils. Among them are the various addictions and unhealthy habits that shackle the human spirit. But Jesus said he had overcome all the evil in the world. Jesus is an overcomer. And he lives within you. So you, too, are an overcomer.

—MARILYN MEBERG (*Assurance for a Lifetime*)

MAKING YOUR LIFE WORK

These commands are a lamp, this teaching is a light, and the corrections of discipline are the way to life.

—Proverbs 6:23 NIV

Everything has a shelf life, my friends. Every cause has not only an effect but a means to be accomplished. That's called being expedient. When we think like that, we get a lot done; and slowly, slowly, our goals are realized. For some of us it will mean hiring a nanny or baby-sitter, having a secretary, using a maid service to clean our houses, or engaging an assistant to keep us on track.

My computer has a funny little quirk: it won't start unless I punch the start button twice. It's been that way since the first day it was up and running. I've had tech people work on it, and it still has the quirk. So I accept it as part of its idiosyncrasies. I've learned what it takes to get the thing started, and that's what I do. It's as simple as that.

Some of our lives are the same way. We have a hard time getting off the start line. I'm suggesting you do what it takes to make your life work. Study your habits and patterns. See what's best for you. Keep pressing ahead, and punch whatever buttons will get you up and running. Once you learn that and keep doing it, many of your battles will be over.

—LUCI SWINDOLL (*Life! Celebrate It*)

JUST IMAGINE!

There shall be no night there: They need no lamp nor light of the sun, for the Lord God gives them light.

—Revelation 22:5

Getting up in the wee hours to experience the first rays of light conquering darkness heartens me. I watch the ebony melt from the sky and drizzle behind the distant stand of trees, and my senses awaken. Those first morning moments when the sun seems to ignite a horizon of hope—a new dawn, a new day, a new beginning—who doesn't need that?

Yesterday can't be altered, tomorrow can't be predicted, and today can't be controlled any more than I can adjust the sun's path. While that could make us feel helpless, I find a deep comfort in the knowledge that the one who placed the sun on its course has lit a distinct path for us. The path is filled with purpose and with the potential for interior prosperity: "You will show me the path of life" (Psalm 16:11).

While on earth, we will encounter both darkness and light, but that will not always be so. A day will come when Christ in all his glory and light will fill every shaded nook and every shadowed cranny, and darkness will be no more. Nothing will be as we now know it, and earth and God's people will experience full redemption. Imagine that. Just imagine!

—PATSY CLAIRMONT (*I Second That Emotion*)

THE PARTY OF FRIENDSHIP

A friend loves you all the time.
—Proverbs 17:17 NCV

Getting an invitation to anything is a special occasion. Whether it comes in a phone call, a letter, an e-mail, or smoke signals, the message is, "Your presence is requested." The excitement is undeniable. An invitation piques our curiosity and starts us imagining wonderful things. It doesn't really matter if it's Cinderella at the ball, a dinner at the White House, or Tuesday morning coffee with your neighbor. We love being invited. Even if we can't attend, it feels good to have been invited.

Every friendship arises out of some kind of invitation. Inviting is active. Inviting says, "I was thinking about you, and I am requesting your presence." Inviting says, "I have made time for you and me to celebrate." Inviting makes a hopeful promise of good times.

To the party of friendship, you must bring a gift. You've been invited, remember? "Your presence is requested." It would be far easier to bring a kitchen gadget. C. S. Lewis cautions us that we may act kindly, correctly, justly . . . and yet withhold the giving of ourselves, which is love. To offer a vulnerable nugget of your soul that has been mined from a deep, sometimes dark, place is more valuable than gold to your friend.

—NICOLE JOHNSON (*Fresh-Brewed Life*)

LEAVING A LEGACY

A good life gets passed on to the grandchildren.
—*Proverbs 13:22* MSG

Are you leaving a legacy that will give your children and grand-children—all those who look up to you—wings to fly? Have your children (no matter what their age) seen evidence that you love, honor, respect, talk to, and rely on the Lord for all you are?

I plan to leave five Bibles with my markings, thoughts, prayers, and notes. I want each of my five grandchildren to know that their grandmother knew the Lord and took notes on what he said! I want them to think about the things they do and who they are because they remember that their grandmother prayed for them and believed in God's plans for them.

I also want them to know they are and were always loved very much. My granddaughter Rachel has had her eye on a star-fish paper weight on my desk since she was about three. She has held it in her little girl hands with wonder and asked if she could have it when she got married. I assured her that she could, and now I keep it in a special place where she can admire it until then. It is valueless in terms of money, but it's a treasure in her brown eyes. It says her grandmother loves her. It's all about leaving a legacy.

—JAN SILVIOUS (*Smart Girls Think Twice*)

GOD'S DAUGHTER

*I will be your God through all your lifetime, yes, even when
your hair is white with age.*

—Isaiah 46:4 *TLB*

Do you know in the deepest place in your heart that you are
loved? I pray you do. And I pray that you understand that God
never takes his eyes off you, that you are not alone. I pray that you
will grasp hold of the truth that because you are God's daughter,
his princess, anything is possible.

I believe with all my heart that God has a dream for your life
that is far greater than any you could dream for yourself. When
God looks at you, he sees a woman whom he passionately loves.
That love compelled him to give his Son to redeem you from the
nightmare of a life spent apart from him. No matter whether any
of your smaller dreams are realized on this earth, God has an
amazing dream for your life that nothing and no one can touch.
God's dream for you outweighs every other dream in your life.

And remember, each one of us is given only one life. Your
days on earth are not a dress rehearsal so that you can come back
and try again. Every life counts. Your life counts. Heaven is
watching to see what you will do with the life you have been
given.

—SHEILA WALSH (*God Has a Dream for Your Life*)

RAIN, RAIN, GO AWAY

This is the day the LORD has made. We will rejoice and be glad in it.
—Psalm 118:24 NLT

Having spent the majority of my life basking in the golden, balmy Los Angeles sunshine, I figured I had the freedom to whine about the weather. Not according to my mother! One morning as I was complaining about the stormy skies, she put me in my place.

"Oh, let me call the 'whaaaaaam-bulance.' Or perhaps you should just order a 'whineburger and French cries,'" my mom said as she rolled her eyes. "Welcome to the real world, sister, where we have all kinds of weather."

All of us must live through some rainy days, both literally and spiritually. Life's dark days give us the opportunity to grow in ways we may not otherwise. But God does not force us to learn through challenges; we must embrace his lessons for ourselves. When the rain pours down by the bucketful, we're often tempted to whine and complain. By giving in to negativity, though, we lose sight of our blessings.

Are you easily irked by long lines, late people, or carpet stains? Are you tempted to whine about the inevitable challenges of life? Don't do it! Today and every day, make it a practice to count blessings, not raindrops.

—LISA WHELCHEL (*Speaking Mom-ese*)

MAKE SURE TO LAUGH

So I realize that the best thing for them is to be happy and
enjoy themselves as long as they live.
—Ecclesiastes 3:12 NCV

For years my family rented a house on Balboa Penisula. During one stay, I invited Luci Swindoll to come down for the evening. As we sat on the end of the dock, Luci asked, "Who owns that little dinghy tied to the end of this dock? Let's get in it and row across the bay!" The next thing I knew, we were sitting knee to knee, zigzagging into the bay.

As I got into the spirit of this crazy adventure, I became increasingly giggly. Suddenly, we were illuminated by a bright light. An amplified voice from harbor patrol demanded to know why we were on the water without a light. Luci shouted that we would make our way to shore immediately. Only as we pulled our cramped bodies out of the dinghy did the searchlight snap off. As the harbor patrol boat moved away, the voice, with muffled laughter, said, "Good night, ladies."

The ability to laugh is a gift God has bestowed upon each of us. You may not be amused by bobbing about in a dinghy, but find out what does amuse you and then enter into it with unrestrained enthusiasm. You'll be amazed at the readiness with which you begin to laugh.

—MARILYN MEBERG (*Choosing the Amusing*)

TRUST IN ACTION

One who trusts in the LORD is secure.
—Proverbs 29:25 NRSV

Do you know what it means to our Father and to Jesus our Savior when you choose to trust him in everything? I love the truth that we can give back to the one who has given everything for us by trusting in his love. It is of course a totally win-win situation, since the one we are being asked to trust is one hundred percent trustworthy, and as we continue to walk with him, we understand that more and more. It's not that we won't ever be tested but rather that testing plus trust is love. A time of testing can paralyze us, but when we mix it with trust, we move out in love.

There is no greater gift we can give God than our trust, and there is nothing more liberating than to do that in prayer. We are invited to bring our lives, our families, our hopes, and our dreams and lay them as a gift before our Father, believing he can be trusted with everything we treasure most. Prayer is the place where we take our hands off our lives—it is trust in action.

Your heavenly Father waits with open arms to hold your treasures. There is no safer place in heaven or on earth.

—SHEILA WALSH (*Get Off Your Knees and Pray*)

THE SOLITARY HEART

O give thanks to the LORD, for he is good; for his steadfast love endures forever.

—Psalm 107:1 NRSV

For those of you out there who live alone, I can tell you from experience that it's important to have a grateful heart about living by yourself. And in many ways, each one of us is essentially alone. We "exist within our own unique epidermal envelope as a separate thing," Thomas Wolfe once wrote.

Living alone has taught me not only to tolerate solitude but revel in it. I've learned to confront my fears and become comfortable with my inner self. In fact, solitude isn't a luxury but a requirement for me now. It gives me good mental health. When I'm alone, I process life's experiences, think through choices, replenish my energy, and face myself without other distractions. Sometimes that's pleasant; sometimes it's not. But it's never without value.

The German psychologist Erich Fromm believes our ability to love others is predicated upon whether or not we can enjoy time alone. He says if we're not comfortable with our own company, we'll never be able to love anybody else out of desire rather than need. That's an enormous thought! A heart of gratitude leads us down many avenues that enhance personal growth and teach us to celebrate life just as it is, without balloons, streamers, confetti, and horns blowing.

—LUCI SWINDOLL (*Life! Celebrate It*)

133

OH, YES YOU ARE!

As each one has received a gift, minister it to one another, as good stewards of the manifold grace of God.
—1 Peter 4:10

I love that God gave us imagination. He knew we would need it to see beyond where we are to what might be. Certainly the dark enemy longs to corrupt the bright light of imagination; so we must put boundaries on where we allow our thoughts to go. Yet we must not ignore the gift of thinking beyond ourselves because that's how we explore creativity and hope.

When imagination is used to explore art, it can be enlightening. We tend to be boxy in our perspectives, but art can help us to take a leap into a bigger world. I believe in the emotionally healing value of creative endeavors. If you're one of those who say as I once did, "I'm not artistic," may I say unequivocally, "Oh, yes you are." Give yourself a chance to explore your creativity; risk making mistakes to find your undiscovered artist.

You may not ever be lauded in an art museum, but your "brush strokes" might take place in the kitchen. Your soufflés may become fine enough to frame; your roast, a tender masterpiece of culinary genius. Perhaps you are a talented musician, jewelry designer, poet, tender caregiver, teacher, photographer, seamstress, hairdresser, inspired letter writer, or decorator. The list is limitless when it comes to all the ways art can be expressed.

—PATSY CLAIRMONT (*I Second That Emotion*)

THE UNLIKELY FIVE

Fear not; you will no longer live in shame. Don't be afraid;
there is no more disgrace for you. You will no longer remember
the shame of your youth.

—Isaiah 54:4 NLT

Each of the women listed in the book of Matthew in the genealogy of Jesus could probably be nominated as least likely to show up in the Messiah's royal line. Five out of five women listed came with *issues*. Rahab was a prostitute. Tamar seduced her father-in-law. Bathsheba committed adultery. Ruth was a Gentile, considered a pagan and an outsider. Then there was Mary, who was just a young, common peasant girl. A nobody. Just another pregnant teenager.

Rarely were women ever mentioned in lineages. Yet God seemed to have made a special place in his heart for these Unlikely Five. I wonder if each woman represents, perhaps, the things that generally hold women back from being used greatly of God. In this list we have sexual sins; we have someone who feels like a newcomer or outsider; and we have a gal who comes from humble means and probably considers herself much too young and insignificant to become anything special. The thing is the New Testament writers did not remember these women for their sins of perceived flaws but rather for the goodness God birthed through them during their time on earth.

I love that! God uses broken men and women.

—SANDI PATTY (*Falling Forward*)

FRIENDSHIP IS FRESH WATER

*These God-chosen lives all around—what splendid friends
they make!*
—Psalm 16:3 MSG

Looking for reasons to celebrate, I uncover gratitude. I realize how much I have to be thankful for. Spending time with my friends allows me to stay in that place of gratitude a little while longer. Celebrating birthdays, victories, answered prayers, and accomplishments lets me savor them before I move on to something else. Throwing a party, even if it's just a cup of coffee shared, is good for the soul.

I am a better wife when I celebrate my friendships. In addition, I am a more contented person when I celebrate my friendships. I become a better friend. It puts a spring in my step, a smile on my lips, and gives me a much lighter heart. I can be by myself, five hundred miles from any of my friends, and something one of them has said will cause me to laugh out loud.

I have exponentially more joy in my life because of them. I bring more joy to my marriage and to my family because of them. Friendship fills a deep well within me with fresh water. When I celebrate my friendships, it's like dropping a huge rock into the well. It splashes that water everywhere, on everyone else in my life.

—NICOLE JOHNSON (*Fresh-Brewed Life*)

EXPRESSING GENEROSITY

A generous person will be enriched.
—*Proverbs 11:25* NRSV

Generosity and kindness aren't meant to be held in reserve for big storms or hard times. Generous living is an art to be practiced, a lifestyle that springs naturally from understanding that God really owns everything, and we are merely conduits through whom he delivers his blessings.

If we're paying attention, we'll notice examples of generosity—and opportunities to express it—all around us. And generosity isn't limited to money. A short note of encouragement, a basket of muffins, a flower left on someone's desk or doorstep, a surprise phone call, or a kind word in passing are all small generosities anyone can give. You don't have to have a lot, just the desire to share your time or skills or whatever God has blessed you with. Sometimes we forget all the tangible ways we can express God's love unless we've been in similar need ourselves. Providing a meal for a family whose mother is sick, volunteering to care for a friend's children while she goes to the grocery store, visiting someone who is confined in assisted living, offering a ride to someone who can't drive—all of these are physical offerings that require only your time, energy, and the willingness to be involved in someone else's life.

—JAN SILVIOUS (*Smart Girls Think Twice*)

GOD HONORED HERE

You were bought at a price; therefore glorify God in your body and in your spirit, which are God's.

—1 Corinthians 6:20

If I could hang a sign around my neck to indicate that I am a believer, I'd want it to read: God Honored Here. I have realized for years, however, that when I am consumed by how I look and what diet I am on or off, "God Honored Here" would not be an accurate statement. More than the waste of money, I regret the time I have wasted in self-punishing cycles. Instead of having on internal running shoes that would take me to a healthy place of honoring God with my body, I kept going in self-defeating circles.

I knew that one of the big issues for me is how I look to others, and I wanted to be free from that compulsion. As I prayed for God to help me find victory to live free from these endless cycles, one phrase kept coming to me over and over again: a long obedience in the same direction, which is also the title of a book by Eugene Peterson that I read many years ago. This phrase captures the heart of what it actually looks like to put on your running shoes and honor God every day in your body.

—SHEILA WALSH (*I'm Not Wonder Woman*)

FIRST CHURCH

We look inside, and what we see is that anyone united with the
Messiah gets a fresh start, is created new. The old life is gone; a
new life burgeons! Look at it!

—2 Corinthians 5:17 MSG

First United Methodist Church in Oklahoma City, the city where
I was born, is more than one hundred years old. Called "First
Church" by its members, it stands across the street from the
national memorial marking the site where the Murrah Federal
Building was bombed on April 19, 1995.

The violent explosion that killed 168 people caused smaller
losses as well. When the front walls of the grand old church collapsed, the beautiful old stained-glass windows were shattered.

Almost before the dust settled, volunteers and church members lovingly collected the fragile shards of glass from the
heaped-up rubble of the collapsed walls. Over the next five years,
they carefully put those pieces back together in totally new creations. Today, wonderful new stained-glass windows glow on the
building's reconstructed façade.

The windows at First church are especially meaningful for
people like me, and for families who feel like their lives have gotten
all cracked up and glued back together—who know what it's like
to be broken and end up in a totally new creation. We are living
out the powerful truth of the inscription on one of the windows:
The Lord takes broken pieces and by His love makes us whole.

—SANDI PATTY (*Life in the Blender*)

STONE-COLD WORDS

> *God's judgment is right, and as a result you will be counted*
> *worthy of the kingdom of God.*
> —2 Thessalonians 1:5 NIV

Have you ever trembled and told a friend something you've done terribly wrong, and then, emotionally hunched over, waited for their stone-cold words of judgment to hit you? But instead you heard the flat thud of grace as their rock hit the ground.

Throwing rocks will never make us more loving. As we clutch and throw our rocks, we reveal our pettiness and our inability to change our own lives. Only when we drop our rocks and choose to love do we become more loving.

So the next time someone trembles in fear and tells you something you really didn't want to know, or you see your sin in someone else's life, or your loved one is braced to feel your stone-cold words, you'll know what to do. Loosen your grip, and listen for the flat thud of grace as you choose love over judgment.

The only one who has the right to throw a rock is the one who has never done any wrong—ever. There has been only one, and only that one can pick up the rock.

And he did. Jesus became the Rock and took care of our wrong for all time. He still stands between our accusers and us. He still lifts our heads and sets us on the path to freedom.

—NICOLE JOHNSON (*Dramatic Encounters with God*)

LIKE AN EAGLE

God loved the world so much that he gave his one and only Son so that whoever believes in him may not be lost, but have eternal life. God did not send his Son into the world to judge the world guilty, but to save the world through him.

—*John 3:16–17* NCV

When God dealt with the children of Israel, he protected them like an eagle caring for his young. Because we also are "a people for God's own possession" (1 Peter 2:9 NCV), part of his chosen because of our belief in Jesus (Ephesians 2:11–16), he hovers over us with the same concern.

He watches and when we are big enough to leave the nest, he stirs it up, forcing us to get out and fly. But he is always ready to catch us on his strong feathers if our weak little wings should fail.

You may be saying, "Well, how can I know that he loves me? I don't always feel it." I understand, but when we recall what he has done for you and me, there is no rational explanation but love. And besides, he not only has said he loves us but he also has shown us.

God sent his Son, Jesus, to let us know that he loves us, just as he showed Israel in so many ways that they were loved and that he could be trusted. He never stops being the Supreme Ruler of the universe, and he never gives up his role as the great Lover of our souls.

—JAN SILVIOUS (*Smart Girls Think Twice*)

FIX YOUR EYES

*Let us run with endurance the race that is set before us, looking
unto Jesus, the author and finisher of our faith.*
—Hebrews 12:1–2

If you are like me, you have been familiar with the phrase "Fix
your eyes on Jesus" for some time, but you may wonder what it
means, what it looks like. When I was a teenager I was stumped
by Christ's command to pick up my cross every day and follow
him. I had no idea how to do that. Did it mean that I should carve
up the breakfast table and drag it around the neighborhood? As
I studied and prayed, I became convinced that it means that
every time my will crossed God's will, I dragged my will back in
line with his. It means doing the things that I know are good and
true, whether I feel like it or not. It means setting my face and
heart toward heaven just as Jesus did. But what about "Fix your
eyes on Jesus"?

I believe that phrase means that we study how Jesus lived,
how he loved, and follow his example. When we find ourselves in
a difficult place, we do what he did: we turn to our Father.

Faith is not wishful thinking or theatrics. Faith is born in us
as we fix our eyes on Jesus and as we recognize the fingerprints of
God the Father all over our lives.

—SHEILA WALSH (*Extraordinary Faith*)

OUR DAY OFF

For in six days the LORD made the heavens and the earth, the sea and all that is in them, and rested on the seventh day.

—*Exodus 20:11* NASB

I'm one of those people who likes to work; I get an adrenaline rush when I'm completing a project. So the Sabbath is tough for me. My husband is an even worse workaholic than I am. One Sunday morning, he woke up and headed straight for our home office. He discovered a tiny yellow note stuck to the monitor. It read, "Don't turn on the computer on Sundays—God." The handwriting was suspiciously adolescent, but he knew the original command was not.

I understand that as Christians living under grace, we are no longer required to keep the Sabbath. At the same time, the Lord commanded the Sabbath for our own good, so why would we want to work ourselves to death? Taking time to rest is a provision directly from God's hands. What's even more amazing is that this is the only commandment God illustrates with a personal example. Can we really say, *God may need to take a break, but I don't?*

Keeping the Sabbath is a matter of trust. Do I trust God enough to believe that ultimately he will enable me to accomplish all the things he deems important enough to do? I can't do everything in my own strength anyway (John 15:5). When I remind myself that anything of lasting value is going to happen by God's power (2 Cor. 3:5), I can relax and take a day off. So can you!

—LISA WHELCHEL (*Taking Care of the Me in Mommy*)

OUT OF NOWHERE

I am the LORD your God . . . and I have put my words in your mouth and hidden you safely in my hand.

—Isaiah 51:15–16 NLT

Whether they surface frequently or rarely, we all have strong feelings that impact us, causing tears to spring up unexpectedly, sending grief sweeping over us "out of nowhere," or pushing us to behave in specific ways. By studying these feelings and by remembering back to the events and issues that sparked them, we gain understanding that helps us cope.

As we acknowledge the damage inflicted on the crucial bonds our hearts innately crave, we also seek desperately to give meaning to our experiences, no matter how grievous the damage. The fact is, the human psyche can withstand almost any assault if we can find purpose in our lives in spite of that assault.

Our supreme purpose and meaning in life are to know, believe, and trust that we are loved by the God who does not "do" throwaways. That knowledge—understanding we are loved and valued by our Creator even more than we can comprehend—makes productive lives possible for all of us.

And here's the most important thing to understand: whether we are abandoned intentionally or due to uncontrollable circumstances, we are the intentional creation of the Lord Almighty. We are hidden safely in his hand because that's where he chooses for us to be, and that's where we *will* forever be.

—MARILYN MEBERG (*Love Me Never Leave Me*)

THE ENERGY GIVER

[God] gives power to the weak, and to those who have no
might He increases strength.
—Isaiah 40:29

The dictionary defines *energy* as the vigorous exertion of power. It has to do with effort, strength, potency, and might. Who has all these attributes? The Lord!

Scripture tells us that God not only has his own power and strength, but he's given that same power to us. He enables us to have energy when we tap into his. David says to God in Psalm 31:4, "You are my strength." And again in Psalm 27:1, "The Lord is the strength of my life; of whom shall I be afraid?" What great verses! What comforting verses! God gives us all the energy we need.

When I'm exhausted and fall into bed at night, I often think I'll never get up the next morning because I'm utterly played out. Or when I have no more strength to take care of a need or do the things that have been assigned to me, I have to force myself to remember my strength comes from God, not from inside me. There's a vast difference.

So, remember—strength doesn't come from exercise; strength comes from waiting on God. Tomorrow is another day, and God energizes us for it . . . no matter our age. Every day that I get older, his strength brings more comfort.

—LUCI SWINDOLL (*Life! Celebrate It*)

NOW THAT'S ART

*Who endowed the heart with wisdom or gave understanding
to the mind?*
—Job 38:36 NIV

We have been made in God's image (from which the word *imagi-nation* derives), and no one outdoes God's artistic flair, which is why people copy his art all the time. From a forsythia bush burst-ing with blooms, to a bowl of green apples, to clear vases of white tulips, they all drip with his creative involvement.

I just came in from my after-dinner walk, and I was delighted to view the beginning of God's Spring Collection. Daffodils, pan-sies, and even a deep-purple hyacinth greeted me. Now that's art. Art inspires, and inspiration beckons us to join in the creative process in all we do.

Color is paramount to art, and the wonderful thing about color is it can be splashed across all of life's offerings: our attitudes, our speech, our clothing, our gift giving, and our emotional lives.

Why are we so moved by a crimson sunset, an ocher-dappled masterpiece, and a fistful of fuchsia peonies? Have you ever become misty over a glorious musical arrangement, a stunning sunrise, or a stirring dramatic performance?

We are hardwired to respond emotionally to the wonder of art. I believe God has given us many elements in this life that help to heal us, inspire us, and remind us of our Creator, as well as enlarge our interior worlds.

—PATSY CLAIRMONT (*I Second That Emotion*)

OUR LIFE AND OUR BREATH

Get down on your knees before the Master; it's the only way
you'll get on your feet.
—*James 4:10* MSG

There is no greater gift that we are given on this earth, after our salvation, than the open line we have directly to the heart of God. Sometimes, all we want to do is kneel. Other times we want to lay on our faces and call on the name of Jesus. There are moments when we want to stand with our faces toward the warmth of the sun or battle against the driving rain as we share our hearts with him. Prayer is our life, our very breath. Share everything you love and everything that troubles you with him. Sing, cry, scream, laugh, dance, and rejoice always, knowing you are in his presence, loved and received.

This doesn't mean every prayer will be answered as we might hope it would, but there is a day coming when this detour will end and we will be home free. Until that day we have our Father who loves us, our Savior who died for us, and the Holy Spirit who intercedes for us when we don't know what to say. And we have each other. When we give our lives to him, we can experience a life where we get off our knees, lift our hands in the air, and pray until we see him face to face.

—SHEILA WALSH (*Get Off Your Knees and Pray*)

WAYS TO CELEBRATE FRIENDSHIP

Love one another with mutual affection; outdo one another in showing honor.

—Romans 12:10 NRSV

+ *Celebrate your spiritual birthday, or someone else's.* Go on a picnic, have a party, or just have a big slice of cake in honor of "rebirth." Celebrate being found by God!
+ *Request the honor of someone's presence.* Practice inviting. Invite your daughter to join you on an errand that you normally do by yourself. Write an invitation to a friend to meet you for a cup of coffee or tea or lemonade, and give her a book, just because. Invite someone to attend church or Bible study with you, and bring cookies.
+ *Plan an extravagant, expensive, special day with a close friend.* Think of as many fun things as possible to squeeze into one day. Give your friend a copy of the expensive day you planned—then do something inexpensive together.
+ *The goal is not to form an exclusive circle of celebration among your friends.* The goal is to celebrate life. To say yes to being more loving, more caring, and more gracious. The choice to celebrate is about us, not about the other person. Like a rock dropped into a well, when celebration begins in your friendships, it will have a ripple effect and touch every area of your life.

—NICOLE JOHNSON (*Fresh-Brewed Life*)

WHO IS YOUR HIGHER POWER?

*Do you not know? Have you not heard? The LORD is the
everlasting God, the Creator of the ends of the earth. He will
not grow tired or weary, and his understanding no one can
fathom. He gives strength to the weary and increases the power
of the weak.*

—Isaiah 40:28–29 NIV

I have heard dear, dear people say, "Oh, I believe in a Higher
Power." I want to say, "If you really know the God who created
the universe, he would be more than a Higher Power to you. He
would be the God of your very life."

When you know that you know that God is who he says he
is, you'll be infused with strength to walk through situations you
never dreamed you'd be able to endure. When you know God
and trust him for whatever you need, you can relax and rely on
his strength to be your strength and his peace to be your peace.

I recently bumped into a good friend at the grocery store.
This woman has faced many tough trials, including chronic illness and financial reversals, but she has a strong trust in the Lord.
As we chatted, she said, "I guess I should be worried about this
latest mess, but I'm not! I trusted God a long time ago, and he's
always come through, so what good would it do to worry now?"
Great point! She knows he is all-powerful, all-knowing, and all-
loving, so she's decided to trust what she knows and see what he
does. After all, he is the Highest Power, and he is her life.

—JAN SILVIOUS (*Smart Girls Think Twice*)

149

ROCK-SOLID CONVICTION

Faith is the confidence that what we hope for will actually happen; it gives us assurance about things we cannot see.
—Hebrews 11:1 NLT

I asked the young Vietnamese girl who does my nails what the word *faith* meant to her. At first she was unsure what I was asking. I told her that I was aware that the girls in the salon prepared a bowl of fruit and set it in front of a small effigy of Buddha. She said they did that for protection and out of respect, for good luck. I asked her if she talked to Buddha, and she gave me one of her big smiles and said something I have heard from her many times: "Miss Sheila, you crazy!"

When we study faith in the biblical context, it has both an active and a passive sense. In an active sense, faith is our loyalty and devotion to God; in a passive sense, our resting confidence in God, in his Word, and in his promises.

Faith is not just what we believe, our doctrine or denominational creed but also and more importantly, a rock-solid conviction that what we believe and whom we believe in are worth staking our lives on; they are real and living.

Christian faith is more than wishful thinking; it is a certainty, a constant assurance based on God's track record in our lives and the lives of the faithful through the generations.

—SHEILA WALSH (*Extraordinary Faith*)

ACHIEVING GREATNESS

"But the greatest among you shall be your servant."
—Matthew 23:11 NASB

I've always looked up to my Uncle Jimmy. He has a deep, abiding faith that is central to every decision he makes, but unless you observed him quietly for a long period of time, you wouldn't necessarily know it.

Every morning, he gets up before sunrise and spends time praying for each member of his family. He impacts their lives with eternal significance, but for all intents and purposes, none of them know. He doesn't advertise his routine. Uncle Jimmy's prayer time is just a special ritual between a father and a Father.

Uncle Jimmy used to visit my nanny each day after his morning coffee and prayers. He would fix her breakfast, take out her trash, mow her lawn, vacuum her floor, and do whatever else she needed help with. Then he would sit down and talk with her.

I believe acts of ministry like Uncle Jimmy's bring a bigger smile to the Lord's face than when I speak before a thousand people, sell books, and bring home an honorarium. We are often tempted to believe that we need to become an author, a speaker, or a missionary in order to serve God. The truth is, though, we can and should serve God without ever leaving our neighborhood.

Instead of searching the world over to find some far-flung ministry, ask yourself this: how does God want me to serve others today? Not tomorrow. What needs to be done right here, right now?

—LISA WHELCHEL (*Speaking Mom-ese*)

151

YOUR CALLING IN LIFE

We love Him because He first loved us.
—1 John 4:19

Some of you may be wondering about your personal calling in life. Being married or not being married can indeed be a calling. So can having children or having no children, working outside the home or being a full-time mom, traveling on a job or staying in an office, working out of your home or being president of something, sewing drapes, cooking at the school cafeteria, finding a cure for cancer, or creating a better meat thermometer. Dare I say, your calling in life lies not in *what* you do but in *who* you are?

Remember this. Scripture says God created us for the express purpose of giving himself the joy of loving us. In being loved, we return that love. That is who we are: persons loved by God. When we return his love, we do it in a spirit of response that produces service to him. That is what our relationship with him is all about. If we do things for God because we are trying to pay him back, we miss the point of the relationship. We are not asked to *earn* the relationship; we are asked to *receive* the relationship.

So what is the call for each of our lives? To receive God's love and return God's love. We can experience that in everything we do.

—MARILYN MEBERG (*Love Me Never Leave Me*)

THE TRUTH ABOUT TIME

There is a time for everything, and a season for every activity under heaven.

—Ecclesiastes 3:1 NIV

Time is my highest priority right now. I never have enough of it. And the truth is, I'll never have enough time because it's all up to God, and he views time differently than I do.

My time has to do with *duration,* a measurable period when something occurs. I don't have enough "duration" during the day. I lack the continuum for everything I want or need to do to actually get it done. It's that simple. But God's timing is in terms of *division;* God operates moment by moment or through seasons or a lifetime or a dispensation. His time is not measurable, because he's eternal and earthly time is temporal.

The reason this is important is because when I look at my life from a human viewpoint, I run out of time. But when I look at it from a spiritual viewpoint, I see that God is in charge of everything; I'm not! Therefore, I will accomplish whatever comes my way even though it may not be written into the schedule of my daily planner.

Realistically speaking, then, I do have enough time. I have all the time God wants me to have and can spend it any way I like. I just need God's help to learn to spend it better.

—LUCI SWINDOLL (*Life! Celebrate It*)

ART EXPRESSIONS

Think about the things that are good and worthy of praise.
Think about the things that are true and honorable and right
and pure and beautiful and respected.
—*Philippians 4:8* NCV

Do you have a favorite artist? What about a favorite classical piece? What flowers thrill your senses? When was the last time you walked through the woods? Have you handpicked a bouquet lately? Or attended a play, ballet, or read a classic? Have you in recent months walked on a beach, skipped rocks on a lake, or photographed a child or a pet?

Sometimes unplugging from our routines and losing ourselves in life's art is the most healing thing we can do for our stretched-out emotions. That's why therapists use handcrafts in recovery programs, doctors recommend vacations, and folks escape to tents, cabins, mountains, boats, and camps with sketchpads, Bibles, cameras, and journals tucked into their backpacks. We seem to instinctively understand that we need art expressions.

We just know if we sit on a pier with a fishing line in the water we might snag a little sanity. Or if we sleep under the stars, we'll air out our musty minds. Or if we float across a rhythmic bay, we'll step back on land calmer and better prepared to handle the tidal waves of obligations on our desks. I personally love to get lost in a museum for a morning and then reflect on what I saw with a friend over blueberry muffins and hot tea.

—PATSY CLAIRMONT (*I Second That Emotion*)

WHO ARE YOU—REALLY?

Your hands have made me and fashioned me.
—Job 10:8

Do you know who you really are? Do you really?

The more I've soaked myself in the truth of God's Word, the more I believe I know who I really am. God has the kindest and most amazingly brilliant methods of affirming who we are to him.

Well, just in case you aren't completely sure who you really are, consider this wonderful list of verses as a daily reminder of what God thinks when he thinks of you—which is, by the way, constantly. Let them lift you up and open your heart to see your true identity.

1. I am God's daughter. (John 1:12)
2. I'm a friend of Christ. (John 15:15)
3. I'm God's coworker. (1 Corinthians 3:9)
4. I'm God's workmanship. (Ephesians 2:10)
5. I can't be separated from the love of God. (Romans 8:35–39)
6. I am free. (John 8:31–32)
7. I am forgiven. (Romans 8:1–2)
8. I can do all things through Christ. (Philippians 4:13)
9. I have been blessed with every spiritual blessing. (Ephesians 1:3)
10. I have Christ's mind. (Philippians 2:5–7)

—SANDI PATTY (*Falling Forward*)

DISCOVERING YOUR PASSION

Jesus said, "Love the Lord God with all your passion and prayer and intelligence and energy."
—Mark 12:30 MSG

I have a friend who says, "The deepest question of our lives is not 'If you died tonight, do you know where you would spend eternity?' That's a good question, and one that must be settled, but the deeper question is 'If you wake up tomorrow, do you know how you will spend the rest of your life?'" A lot of us aren't afraid of dying. We're afraid of living. We don't know what we are living for. We know that Jesus will be there for us when we die, if we have a relationship with him, but we don't understand what kind of life he is calling us to today.

There is something that God is calling you to do. You know it. You've always known it. You may not know exactly what it is, or what shape it will ultimately take, but it is unique to you and it is why you were put here on this earth. I don't think this passion is just handed to us like a gift. I think it is revealed in us over time like an excavation. Everything extra gets chiseled away.

Uncovering God's purpose for your life and following it will lead you to the greatest satisfaction there is.

—NICOLE JOHNSON (*Fresh-Brewed Life*)

BE QUIET AND LISTEN

Be still, and know that I am God; I will be exalted among the nations, I will be exalted in the earth.

—Psalm 46:10 NIV

Taking time to listen to God and to discern what he's calling us to do is a discipline we all can embrace. Sometimes in our great need to be heard we forget that listening allows God to be heard. I believe I've learned more in the silence, listening to him, than I've ever learned as I prayed and begged him for answers. At times I wasn't even asking the right questions, but when I quieted my mind and listened, really listened, I heard what I needed to hear.

Contemplative listening is a rich experience for those willing to make time to be still in God's presence. Set aside ten minutes and just be quiet. Turn off the music, the phone, and the television. Be quiet and invite God to speak to you in your spirit. As you grow comfortable with the silence and learn to hear God's voice, I think you'll want to set aside longer periods of time in which you deliberately listen for his counsel.

When I actually get quiet and listen, I find that God usually has something to tell me about myself. Sometimes when I think I have things all figured out, he reminds me that his ways are not my ways and his thoughts are far better than my best ideas.

—JAN SILVIOUS (*Smart Girls Think Twice*)

WHEN THINGS DON'T MAKE SENSE

Jesus said to him, "Have you believed because you have seen me?
Blessed are those who have not seen and yet have come to believe."
—John 20:29 NRSV

If you are like me, you want life to be more black and white than gray. I like things to make sense to me. I want to be able to understand what God is doing, but that's not always the case. Sometimes the plans we have made, the hopes and dreams we carry, fall apart at our feet. Are you in that place now? Do you wonder if God has abandoned you, or if you have missed God somewhere along the path?

It is the loneliest place on earth as a believer to feel as if God has left you or to live with the taunting voice that says you have blown it and missed God's best for your life. I pray that each of us will receive a clearer picture of what it means to walk by faith, no matter what sight tells us. Perhaps that is the whole point of faith: that we follow God faithfully when nothing makes sense anymore.

I've faced some of those dark days when things didn't make sense. Surprisingly, they made me take a much deeper look at faith than I had ever done. Is that where you find yourself? Cling to your faith—don't give up! God is faithful!

—SHEILA WALSH (*Extraordinary Faith*)

TEMPLE WORSHIP

> *You should know that your body is a temple for the Holy Spirit*
> *who is in you. You have received the Holy Spirit from God. So*
> *you do not belong to yourselves, because you were bought by*
> *God for a price. So honor God with your bodies.*
>
> —*1 Corinthians 6:19–20* NCV

We must take care of ourselves, ladies—and that includes taking care of your body. If not for yourself, then do it for your family. If not for your family, then do it for the Lord. You may have heard "your body is a temple for the Holy Spirit" a million times, but sometimes we get so familiar with verses that we no longer pay attention to what they are saying. That is why I like to look up passages in many different translations. I used the New Century Version on this one. Doesn't it just spell it out for us? It is an act of worship to take care of God's temple.

We really don't have a choice about whether we have time to go to the doctor or the money to take vitamins, or whether we should go to bed at a decent hour. If it is good for our bodies, we should do it. I think we've all heard tragic stories of women who were so busy taking care of everyone else, they failed to take care of themselves until it was too late. Let's make sure we don't make the same mistake in the name of laying down our lives for others.

Jesus made the ultimate sacrifice of laying down his body to redeem ours. What a great way to say thank you by taking care of the gift he gave us.

—LISA WHELCHEL (*Taking Care of the Me in Mommy*)

159

EXPECTATIONS

"My thoughts are not your thoughts, nor are your ways My ways," says the LORD.
—Isaiah 55:8

We all have expectations of God. For one thing, most of us think it makes sense to be rewarded for good behavior. We expect God thinks that too. When we're good, doing all the "right things," we expect God to notice and protect us as well as reward us. When he does not always do that, we may be tempted to grumble, but we won't grumble loudly or noticeably because that would not be the right thing to do. We wait, though. We wait for our reward.

I've needed to abandon my expectations of God. I know all that great scripture about God's ways not being my ways, but it's hard for me to swallow the fact that he does not always seem fair. (I know. I'll never get a reward for talk like that.)

Now I too know what I didn't know then. By abandoning my expectation of God and realizing I can't coerce his mystery into a predictable formula based upon the merit system, I free up more space in my mind for his ways. And because his ways are not my ways, I have to choose to let him be God and rest in his invitation to trust him. I don't always do that well, but I know it is the only path to peace.

—MARILYN MEBERG (*Love Me Never Leave Me*)

RENEWED DAY BY DAY

Outwardly we are wasting away, yet inwardly we are being renewed day by day.

—2 Corinthians 4:16 NIV

Scripture teaches us to number our days and to apply our hearts unto wisdom. It also says even though we're "wasting away" on the outside, we are being renewed inwardly day by day. Those two verses say a lot about the aging process. It's a lifelong journey that has neither a clear beginning nor clear ending. But there are signs along the way that one's body is changing. We see our hair turning gray. Wrinkles show up in our faces as they become seasoned and worn with time. We do things more slowly and deliberately. These are the signs of the outside wasting away.

But it's the inside that's being renewed daily. And *that's* what we want to concentrate on. This is the secret of happy aging. Although obvious signs of physical changes are known to all of us, life's journey takes us beyond the obvious. It reaches inside and teaches us lessons we can only learn with our mind, spirit, and heart. The outward appearance becomes secondary to a far more endearing beauty and strength. The physical appearance of youth may be gone, but the capacity to love, experience, enjoy, share, and create grow even stronger. Therefore, these are the areas we must learn to stop and ponder.

—LUCI SWINDOLL (*Life! Celebrate It*)

AN ART TOUR

He has made everything beautiful in its time.
—Ecclesiastes 3:11

Have you ever stepped inside a painting? In your imagination, I mean. It's wonderful to find a painting you love and then to study it. Sit, observe it, and then ask yourself what you like about it: the subject matter, the color palette, the artist's style? Then mentally enter the picture and try to imagine what the artist was thinking, what time of day you think the picture was painted, where the light source originates, what the people in it are doing, how you think they feel (tired, bored, joyful, in love). And before you leave the museum, visit the gift store and buy postcard-size pictures of your favorite paintings to refer to later.

Then, when you get home from your art tour, expand your experience by researching the artists you most appreciated. Just Google the artist's name and learn who inspired him or her and what struggles the artist faced. You might want to check online for Mary Cassatt, Pierre-Auguste Renoir, George Seurat, or Thomas Eakins. Or you may prefer Ansel Adams's black-and-white photography or the sculptures of Michelangelo or Bernini, and then there always are those who become ardent Pablo Picasso fans. Find your interests and explore them. Not only will you broaden your mind but also just think how impressed your friends will be.

—PATSY CLAIRMONT (*I Second That Emotion*)

GOD-WIRED FOR FELLOWSHIP

Love the family of believers.
—1 Peter 2:17 NRSV

Women need women friends, even if they have a great marriage. The rub can happen when we, for a variety of reasons—pride, shame, mental exhaustion, independent personality—tend to think, *All I need is God and no one else.* In essence we hibernate, acting like monks without a monastery.

But cloistering ourselves away from others isn't the way of true spiritual healing. God is there to fill our God-voids for sure, but he created human beings to fill our need for human connection. In Eden, God gave Adam a human helpmate right after declaring, "It is not good that man should be alone." God did not create us to thrive without each other, so never assume that you are somehow weak if you feel you cannot make it alone, just you and God. You weren't created to do life by yourself. Most of us tend to get a little crazy when we are alone for too long: introspective or edgy or sad. Our physical bodies are wired to push us toward the cure—being with supportive people.

I encourage you to proactively seek out women who like to do (or talk about) the same things you enjoy. Do it on a regular basis until your comfort level with them increases.

—SANDI PATTY (*Falling Forward*)

EMBRACE YOUR LIFE

Celebrate God all day, every day. I mean, revel in him!
—*Philippians 4:4* MSG

Do you realize that the quality of each day is determined by one thing—your attitude toward it? Don't miss the life that is right in front of you. If you don't think enough meaning exists in your life, create it. Don't just run errands; use the opportunity to meditate. Pray for the businesses in your community you have to visit. Your bank and your dry cleaners both could use your prayers. You are on God's agenda now. He has given you meaning and purpose; splash in it. Don't just eat a quick bite; "dine instead." Even if it's peanut butter and jelly by yourself. Take it outside, savor the taste, enjoy the moment, breathe in the beauty. Look for the extraordinary in the ordinary.

In your drive to work or to take care of chores, think of all the things you pass, yet don't notice every day. Someone crying in the car next to you, the sunrise, a cornfield bringing forth first-fruits, the new shrubs in the neighbor's yard. Opportunities to minister, chances to have your breath taken away by beauty, a great idea for a new business.

Celebrate the significance and wonder of life. Don't wait until it hits you over the head. It's already there; waiting for you to embrace it.

—NICOLE JOHNSON (*Fresh-Brewed Life*)

KNOWING GOD

The people who know their God shall be strong, and carry out great exploits.
—Daniel 11:32

When you know God—really know his character based on his Word, his past actions, and his promised intentions toward his people—you will be a strong, smart, settled woman of God.

In fact, what you know and believe about God is the foundation for every decision you'll make. You may have a good head on your shoulders and certainly you draw on your intelligence and common sense for guidance. But if you're truly smart, you'll recognize that all wisdom originates with and is given by God.

For all of our experience, logic, theories, and intelligence, there remains so very much we don't know and can't know as limited, finite human beings. Just about the time we figure out one situation, we're confronted with fresh questions from another direction. The best we can do when the answers aren't clear is to go with what we do know and rest in the fact that what we don't know is somehow wrapped up in the mystery of the God we trust. We can rely on him to show us ways we could never devise ourselves and answers we could never conceive on our own.

Thank God, we know who he is and who we are not.

—JAN SILVIOUS (*Smart Girls Think Twice*)

START WHERE YOU ARE

The Lord said, "If you have faith as a mustard seed, you can say to this mulberry tree, 'Be pulled up by the roots and be planted in the sea,' and it would obey you."
—Luke 17:6

Perhaps as you look at your own life, you feel as if you have no faith at all. I think of the words of Mary Graham, president of Women of Faith, that faith is not about our mustering up huge reserves of mountain-moving power but about leaning on Christ, trusting our Father, and taking one more step. We start with what we have. We bring the tiniest seed of faith that God has placed in our spirits, and God honors that faith. If we spend our time looking at the mountain, we will be overwhelmed, so we nurture the seed that God has planted in us.

I received a letter from a woman who wanted to talk to her neighbor about Jesus but felt overwhelmed at the thought of leading another to faith. I asked her, "What seems doable to you?"

"I could invite her in for coffee," she suggested.

"That's a great beginning," I said.

After that she wrote and told me that she believed she could invite her neighbor to a concert at her church. Then when the neighbor responded warmly to that, she invited her to a Sunday service. A few weeks later, the neighbor gave her life to Christ.

My point is, start where you are and leave the rest up to God. Just take the first step.

—SHEILA WALSH (*Extraordinary Faith*)

NOT JUST A LAST RESORT

Don't fret or worry. Instead of worrying, pray. Let petitions and praises shape your worries into prayers, letting God know your concerns.

—Philippians 4:6 MSG

I felt like a pretty good parent when I was bigger than my kids. I felt much safer when I believed (rightly or wrongly) that I had more control over their lives. But the older they get, the harder it is for me to convince myself that I can truly "direct" their lives.

Part of parenting teenagers is letting them grow up and make decisions—even if those choices are wrong. It's terrifying knowing there is no guarantee that my children will choose to follow Jesus. So I've learned to redirect my parenting passion. Now, when I'm tempted to lecture my children, I try to pray for them instead.

Prayer is a powerful tool that allows us to communicate with the living God. It is not something to be taken lightly or used occasionally. After all, I can only control so much from the outside in. Our heavenly Father does *his* work from the inside out. It's heartening to see God work in my kids' lives, and I'm so thankful I can help by praying for them.

Is prayer an integral part of your life, or is it a hit-or-miss habit? Make no mistake: the quality of your spiritual life will have a direct impact on those you love. Prayer changes things and people, so pray constantly. God is listening, and God wants to hear from you!

—LISA WHELCHEL (*Speaking Mom-ese*)

OUR MYSTERIOUS GOD

Trust the Lord with all your heart, and don't depend on your own understanding.

—Proverbs 3:5 NCV

I've never liked secrets unless I'm in on them. God has not let me in on some things he knows, and—in love—means to accomplish for my good. There is an odd sort of comfort to that in spite of my wanting to know his secrets that pertain to me. I'm invited to rest in his mystery and in his love.

So then, how am I to live in harmony and peace with a God who holds secrets and whose mystery I'll never fully understand? I must first realize this truth. I'm not meant to understand it all. If I did, trust would not be necessary. Understanding would be all I need, but trust is what God needs.

Trust comes to me when I remember what God says about his love for me. Trust also comes as I recognize that his love provides a promise about my circumstances that don't always change when I want them to. His purpose for me is that I love and trust him in all things. His purpose for me is that I stay in constant touch with him through prayer, no matter what I'm asking for. His invitation is always, "Come unto me, . . . and I will give you rest" (Matthew 11:28 KJV).

—MARILYN MEBERG (*Love Me Never Leave Me*)

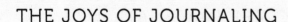

THE JOYS OF JOURNALING

Reflect on what I am saying, for the Lord will give you insight into all this.

—2 Timothy 2:7 NIV

I counted my journals today. There are fifty-four. Some are travel journals from different trips and excursions through the years, but most are daily journals in which I've recorded activities, thoughts, ponderings, and concerns. By writing them, I've wanted to leave a trace that I've crossed life's threshold and hopefully made a difference in someone else's life.

There are numerous times I've reread those journals and thought about the moment this or that was written. I've pondered stories of my past. I've cried over pictures of those I loved who are no longer with me here on earth. I've laughed over antics by which my friends made me happy. I've read scriptures that meant something very meaningful to me at a particular time. I've remembered how I felt in an embarrassing moment or time of deep sadness. I've spent *hours* reflecting in those pages—tracing the route that a particular memory first took through my senses—and I'm richer for it.

I could talk all day about the benefits of keeping a journal, but that may not work for you. Primarily, I'm suggesting you think back, remember, be still and thoughtful about where you've come from, what you've come through, and why it's important.

—LUCI SWINDOLL (*Life! Celebrate It*)

RELEASING THE IMAGINATION

*So God created man in His own image; in the image of God He
created him; male and female He created them ... Then God
saw everything that He had made, and indeed it was very good.*
—Genesis 1:27, 31

What turns the crank on your imagination? Perhaps stimulating
conversations do. I've found intentional chat sessions helpful to
stretch my mind in problem solving. That's a healing form of art, for
sure. When someone helps me to see beyond my stuck place, it
paints my world with perspective. Maybe you're a songwriter. What
a holy exercise. And oh, how it pleases the Lord when we sing to
him. Perhaps you prefer to twirl your imagination wheel by teaching.
We all applaud those who impart life-giving information with zeal.

Here's an idea: sign up for a class just outside your comfort
zone. Maybe a cooking class, book club, stained-glass demonstra-
tion, writing seminar, or pottery or dulcimer lesson. Some of these
only require an evening but could enhance and expand your creative repertoire and surprise you with your untapped potential.

Artistic endeavors can be therapeutic to our uptight bundle of
emotions and crucial for our mental health. If you're already over-
obligated, please don't join a class. Instead, take a nap. Really. Then,
when you are well rested, figure out what you can do to thin your
uptight must-do list to make sane space for art. It will make you
more ingenious, fun, textured, and more satisfied with your trek here
on this wondrous, spinning kaleidoscope called God's green earth.

—PATSY CLAIRMONT (*I Second That Emotion*)

FELLOW SOJOURNERS

*Therefore comfort each other and edify one another, just as
you also are doing.*

—*1 Thessalonians 5:11*

After a crisis, or the beginning of recovery or a major transition,
it is especially vital to begin creating a network of mutually supportive sojourners. Even Jesus, in his darkest moments in
Gethsemane's garden, confessed the need to have his friends
nearby. If God's Son needed friends during his hour of crisis, we
would be silly to say that we don't.

What holds us back from reaching out and connecting? Fear
of rejection, perhaps. Or the thought that our dilemma or grief is
so unique that there will be no one out there who will really
understand or care. We know others are busy with full lives and
assume they do not have time for us.

But what I've discovered is that, in general, quite the opposite is true. Most people are "God-wired" deep within to want to
help others who are in pain in any way they can, especially people
who have traversed a path similar to yours. Follow up on any
leads you come across until you find someone whose thirst for
healing has been quenched and is now delighted to hold your
hand and show you where she found the living water.

—SANDI PATTY (*Falling Forward*)

June 20

TRUST MUST BE GIVEN

Those who are attentive to a matter will prosper, and happy are those who trust in the LORD.
—Proverbs 16:20 NRSV

Trust is like faith. You cannot see it; you just do it. It must be given. Here are some other words from the thesaurus for *trust*: confidence, belief, credence. To trust is to "depend on, rely on, bank on, build on, count on." You cannot trust without moving out of your head. You cannot depend on someone or build on something with mere knowledge. The soul must be part of the equation. The words call us to action, not inspection. The word *on* is significant as well. You can't merely rely. You can't depend by yourself. You can't build in air. There is a requirement of someone or something else that moves us out of ourselves.

We can know, yet not do. We can gather facts, and give nothing in return. We can observe all day long without ever caring. But we do not trust if we don't care. We do not give to something if we don't trust it. And if we say we trust the truth, and yet do nothing with it, it reveals we have not trusted it at all. Trust requires something of us. Trust holds the feet of knowledge to the fire of action.

—NICOLE JOHNSON (*Fresh-Brewed Life*)

DEEP ASPIRATIONS

Jesus replied, "The seed cast on good earth is the person who hears and takes in the News, and then produces a harvest beyond his wildest dreams."
—*Matthew 13:23* MSG

Let's talk for a moment about holding onto your dreams. The word *dream* can be defined as a "wild fancy or hope." It can also be defined as a "reverie, a trance, or a state of abstraction." The Webster definition I am using is that a dream is "a deep aspiration." I'm also using the word in relation to God's plans for our lives; God has deep aspirations for us, which I often refer to as his dreams for us. God knows what he's doing when he places his desire in our hearts to do what he has ordained for us from the beginning of time.

People's experience with personal dreams is as varied as the people themselves. No one's dream history is the same as another's, and yet we all know what it is to have dream yearnings. I think the very existence of those yearnings ties into God's personal dreams for our lives. He placed within us an awareness of certain preferences and in the awareness of those preferences we can find our dreams and motivations. In other words, he places the dreams, and we live them out. When we do, there is internal peace.

—MARILYN MEBERG (*Love Me Never Leave Me*)

THE PARADOXES OF FAITH

Jesus said, "If you try to hang on to your life, you will lose it. But if you give up your life for my sake and for the sake of the Good News, you will save it."

—Mark 8:35 NLT

It was a beautiful Indian summer day, and I was sitting in the back of a church I had never attended before. As I listened to the old traditional hymns washing over me, I felt I was healing from my dark night of depression. The pastor said, "Some of you in here feel as if you are dead inside. Christ is here in all his resurrection power. If you will simply call on him, he will reach into that place and pull you out."

Quickly, I ran up the aisle and lay flat on my face in front of the altar. It was the first time I had gone to God empty-handed. Before I'd always gone with a new book or a new record or a new something I'd done to make God love me. I felt like I came as a filthy, broken, bedraggled orphan. "There's not a thing in the world I can do to make you love me," I said to God, "but I also realize there's not a thing in the world I can do to stop you from loving me." I felt such peace.

Christ reached down that day and gathered me to his heart. It's one of those great paradoxes of faith—you give up control and yet you feel so free.

—SHEILA WALSH (*Life Is Tough But God Is Faithful*)

LEARNING TO TRUST

Whoever trusts in the LORD shall be safe.
—*Proverbs 29:25*

As Christians, we are the beloved of God. We can stake our claim on that promised land. We can choose to trust it and allow it to change us, or we can mistrust it. Not trusting it doesn't make it any less true. It simply makes it untrue for us. It keeps us locked out of the freedom of experiencing God's embrace. It's like being invited to a party and mistrusting the invitation. The party is going on with or without us. Should we choose not to attend, we are the ones who lose.

Understanding who we are in Christ intellectually will not change us unless we *trust* that identity in the core of our being. We are completely and totally loved and embraced in the arms of God. Allowing that relationship to transform us is the key.

Does trusting God come easily to you? Or do you struggle? Giving yourself in relationship to God affords you the opportunity to enter into a relationship with a spiritual foundation to build on and with someone who will never fail you. Once you've learned to trust him, you can better trust others.

—NICOLE JOHNSON (*Fresh-Brewed Life*)

THERE IS ALWAYS A REASON

As Jesus was walking along, he saw a man who had been blind from birth. "Rabbi," his disciples asked him, "why was this man born blind? Was it because of his own sins or his parents' sins?" "It was not because of his sins or his parents' sins," Jesus answered. "This happened so the power of God could be seen in him."

—John 9:1–3 NLT

Not all difficulties result from bad choices. In the passage above, Jesus spoke clearly on this subject when the disciples mistakenly made a broad assumption about a man born blind. Picture yourself standing among the disciples, listening and concentrating in this teachable moment. Jesus' words were simple and straightforward. The man's condition was not a consequence of someone's choice; he was just blind. But there was a reason.

There always is a reason for whatever challenge or opportunity we face, although we may not know it on this earth. When we face circumstances beyond our control, we are given the option to respond with wisdom or to react with folly. What we choose will determine the course of our lives.

Of course, not all of our choices will turn out as we hope. That's life. Sometimes there simply is no perfect choice. The best we can do is Stop, Look, Listen, and Look Again at the possible consequences of each option—then make the wisest choice we can, leaving the rest in God's capable hands. There is great relief in knowing that God sees and God cares and, ultimately, God is in control.

—JAN SILVIOUS (*Smart Girls Think Twice*)

IT WILL RISE AGAIN!

I know, LORD, that our lives are not our own. We are not able to plan our own course.

—*Jeremiah 10:23* NLT

What happens when we're not obedient to God's original dream for our lives? What happens when we choose a direction other than the one that fulfills God's dream—when we abandon the dream and try to comfort ourselves in pursuit of something else? Does that mean God also abandons his dream for us?

One of my favorite things about God is that he is stronger than I am, smarter than I am, and cares more about everything and everyone than I do. That means nothing, including my misguided determination to follow my own plans or my willful disobedience to do his will, is going to derail God's plan.

It *will* rise again because God will always prevail.

There again is the mystery of God: He does allow us to do stupid things, but just as the good shepherd goes after one lost sheep, God goes after us. He has a dream for our lives; that dream will prevail because he does.

If you're not following God's plan for your life, change course! If you've abandoned your dream, reclaim it. God is in the business of turning ashes into beauty.

—MARILYN MEBERG (*Love Me Never Leave Me*)

COMPASSION POURED OUT

*If there is any consolation in Christ, if any comfort of love, if any
fellowship of the Spirit, if any affection and mercy, fulfill my joy
by being like-minded, having the same love, being of one accord,
of one mind.*

—Philippians 2:1–2

The desperate plight of two young prostitutes I'd seen on a TV show
so touched my heart that I decided to talk about them during a concert. Midway through, however, I was so overcome with emotion
that I got down on my knees, right there and began to pray.

When I looked up, the whole front of the church was filled with
people who had come forward to kneel or fall flat on their faces. I
could hear people asking God to forgive them for their apathy and
unconcern. I ended the evening with a song and prayer, but that
didn't end the evening at all. God was there, speaking to people.

A Vietnam veteran was bitter and angry because he'd come
home and found people who didn't seem to care. But he found
Jesus that night and was able to forgive.

A little eight-year-old girl said to me, "I love the Lord. My mom's
not a Christian; will you pray with me?" So I joined hands with her
and her little friend, and the three of us prayed for her mother.

Young couples having trouble with their marriages came forward to talk. One person after another reached out to communicate
with God—and to be honest and real, totally open to him. Now
that's a concert!

—SHEILA WALSH (*Life Is Tough But God Is Faithful*)

ANYONE FOR DESSERT?

*You show me the path of life. In your presence there is fullness
of joy; in your right hand are pleasures forevermore.*
—Psalm 16:11 NRSV

Pleasure has many forms: beauty, laughter, solace, companionship, solitude, love. Even giftedness. It can be playful, sensual, enriching, or frivolous. Even worshipful. Sometimes when I'm praying, I thank the Lord for the pleasure of his company. I love knowing he is with me, that he cares about me and he makes my heart feel grateful, content, and full. All of those thoughts bring me pleasure, and I want him to know that from my heart. I want to tell him.

What is your most pleasant feeling? Mine is relief. I love that feeling more than any other. When I'm hungry, eating brings relief. When I'm tired, sleep gives relief. When I'm lonely, companionship gives relief. When I'm standing in a long line wearing bad shoes, even an inadequate place to sit feels wonderful. Anything uncomfortable that finds relief gives the feeling of pleasure. And nothing on this earth is more wonderful than something that relieves my soul. This is what I'm talking about. Someone has said, "Work is the meat of life; pleasure is the dessert." Pleasure is a wonderful, delightful, enjoyable feeling, and I believe we should stop for it in life. It makes our time on this earth sweeter and easier to bear.

—LUCI SWINDOLL (*Life! Celebrate It*)

TRUST'S SILVER LINING

Those who trust in the LORD are like Mount Zion, which
cannot be shaken but endures forever.
—Psalm 125:1 NIV

Everyone has a story of how trust was broken and why he or she can't trust. Not trusting comes naturally. Actually trusting came first, and then sadly we learned to distrust. Once we distrust, it is hard to go back to trusting again. But the path of enriching our relationships is a way of trust.

But what about people who aren't trustworthy? Are we supposed to trust even when we might get hurt? What if someone has let us down? How can we trust that person, and should we? When we distrust we hurt ourselves. If we trust someone and that person lets us down, were we wrong for trusting? Or was that person wrong for letting us down? Just because we trusted someone doesn't make us foolish. If anything, we can be proud of the fact that we trusted.

It's much like that with love. When we love someone who doesn't love us, are we fools? Or are we better people for having loved, even if that love wasn't returned? When we learn to trust others, we are changed in the process. We trust because of what it does for us, not because of what it does for the other person.

—NICOLE JOHNSON (*Fresh-Brewed Life*)

PARTNERING WITH GOD

*To him who by the power at work within us is able to
accomplish abundantly far more than all we can ask or
imagine, to him be glory in the church and in Christ Jesus to all
generations, forever and ever.*

—Ephesians 3:20–21 NRSV

One of the most gracious ways God receives our love is to make us partners with him in doing those things that make the world a better place. We already know God could get things done without us, but he wants us to be a part of everything he does. God places dreams and plans within us as motivators to accomplish his already conceived dream plan. So we do together what he could do alone.

When Jesus established his earthly ministry, he chose twelve disciples to partner with him. They not only had a relationship with Jesus, they ultimately spread the news that he was the Son of God. When they didn't understand his miracles, Jesus explained them. When they didn't get the meaning of his parables, Jesus taught them. He also taught them how to love and how to live in the divine reciprocity of give-and-take. All that helped them later to establish the Christian church after the resurrection of Jesus and his return to heaven.

God's concept of partnering is a tremendous relief to us because we realize it is not we who are fully responsible for the results of our efforts to serve. Our internal engine is powered by him—not just by ourselves. We serve and work together.

—MARILYN MEBERG (*Love Me Never Leave Me*)

181

BAPTIZED IN LOVE

The Lord is near to those who have a broken heart, and saves such as have a contrite spirit.

—Psalm 34:18

I was walking through the mall the other evening, flipping through the pages of a new book I had just purchased. I became so interested I almost walked into the tiny wheelchair of a little girl who couldn't have been more than four years old. My heart ached as I looked down at that little child, and I thought, *Lord, how I wish I had the faith of a mustard seed to look into the eyes of this little girl and say, "In the Name of Jesus Christ of Nazareth, rise up and walk!"*

I long to see God's power and glory strewn across people's lives rather than the wreckage and chaos that is so often there. I do believe with all my heart that a new Christian leadership has emerged during the last decade. I believe they are people who have been baptized in love, people who have had their hearts broken.

You can tell when you're in the company of those who have been through deep water. They have been through the very valley of the shadow of death, but they have walked every step of the way holding on to Jesus' hand. And they have emerged on the other side with a brighter light, a more tender heart, and a loving, outstretched hand for others.

—SHEILA WALSH (*Life Is Tough But God Is Faithful*)

POST IT!

Thy word have I hid in mine heart, that I might not sin against thee.

—Psalm 119:11 KJV

In Deuteronomy the Lord instructed the Israelites regarding how they were to respond to God's counsel: "And these words which I command you today shall be in your heart; you shall teach them diligently to your children, and shall talk of them when you sit in your house, when you walk by the way, when you lie down, and when you rise up. You shall bind them as a sign on your hand, and they shall be as frontlets between your eyes. You shall write them on the doorposts of your house and on your gates" (Deuteronomy 6:6–9).

If I condensed those verses down for someone, I would suggest that person place God's Word like memos, first inside, then outside of herself. Memorize it. Study it. Sing it. Rehearse it. Teach it. It will do her well, and it will secure her people. (You got people? I got people, people I want to know his Word.)

Psalm 119 is a good starting place for Post-Its. Select your favorite verses and write them in your journal, pen them in calligraphy and frame them for your walls, tape them to your mirror, magnetize them to your fridge, and most importantly walk in the light they will add to your path.

—PATSY CLAIRMONT (*I Second That Emotion*)

NO SMALL TEST

The LORD is the true God, he is the living God, and an everlasting king.

—Jeremiah 10:10 KJV

I always feel like I want to stand up and cheer when I read Matthew 16, where Jesus asks the disciples, "Who do you say I am?" Simon Peter, apparently with hardly a thought, steps right up and answers boldly, "You are the Christ, the Son of the living God" (verses 15–16).

Peter got this one right—and it was no small test. Upon this answer, Jesus told Peter two amazing things. First, this truth had been revealed to Peter directly from God himself—it wasn't just earthly wisdom, it was truth that came straight from the Holy Spirit. Second, Jesus said that based on this confession, Peter would be the rock upon which he would build his church. Peter's answer to the question revealed Christ's true identity, and believers ever since have been making the same confession of faith.

The truth of Christ's identity and the truth of who God really is are the truths that outweigh everything else. When you are struggling to revive your life after a tough time, you can fall forward into the truth of who God is. Who *we are* becomes less important in the face of *who God is*.

—SANDI PATTY (*Falling Forward*)

FANNING THE FLAME OF HOPE

The LORD is good to those who hope in him, to those who seek him.

—*Lamentations 3:25 NCV*

Hope is not a positive mental attitude. I have hope but I'm not always positive. There is no way to conquer despair with happy thoughts. Hope has real strength, but not strength of its own. The power of hope comes from the truth it hopes in; no matter what the outcome, I can have life, because the loving, merciful God of the universe is good and he is looking after me. So if I fan the flame of hope every day, I win.

Now I can smile, a lot. Living with real hope is like discovering a savings account that was started for me before I was born. It frees me to laugh more and make jokes about things—even painful circumstances. Hope also allows me to cry my eyes out when I need to.

No one who fights with her hope in the Lord ever loses the last round. No matter what you may be facing, today is only one chapter, not the complete book of your life. No adverse circumstance can claim your spirit.

Rest assured, when the battle that is raging is over, your life will still be with the one in whom you've put your hope. Can you imagine his hand in yours, raising it in victory?

—NICOLE JOHNSON (*Stepping into the Ring*)

CREATED FOR A SPECIFIC JOB

*Now all of you together are Christ's body, and each one of you
is a separate and necessary part of it.*

—1 Corinthians 12:27 NLT

The first time I met author and speaker Beth Moore, I was ecstatic. My husband and the kids got sick of hearing me talk about it. To me, meeting Beth was more exciting than going to a presidential inauguration or shooting hoops with George Clooney. She looked younger, prettier, and even tinier than she does on her videos. (If I didn't love her so much I would hate her.) We enjoyed a delightful conversation, a delicious meal, and split a piece of sugar-free cheesecake.

It was an absolutely fabulous evening, but I must confess that over the next couple of days, I struggled with wishing I could be more like Beth Moore. I told God, *I want to be that deep into Bible study. Better yet, I want to be that deep, period.* Next to the obvious intensity of her relationship with God, I felt downright shallow.

But then God gently chastised me by reminding me that we are all unique parts of the body of Christ. Sometimes we need a stronger, more intense touch from God—like iron sharpening iron—and sometimes we need a softer touch from him—the kind that gently strokes our weary cheek and wipes away our tears.

Friend, I hope you never wish to be me. The world doesn't need another Lisa Whelchel. God created you for a specific job at a specific time that nobody else can fill—not even Beth Moore.

—LISA WHELCHEL (*Speaking Mom-ese*)

NEVER MEANS NEVER

Be strong and of good courage, do not fear nor be afraid of them; for the Lord your God, He is the One who goes with you. He will never leave you nor forsake you.

—*Deuteronomy 31:6*

When we find ourselves in the greatest places of testing, the Lord tells us over and over and over and over and over: "I will be there!" When I face new trials, I look back at God's track record in my life, and God's faithfulness increases my faith. When he says, "I will never leave you, *never* means never!"

As you look at your life today, my prayer is that you will take some time and write out for yourself what God's track record is with you. Consider:

+ When did you come to faith, or have you yet?
+ What do you trust about God today that you may not have trusted him for some time ago?
+ Can you look back and see God's hand at work now in situations where you could not see it before?
+ Do you love God today more than you did a year ago?
+ Do you believe he loves you?

I believe that God's love for us is overwhelming and his faithfulness unending. Whatever you are facing right now, be it the worst of times or the best, remember you are loved by a God who spared nothing of himself to show his faithfulness.

—SHEILA WALSH (*Extraordinary Faith*)

OUR "IN THE BEGINNING" RELATIVES

I bow my knees before the Father, from whom every family in heaven and on earth takes its name.

—Ephesians 3:14–15 NRSV

The Bible is the best family album going. It's all about our family tree, our "in-the-beginning" relatives. For example, I know for sure I'm related to Moses. He started off his life as a basket case, for heaven's sake; of course we're kin!

But quite honestly I've been a Jonah as well. Like him I ran away and got in over my head. And I've certainly known a number of folks who would have relished the idea of throwing me overboard.

The Word is part of our heritage so that we might see that since Eden we've been in need of a Savior. God gives us his family, which deepens our connection with each other. Without fail when I study the Scriptures I find snapshots of myself in those who came before me. I have Eve tendencies and hide when I'm afraid, I have been a Naomi bitter with heartbreak, I have been an impetuous Peter with more words than sense . . . and I've been a Paul encountering Christ and experiencing a changed life.

Reading Scripture will help us to get a grip on our genealogy. Once we're adopted into God's family, we, like Ruth, can say, "Your people shall be my people" (Ruth 1:16).

—PATSY CLAIRMONT (*I Second That Emotion*)

THE SKY'S THE LIMIT

I praise you, for I am fearfully and wonderfully made.
Wonderful are your works; that I know very well.

—Psalm 139:14 NRSV

If you respond to the fact of God loving you as the reason you were born, the sky's the limit in how you conduct your life. God's love gives you purpose; it gives you a great depth of meaning. You then partner with him as you experience that meaning and how it is to be communicated.

Meaning for life comes when you realize God made you because he wanted to. First John 4:10 states, "It is not that we loved God, but that he loved us." God made the first move; you choose whether to make the next one.

I hope you see the profound love principle at work that prompted God to create you. Psalm 139 describes how carefully he watches over the processes that knit you together in your mother's womb. We are not mass produced. We are one-of-a-kind creations over whom God always has a loving and watchful eye. He calls us by name. He knows how many hairs are on our heads. He knows when we stand up and when we sit down. He is never indifferent to any hurt, challenge, or joy we experience in life. His ear is ever inclined toward our voice when we call out to him.

—MARILYN MEBERG (*Love Me and Never Leave Me*)

MY HEART IS NEVER OLD

Rejoice that your names are written in heaven.
—Luke 10:20 NIV

Everything has a shelf life. There will come a day when my life will end as I know it. Do I have a will or a living trust? Are the bills paid? Do I owe anybody money? Have I done the best I could? All these are little "housekeeping" duties. As sure as night will come, so will my death. Am I ready for that?

I know for a fact where I will go when I die, and I believe God's Word on that subject is absolutely true. Nevertheless, I do wonder about some things. Will anything about death hurt? Will I go right into the throne room with Jesus? Will I see people right away who have gone before? What age will I be when I get there?

I don't know any of those things for sure, and I'm curious about them. But I do know I'm going to heaven, and I'm ready.

In short, I'd like to live forever. And I will—not on this earth, of course, but in heaven. Until then, I want to be looking for new possibilities, trying new things, and enjoying new friends, ideas, and accomplishments. No matter how many years I live on this earth, my heart will never be old.

—LUCI SWINDOLL (*Life! Celebrate It*)

TAKING HOLD OF SALVATION

I will greatly rejoice in the LORD, my soul shall be joyful in my God; for he hath clothed me with the garments of salvation, he hath covered me with the robe of righteousness.
—Isaiah 61:10 KJV

For many years, I was controlled by the hidden places in my life. I thought I was suffering alone, but over the years I've learned that my story is not unique. Many people have secret places where they hide and lick their wounds. They choose to live a life of denial and doubt rather than be honest with themselves. Sometimes they are unaware of what they're hiding, or why.

For so many of us, it takes years to come face-to-face with the fears that lurk in our past. We bury them so deeply because we are convinced that if they were released they would overwhelm us. We don't allow ourselves to think about them even for a moment, but their long shadows cast a dark cloud over our minds nonetheless.

The Greek word for salvation means "to save, to heal, to make complete." That is what happens at the cross. The Father is committed to shining his light into the darkest corners where fear and sorrow lurk and bringing peace.

I was able to walk away from the past, reveal those hidden places. With God's help I was able to focus on what God was going to do with my future. I allowed his love to set me free. You can be free, too, my friend.

—SHEILA WALSH (*Life Is Tough But God Is Faithful*)

WHAT MATTERS

*Jesus Christ is the atoning sacrifice for our sins, and not only for
ours but also for the sins of the whole world.*

—1 John 2:2 NIV

When I'm having trouble accepting my own failures and foibles, I
am helped by focusing on some of the "I am" statements of Jesus
in the book of John. I find comfort in knowing that all my "I am"
statements ("I am a failure"; "I am unworthy"; "I am a loser"; "I
am tired") are insignificant. What matters is what Jesus says *he* is.

- ✦ He is the Bread of Life, and if I come to him, I will not be
  hungry (6:35).
- ✦ He's the Light of the World, and with him I'll never be in
  darkness (8:12).
- ✦ He is the Gate, and if I enter through him, I'll be saved (10:9).
- ✦ He is the Good Shepherd who laid down his life for me,
  one of his sheep (10:11).
- ✦ He is the Resurrection and the Life, and if I believe in
  him, I will never die (11:25).
- ✦ He is the Way and the Truth and the Life, and through
  him I will get to the Father (14:6).
- ✦ He is the Vine and I am a branch, and if I remain in him, I
  will bear much fruit (15:5).

Now I ask you, is that some amazing truth or what?

—SANDI PATTY (*Falling Forward*)

THE HEART OF A PRINCESS

*Jesus said, "Do not fear, little flock, for it is your Father's good
pleasure to give you the kingdom."*
—Luke 12:32

It wouldn't be so hard to have the heart of a princess if we lived
in a fairy-tale world. The birds would wake us in the morning,
we would have beautiful clothes laid out for us every day, a song
would always be on our lips, and our good fairy godmother would
be there to make certain our dreams always came true.

And in the real world it wouldn't be so hard to give up hope
instead of struggling day after day to keep our dreams alive,
because in this not-so-fairy-tale world, life is hard.

Just when it seems we must settle for one of the two extremes,
faith shows us another way. It illuminates a new place—an invisible kingdom that can only be seen with the eyes of the heart.
It's a place where our glimpses of the goodness of fairy tales can
fit into a different view of reality. And it's where the realities of
the so-called real world are framed in a way that lightens the
darkness and removes the cynicism.

In the invisible kingdom we'll discover that the unseen dreams
to come are bigger and more powerful than the small ones we've
held so tightly in the past. We'll get new dreams—full of the kind
of hope that is far stronger than despair.

—NICOLE JOHNSON (*Keeping a Princess Heart*)

NO OTHER GODS

"The most important [commandment]" answered Jesus, "is this . . . Love the Lord your God with all your heart and with all your soul and with all your mind and with all your strength."

—*Mark 12:29–30* NIV

God knows that when we begin to seek answers for our lives, there always will be some substitute god enticing us away from him with the promise of peace and prosperity. That's why he warns, "You must not have any other god but me" (Ex. 20:3 NLT). It breaks his heart when we look to other sources to fulfill his role in our lives. It brings him to anger when we choose to worship other people, other philosophies, or other providers when he is the One who started our hearts beating in our mothers' wombs before they even knew we were there.

Years ago I became involved in the study of reincarnation. But then I encountered the Scripture that says, "Each person is destined to die once and after that comes judgment" (Heb. 9:27 NLT). That verse brought truth to my deluded soul and set me back on the right course.

Have you, too, gone after other gods, maybe bought into one of the do-it-yourself philosophies? If so, this girl understands. The good news is that the God who is jealous for our affection and allegiance also is merciful and forgiving of our folly. He waits with open arms to take us back.

—JAN SILVIOUS (*Smart Girls Think Twice*)

THE BACK OF THE TAPESTRY

The Lord is my helper; I will not be afraid. Jesus Christ is the same yesterday and today and forever.

—Hebrews 13:6, 8 NIV

When the world asks if there is any hope, we can say, "Absolutely!" If you happen to be questioning this, I'd like to tell you about an illustration Corrie ten Boom used on many occasions. As she spoke, she would hold up the wrong side of a tapestry for her audience to see.

"Isn't this beautiful?" she would ask.

As the people looked at the back of the tapestry, all they could see were threads crossed at odd intervals, knotted in places, looking clumsy and disjointed. It was, to be blunt, ugly.

The audience would stare back at Corrie, not knowing how to respond to her question. Corrie would be silent for a few moments, and then she would say as if in a moment of great insight, "Oh! Yes, of course. You can't see the tapestry from my perspective." Then she would turn the piece of cloth around to show the front, and there would be a picture of a beautiful crown!

At times, life makes no sense. It seems disjointed, distorted, and ugly. But if we surrender our little view of life for God's much grander portrait, we will always be able to hold our eternal hope in Jesus Christ.

—SHEILA WALSH (*Life Is Tough But God Is Faithful*)

THE REASON YOU WERE BORN

The LORD your God goes with you; he will never leave you nor forsake you.

—Deuteronomy 31:6 NIV

We have all had our hearts broken by someone who did not choose us, or by someone who rejected our offer to love that would have brought the fulfillment of a relationship. Some of us have even said under our breath. "It's your loss. I would have been good for you. We could have had a great life together, but . . . oh, well."

God never says, "Oh, well." He is relentless in his love pursuit of us while at the same time honoring our right to say, "No. I'm not interested."

How blessed we are that, in the cocooning security of God's choice to love us, we also have his promise to *never* abandon us. He will not desert us; He will never choose against us. No human being in our lives can make such a declaration of steadfast love. Only God can; only God does. Let's remember yet again Isaiah 41:9, which promises, "I have chosen you and will not throw you away."

My prayer for you is that you choose to accept the very reason for which you were born and that you rest in your place of one whom God will never abandon . . . never throw away.

—MARILYN MEBERG (*Love Me Never Leave Me*)

SINGING THE SONG IN YOUR HEART

Each one should use whatever gift he has received to serve others, faithfully administering God's grace in its various forms.
—1 Peter 4:10 NIV

Being creative is to find your own voice inside yourself, to identify your own ideas and aspirations. It means singing the song that's in your heart, to your own melody. You're the only one who can hear it, because it's coming to you from God. If you look at this song with your intellect, it goes away because it doesn't respond to your mind; it responds to your heart.

Consider Henri Matisse, the famous French artist who painted in oils. When he was an old man, he became very ill and was confined to a wheelchair or his bed. He was too weak to hold a pen or brush, so he took a pair of scissors and cut out designs and life forms. He created a new way of thinking and looking at art and life. He sang the song that was inside him and found a new, creative voice.

I have a framed print of a cut-out by Henri Matisse on my living room wall; I bought it at the National Gallery of Art in Washington, D.C. It's a great reminder to me that life is still flowing through my veins, and I must continually stop to create what I hear inside my heart.

—LUCI SWINDOLL (*Life! Celebrate It*)

GOD'S FRIEND

Jesus said, "I no longer call you servants, because a servant does not know his master's business. Instead, I have called you friends, for everything that I learned from my Father I have made known to you."
—*John 15:15* NIV

You remember the story of Job, don't you? As this incredible Bible story unfolds, we see that there is more between this man and God than an employer-employee relationship. He was God's servant, true, but he was also God's friend. Throughout his entire ordeal, Job's reactions prove that he did not serve God for what he could get out of him but for what he could give to him from the very core of his being. Job did not serve God out of fear or duty. He served God out of love, and so it should be between friends.

At times it is easy for us to get caught up in Christian "service." We can become members of every committee and attend every prayer group. Wherever there is a job to be done in the church, we will be there. We may run ourselves ragged doing things for God and lose him in the midst of it all.

Serving God is important, even vital, but it should never come ahead of realizing that he is first of all our Friend, and without his friendship, life is an empty treadmill. Christianity is not an employer-employee contract; it is a relationship between a loving heavenly Father and his children.

—SHEILA WALSH (*Life Is Tough But God Is Faithful*)

198

THE ROAD TO EMMAUS

*The same day two of them [disciples of Jesus] were walking to
the village Emmaus.... They were deep in conversation, going
over all these things that had happened. In the middle of their
talk and questions, Jesus came up and walked along with them.
But they were not able to recognize who he was.*

—Luke 24:13–16 MSG

As we continue on our journeys, each of us on an individual path,
my prayer is that we will recognize Jesus when he comes to walk
alongside us. Unlike his disciples who were trudging along on the
road to Emmaus but didn't know the resurrected Jesus was traveling with them, may we listen studiously and take notes as he
explains to us some of life's complexities. He does that for us
through his Word, his Spirit, his people, and his creation.

Along our way we mustn't allow our sorrows to disable us, but
instead we must filter them through God's plan and mercies, which
will add depth to our heart's content. God made us gals emotionally
wealthy, giving us the potential to be prosperous in our dispositions
and intuitions. We all have regrets, but we must learn to receive
what Christ offers freely: forgiveness. And we must realize that Jesus
redeems our failures for his divine purposes.

Expect life to be joyful and rugged. Let's be wise enough to lean
into what comes our way. If God has allowed it, it comes with purposes we may not understand . . . yet. Follow the narrow road; it leads
to the widest joy. Along the way, enjoy your rich emotional design.

—PATSY CLAIRMONT (*I Second That Emotion*)

SHIFTING MY FOCUS

*In him we have redemption through his blood, the forgiveness
of sins, in accordance with the riches of God's grace that he
lavished on us with all wisdom and understanding.*

—Ephesians 1:7–8 NIV

I'm not ashamed to tell you that there was a time when I was
desperately in need of forgiveness. As my accountability group
walked me through the long months of restitution and restoration, I asked forgiveness from God and from each individual who
had been hurt by my actions. By the time my restoration process
was declared finished, I was assured that I'd been fully forgiven.

But I still had two problems: (1) I didn't *feel* forgiven, and
(2) I still had to deal with the consequences, which kept my
weaknesses right in front of my face.

Then one day it dawned on me that my focus was blocking
my ability to forgive myself. I was focusing on my junk—my lack
of worthiness to receive forgiveness. And in doing so, I was actually ignoring God's beautiful gift of his Son. I needed to shift my
focus to Christ on the cross. Like the song says, "Turn your eyes
upon Jesus, look full in his wonderful face."

If you struggle with forgiving yourself or someone else,
remember that Jesus died for all of us equally. As you focus on
the beauty of his redemptive sacrifice, your heart wells with gratitude. Paralyzing guilt or energy-sapping grudges flee "in the light
of his glory and grace."

—SANDI PATTY (*Falling Forward*)

WITH THANKSGIVING

Do not worry about anything, but in everything by prayer
and supplication with thanksgiving let your requests be made
known to God.

—*Philippians 4:6 NRSV*

I spent some time with Ruth Graham in her lovely mountain home in North Carolina in 1991. On that evening, I asked Ruth how she handled the tough days as a young wife and mother. How did she respond when she was, at times, pushed into an unsolicited spotlight? Her answer was simple yet profound.

"Worship and worry cannot exist at the same time in the same heart," she said. "They are mutually exclusive."

Ruth then told me about a time when she awoke in the middle of the night, concerned about one of her children. Unable to sleep, she got out of bed and picked up her Bible. Ruth soon realized that the missing ingredient in her heart at that time was thanksgiving, so she began to thank God for this son, for his life, for the joy he had brought to their home. Her burden lifted.

We can pray and make our requests known to God, but we have to trust that God will answer our prayers. Thanksgiving helps us do that. When we pray with thanksgiving, we are saying we believe he will answer us and provide for our needs or for the needs of those we love—and we will be happy with his provision.

—SHEILA WALSH (*Life Is Tough But God Is Faithful*)

FAIRY TALES

May the God of hope fill you with all joy and peace in believing,
that you may abound in hope by the power of the Holy Spirit.
—Romans 15:13

Long before I knew the stories were called fairy tales, I loved them. It would be years before I understood how fairy tales are different from other stories, but in my earliest memories, my heart soared when I heard the words "Once upon a time . . ."

Fairy tales are still very precious to me, but for far deeper reasons. Many of the tales provide direct glimpses into the way the world should have gone, delightfully confirming a deep suspicion that life should be different.

Fairy tales are like a pair of glasses—not the rose-colored kind that make everything look wonderful, but the kind that bring reality into focus. Like good bifocals, they help us discern the way the world really is up close, without losing the bigger picture of the way the world was intended to be.

The world of fairy tales sharply reveals that what we see around us is not all there is. There is more, much more. Fairy tales suggest and give glimpses of a very different, invisible kingdom—a world that lives between the illusions of the perfect and the real worlds. Fairy tales offer hope. And hope, like nothing else in the world, inspires us and motivates us to keep going.

—NICOLE JOHNSON (*Keeping a Princess Heart*)

OUR PLANS, HIS PLANS

The mind of man plans his way, but the LORD directs his steps
—Proverbs 16:9 NASB

My husband loves the band Avalon. When I heard they were coming to Dallas, I planned a surprise date for us. I even bought Avalon's latest CD and planned to have the waiter present the CD with the bill.

Well, nothing went as planned. There was a terrible accident on the freeway, so it took two hours to get to the restaurant. By the time we arrived, it was too late to eat, so I had to tell Steve about the surprise. I was disappointed, but we made the most of it by eating fast food before heading to the concert. I had reserved seats up front and arranged for us to meet the band after the concert. When we arrived, I discovered that my e-mails hadn't gotten through, so we ended up sitting eight rows from the back.

Since the concert started at seven, I had told the babysitter we would be home by ten. I didn't figure on there being two opening acts. Avalon didn't go onstage until after nine! We were only able to hear a few songs before we had to leave. Fortunately, after two hours of listening to very loud music, we were ready.

There is an old Jewish proverb that says, "If you want to give God a good laugh, tell him your plans!" How true. Everyday life is filled with surprises. But even when our plans get derailed, God remains faithful, and his plans are never derailed.

—LISA WHELCHEL (*Speaking Mom-ese*)

LET GO AND LET GOD

I can do everything through him who gives me strength.
—Philippians 4:13 NIV

The love of God is the key to trusting him enough to let him "do it." Do what? Everything! Absolutely everything. The joy of responding to God's love for us comes in the partnership he offers us in overcoming our difficulties. We are not alone in them. He partners with us by providing the wisdom and strength—and even abstinence from those life issues that threaten to derail us. In our love for him, in our trust of him, we receive from him all we are not. This is what it means to "let him do it." He invites us to climb off the treadmill of self-effort and rule keeping.

Letting God "do it" is not a passive action. We partner with him. He has the power; we do not. We recognize his power, and in our powerlessness we pray, "Jesus, help me!"

That he *will* help us is a given. God plays the major role while we rest in who he is and what he has done and in the knowledge that we were, are, and will always be the focus of his love. And that powerful love is what brings us from death to life.

—MARILYN MEBERG (*Assurance for a Lifetime*)

I'VE GOT QUESTIONS

You have preserved me because I was honest; you have admitted me forever to your presence.
—Psalm 41:12 TLB

Questioning God sounds blasphemous to some people. They might say, "How dare you? Who do you think you are, that you can come before God and question him?" But I don't think being honest with God is blasphemous at all. I believe God wants us to be honest because he wants a real relationship with us, not something plastic or halfhearted.

I sometimes ask myself how it must feel to be God and love people with a passion so great that you would give your only Son to hang on a cross. How must it feel to know that that kind of love is the very essence of your being, and yet day after day you can see that your children are hurting, but they never open up. They are never honest.

I believe God much prefers to have his children come before him and say, "God, this makes no sense to me. I hurt so badly. I just don't understand. I don't think I'll ever understand, but, God, I love and trust you, and I rest in the fact that you know how I feel. You've been there. I can't understand what is happening to me, but help me to glorify you through it all."

—SHEILA WALSH (*Life Is Tough But God Is Faithful*)

FINDING YOUR *QUERENCIA*

> *Those who hope in the* LORD *will renew their strength. They will soar on wings like eagles; they will run and not grow weary, they will walk and not be faint.*
>
> —Isaiah 40:31 NIV

My grandmother refused to get buried under the load of care she had as a mother, a wife, a church member, a grandmother, and a human being. Every one of those callings has problems attached to it. So how did she do it? She had her own *querencia*. In Spanish, this word can mean a favorite and frequent place of rest.

We human beings have an undefined place of peace that God offers to us. By shifting the weight of tough stuff off our shoulders onto God's, we find that place to relax. It's still a jungle out there, but we unconsciously find that quiet place—our *querencia*—where we stop grinding out life's maddening pace for a few minutes. This spot is inside us, and God makes it available so we can pause and catch our breath. Laugh. Sing. Think. Pray. Everyday rhythms and patterns of life keep going, but we're not going with them. We're listening to the beat of a different drum.

Find your own *querencia*—and go there. If you are overwhelmed by a problem that seems impossible to solve, don't! Shift the weight of your problems to God, and the rest of your life and your family will be the richer for it.

—LUCI SWINDOLL (*Life! Celebrate It*)

TRUDGE OR HIGH-STEP

Since we live by the Spirit, let us keep in step with the Spirit.
—Galatians 5:25 NIV

The Bible speaks of footwear, but even more of our walk. Genesis mentions Adam and Eve's barefoot walk with the Lord in the cool of the evening. The Bible closes with the dramatic account of John's vision of the Son of Man in which his feet are like fine brass. Scripture reminds us of the importance of where we walk, how we walk, and with whom we walk.

Life is so textured, full of nubs like a bolt of tweed fabric, interesting and unpredictable. We are walking down a delightful path when, without warning, we find ourselves on a path we never would have chosen. Then our choice becomes whether we will trudge or high-step our way to the finish line.

Loss opens a walkway to what really matters in life. It presses us to see and feel in ways we hadn't previously considered. And while loss doesn't seem like a friend, it often brings refining touches to our character. It can hone compassion toward others, it can move us beyond fear, it can help us to determine a clear-cut path, and it can deepen our dependence on God.

My tendency is to pull on track shoes and sprint in the opposite direction of loss. But I am learning ever so slowly to lean into it and lift my heels.

—PATSY CLAIRMONT (*All Cracked Up*)

THE TRUST FALL

The LORD upholds all who fall, and raises up all who are
bowed down.
—Psalm 145:14

Have you ever been in a corporate or retreat situation where you had to take part in "trust-building exercises"? Sometimes you're led blindfolded by someone and you have to trust they won't bash you into a wall or send you tumbling down a flight of stairs. I don't know about you, but I just hate those things, because trusting someone else means giving up control.

But sometimes I need a visual picture, to help make overused phrases like "Just trust in God" come to life. One of the most common of those dreaded corporate team-building exercises is called the Trust Fall. So when I have no idea *how* to trust God in a given situation, I think of myself climbing up on a ladder to get in position to fall, with God's strong and mighty presence waiting below. And then I mentally do the Trust Fall into his arms.

When I have to perform onstage and I'm beyond tired, and I really just want, with all my aching bones and heart, to go home and put on a robe and fuzzy slippers and sleep for a week, I pray, "Lord, you know I'm out of gas. I'm going to do the Trust Fall into your arms right now." And then I simply let go. He never fails me.

—SANDI PATTY (*Falling Forward*)

CHOOSING TO FORGIVE

Jesus said, "Our Father in heaven ... forgive us our debts, as we forgive our debtors."
—Matthew 6:9, 12

I once had a friend who lied about me to my two closest friends, and I could not defend myself without betraying the trust of someone dear to me. I spent many sleepless nights and wept many bitter tears, feeling helpless and betrayed. But in the midst of it all, I was faced with Christ's command to forgive so that my heavenly Father would forgive me.

When we refuse to forgive, we are setting ourselves up as a judge and demanding that others be perfect—something we can't do. God will judge and demand perfection of us when we judge others.

When we forgive, we see through other people's behavior to their need. We recognize their guilt and at the same time see our own. We realize that we won't find justice in this world—it doesn't live here. So we give up the fruitless, heartbreaking search for it, and we give mercy to those who have wounded us.

In my case, I asked God to bless the friend who had wronged me. I asked him to pull her close to his heart, believing that she had to be pretty miserable herself to lie about someone. I remembered my own need and was finally able to choose to forgive.

—SHEILA WALSH (*Life Is Tough But God Is Faithful*)

209

A SIMPLE ACT OF LOVE

Live a life of love, just as Christ loved us and gave himself up
for us as a fragrant offering and sacrifice to God.
—Ephesians 5:2 NIV

The deepest identity and worth that my heart longs for will never be found in human applause. Although it feels good most of the time, it is far too short-lived. The deepest satisfaction of my heart is found in the faith to work and build and love for a greater purpose than my own.

When I see an unselfish, simple act of love, I am deeply moved. I am left speechless by the silent sacrifices love makes without ever drawing attention to itself. Often my hardened heart is reduced to liquid when I see a daughter wiping the drawn mouth of her parent or a wife sitting by the bedside reading to a husband who can no longer see, or a friend helping a co-worker in a wheelchair get situated into an airplane seat. Through my tears, I want to stand and applaud the beauty of their sacrifice. It is a building in progress and it encourages me to keep going. Some people might be looking around to see who is watching them, or complaining about the task at hand, or even doing nothing instead of giving selflessly. I am fully convinced that invisibility is love's most beautiful costume, given only to its choicest of servants when they are really serious about serving.

—NICOLE JOHNSON (*The Invisible Woman*)

THIS IS YOUR TIME

You saw my body as it was formed.
All the days planned for me
Were written in your book
Before I was one day old
—Psalm 139:16 NCV

God, who is eternal, who has no beginning and no end, thought it important for us to live in increments of time. Daylight and dusk, phases of the moon, and seasons of the year affect our lives in ways we sometimes don't even realize. But God had a purpose in creating the dimensions of time.

The psalmist David understood this when he said all our days were planned for us. I love those words. They bring such order to my mind. Our days and seasons are not just haphazardly thrown together; they are appointed, they are expected, and they are the canvas on which we draw our lives.

Smart Girls love the differing seasons of life. They don't try to hang on to the past, and they don't dread the future. They embrace each day they've been given in any particular season and appreciate it for what it is. In every season, no matter its challenges, you can find something good; you can find ways to enhance your life and the lives of others. Even in those seasons that feel a little uncomfortable, look for lovely, interesting, meaningful, kind things to do, and you'll be amazed by the opportunities all around you.

—JAN SILVIOUS (*Smart Girls Think Twice*)

REMEMBERING

> *A book of remembrance was written before Him for those who*
> *fear the* LORD *and who meditate on His name.*
> —*Malachi 3:16*

I am convinced that one of life's most easily accessible sources of cheer is to remember some of the off-the-wall, crazy things that happen to us. It doesn't have to be a Big Moment, just something zany and fun. Sometimes those memories are bittersweet as we recall an out-of-the-ordinary moment with a loved one who is now gone. But those times nevertheless provide cheer because that was the emotion felt when the experience occurred. That original cheerful feeling will always remain attached to that memory.

Pleasant memories can give us an immediate cheer-producing mind switch. We don't have to wait until we're seventy to do it! Those memories can be as recent as this morning or as distant as thirty years ago. All that matters is that the quirky memory cheers you.

Incidentally, the whole "remembering" thing is a biblical concept. God was continually urging his people to remember what he had done for them as a means of encouragement. He wanted them to remember that he was their rock and their redeemer.

For us believers, remembering starts out by recalling God is the source of our cheer. From that foundational position, we can move into the human realm and remember those experiences that were cheer producing.

—MARILYN MEBERG *(I'd Rather Be Laughing)*

THE CRUCIBLE OF DOUBT

What if some did not believe? Will their unbelief make the faithfulness of God without effect? Certainly not!
—Romans 3:3–4

I find that those who walked with God in the Old Testament seem far more honest than some of us today. The psalmist David, for example, was brutally honest with God. The prophets poured out their hearts to God; Job railed against God. Those who were able to bring their doubts and fears, however raw, into the presence of God, and who truly wrestled with their faith, found a faith that could withstand anything.

The apostle Peter was pretty sure that whatever Jesus needed, he was the man for the job. But as he faced the greatest failure of his life, he was about to be transformed . . . into a man of faith.

Doubts unexpressed isolate us and drive us from the heart of God. God's heart is big enough to carry whatever burden you are bearing.

Do you doubt that God loves you?

Do you doubt that he cares?

Do you doubt that he will see you through any and every circumstance?

Do you doubt that he even exists and that faith is real?

I encourage you to bring your doubts to him. He can be trusted with your questions.

—SHEILA WALSH (*Extraordinary Faith*)

IT CAME TO PASS

The darkness is passing away and the true light is already shining.
—1 John 1:8 NCV

If shifting the weight and clearing your head fail to provide a measure of relief, then remember this: whatever difficulty you're facing today has only come to pass. You know how great literature as well as Scripture often reads, "And it *came to pass* . . ."? That's what I'm talking about. Whatever your burden at the moment, you can be sure that it, too, will pass. One day, it will be no more!

The word *pass* is a wonderful word. In my dictionary, it has twelve different meanings. And while each is interesting, and most of us have used the word in all its meanings at one time or another, it's the first definition to which I refer here: "to proceed; to go away; to depart."

Whatever burden you're facing at the moment *will* depart. It's just a matter of time. It came to pass—and it will. But it's between those two moving targets—*came* and *pass*—that we need to look for humor, isn't it?

When we accept the inevitability of trials and suffering and their mandate for living fully wherever we are and whatever we're doing, a great part of the battle has already been won by someone much stronger and braver than we.

—LUCI SWINDOLL (*Life! Celebrate It*)

A PICTURE OF COURAGE

Lord, you are my shield, my wonderful God who gives me courage.
—Psalm 3:3 NCV

Don't you just love great stories of courage? There's nothing better than grabbing a bowl of popcorn and sitting down to watch a movie about brave people standing up to evil and winning. When the Narnia movie came out, based on C. S. Lewis's classic book *The Lion, the Witch and the Wardrobe,* our family got a chance to enjoy a "good versus evil" battle.

Like wishy-washy Edmund at the beginning of the movie, I've never thought of myself as a particularly courageous person. I don't jump out of airplanes, and I'm not going to climb Mount Everest. I don't even like spiders! Bravery? That's for other people, right?

Wrong.

With the amount of courage it has taken to get through the trials of the last dozen years . . . well, some days I wished all I had to do was *just* climb Mount Everest. All the times my heart threatened to wilt under the strain of holding my head up high; all the times I wanted to give up and hide out in my bedroom forever; all the times I nearly cowered under all the lies the enemy was trying to feed me—these were moments that required me to suck it up, get a backbone, grab on to God's strength, and be a picture of courage.

—SANDI PATTY (*Falling Forward*)

CLOAKED IN HUMILITY

As God's chosen people, holy and dearly loved, clothe yourselves
with compassion, kindness, humility, gentleness and patience.
—*Colossians 3:12* NIV

Everyone—and I include myself—wants to be a servant until we're treated like one. I want to look like a servant, but not have to suffer. And if I have to suffer, I would like to be exalted for my servanthood. I have no idea how many years Mother Teresa worked invisibly in the streets of Calcutta before anyone ever knew her name, but I'm certain it was decades. When she came to renown ironically her name was not the one that mattered. She walked among the poor, cloaked in humility, completely disguised as Jesus. Disappearing among the poorest of the poor, she made them visible with her quiet, strong love.

It is possible that the opposite of love is not hate or even apathy, but showy, self-serving acts. Talking or writing about how much you love, demanding your right to be loved, or being loud and brassy about the way other people don't love will never reveal love's truest essence. The greatest demonstrations of human love in history stand in direct opposition to such circus acts, in the way they are freely and quietly given. They humble us all, and by their power they change the world.

—NICOLE JOHNSON (*The Invisible Woman*)

TWO OPTIONS

We walk by faith, not by sight.
—2 Corinthians 5:7

I used to think that I had just two options in my life:

1) I could live with full abandon and passion, pour out my life and heart to God and to others, take risks, and give generously of heart and spirit. If I did that, I set myself up for disappointment and loss, for heartache and rejection.

2) I could live cautiously, care about others but not too much, love what I do but not too much, give what I have but hold back some reserve. If I did this I would feel safe; not so alive, but safe.

For years I chose option 2, and I think part of me despised that. As believers we are not called to live safe, small lives. We are called to live as Christ lived, to love as he loves.

But here is the dilemma: we can live that way only by faith!

If we do not trust that God is good—that he is in control all the time, no matter what is going on; that whatever we pour out in his name, he will pour back and more into our spirits—we live lesser lives. We know intrinsically that we were created for more!

—SHEILA WALSH (*Extraordinary Faith*)

THE BEAUTY OF THE LORD

So God created people in his own image; God patterned them after himself.

—Genesis 1:27 NLT

What is the purpose of a gorgeous sunset? Is there a reason a genuine smile is so beautiful? Why is the smell of dawn so intoxicating? Can you tell me the rationale behind creating koalas so cuddly? And what's up with clothing the lilies? There are probably logical explanations for these questions. But let me ask you: could beauty for beauty itself be enough of an answer? I think so.

We all appreciate beauty, and in my personal opinion, it is part of being created in God's image. I believe we reflect God when we appreciate and exhibit beauty. Psalm 90:17 says "Let the beauty of the LORD our God be upon us" (NKJV). God's glory is revealed in His creation, and enjoying its beauty is an act of worship.

I really admire women who have the gift of beauty. You know the ones I'm talking about—even if they are wearing jeans and a T-shirt, they look like they stepped off the screen from a commercial. Their houses are filled with frames and trinkets that somehow look eclectic rather than cluttered. When they give a present, the wrapping is more beautiful than the actual gift.

I've learned over time that making time for a little beauty can go a long way. Whether it's dabbing on some lip gloss, cutting fresh flowers, or getting a pedicure, remember that enjoying the beauty of God's creation can be an act of worship.

—LISA WHELCHEL (*Taking Care of the Me in Mommy*)

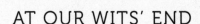

AT OUR WITS' END

God's love will continue forever.
—Psalm 52:1 NCV

I have some good news: when our backs are against the wall—
when we cry out to the Lord—he is there. God is always at our
wits' end. How do we know? Because God is wherever we are.
His promise is to never, ever leave us. Wherever we may wander,
in foolishness or fear, God stays with us and brings us out of our
distresses, because his love for us endures forever.

So what's the problem? Why can't we simply settle into the
biblical drumbeat message that God's love endures forever? I
believe the problem lies in the contrast between what we believe
and what we think. In our hearts we believe that God's love
endures forever, but in our heads we sometimes think in a way
that creates roadblocks to faith. This faulty thinking leads to
shaky faith. Then that shaky faith puts our backs against the wall.
It keeps us at our wits' end.

God wants you to have a faith that is practical and within
your grasp. His intent is to meet you where you are in your faith
need and to lovingly show you what it means when he tells you
he will bring you out of your distresses.

—MARILYN MEBERG (*God at Your Wits' End*)

LIFTING OUR SPIRITS

A merry heart does good, like a medicine.
—*Proverbs 17:22*

I love being around people who seem to have nonsense in their veins. They're the ones who erase tension in business meetings, liven up a schoolroom or office discussion, and relieve boredom wherever they go. If you have someone like that in your life, you need to stop right now and thank God, because that person is a beautiful gift straight from heaven. Anne Lamott says, "Nothing gives hope like laughter. It moisturizes the soul." The difficulties of life break down into manageable sizes. It's a "momentary anesthesia of the heart," to quote French philosopher Henri Bergson.

Interestingly, research shows that laughter itself serves no biological purpose. It's a reflex action, sometimes called a "luxury reflex," unrelated to humanity's struggle for survival. Yet the emotional service it provides can't begin to be measured. According to the Bible, laughter is good medicine—and we've all experienced a healthy dose of that medicine when we didn't even know we were sick. Laughter lifts our spirit and drops the fever. Somehow, it opens the windows to our soul, letting in light and fresh air. A friend of mine used to say, "Laughter is kind of like changing my baby's diaper—it doesn't solve any problems permanently, but it certainly makes things more enjoyable at the moment."

—LUCI SWINDOLL (*Life! Celebrate It*)

WHAT ABOUT HOPE?

Be strong and take heart, all you who hope in the LORD.
—Psalm 31:24 NIV

According to the apostle Paul, three things will continue forever: faith, hope, and love. Paul makes it clear that the greatest of these is love, and we all agree. But what of the other two?

We know faith is crucial. Without faith it is impossible to please God or to hang on when life is tough. Doubt can creep in so easily, and the only answer is to remember that Jesus is worth it all.

But what about hope? In our haste to be sure we have faith and love, do we sometimes fail to give hope its proper due? Without hope, life is a sorry game, played without enthusiasm or joy.

In this, the twenty-first century, people wonder what our real chances are. Is there any hope?

Those are legitimate questions, and I believe that only Christians have the legitimate answers. When our dreams seem to go sour or remain unfulfilled, hopelessness can dominate our lives—or we can hold on with open hands, knowing that we have hope because God is faithful.

—SHEILA WALSH (*Life Is Tough But God Is Faithful*)

HOPE IS A DIAMOND

No one whose hope is in you will ever be put to shame.
—Psalm 25:3 NIV

Hope, that glorious light at the end of the tunnel, is a multi-faceted, brilliant dimension of life. If you've ever experienced hope or observed it in another person, you know that it's indescribable yet undeniable.

But hope often is unearthed in the dark mines of hospital wards, funeral parlors, senior homes, rehab centers, prison cells, abuse centers, counselors' offices, every arena of life. Hope can seem elusive and outside of our price range when, in fact, it's available to pauper and prince alike, thanks to Jesus.

I wish I could wear my hope as a pendant so all who see it might be drawn to my dazzling Christ. But isn't that what happens when we live out our faith in spite of hardships and opposition? What looks impossible suddenly glistens with hope, and others come to observe and ask questions.

Ever notice how a dark velvet backdrop enhances a diamond's qualities? So, too, does hope shine on a backdrop of pain, failure, and loss. Like Corrie ten Boom's life, which included a death camp, or Mother Teresa's, which included the poverty and sicknesses of India. Their diamond-studded lives continue to glitter and refract Christ's hope. What unlikely candidates they must have appeared to be. Yet that's what hope is—the unlikely, even the impossible, becoming the absolute.

—PATSY CLAIRMONT (*All Cracked Up*)

A HEART OF THANKFULNESS

In everything give thanks; for this is the will of God in Christ Jesus for you.

—*1 Thessalonians 5:18*

A five-year-old girl was asked to say the blessing at Thanksgiving dinner. She began by thanking God for all her friends, naming them one by one. Then she thanked God for Mommy, Daddy, Brother, Sister, Grandma, Grandpa, and all her aunts and uncles. Finally, she gave thanks for the turkey, the dressing, the fruit salad, the cranberry sauce, the pies, the cakes. Then she paused. After a long silence, the young girl looked up at her mother and asked, "If I thank God for the broccoli, won't he know I'm lying?"

Have you ever felt that way? We know we're supposed to cultivate a heart of thankfulness. But let's be honest: there's a bunch of broccoli in our lives that is really hard to give thanks for.

Amazingly enough, by cultivating thankfulness for God's work in me as I try to glean the lessons of loss, I've even come to be thankful for the trials I've experienced. I know that through them God has made me into the person I am today, a new and hopefully improved version, full of much more grace and love. Being thankful for everything—intentionally nurturing a heart of gratitude—is a way to bolster your faith on a daily basis. And (broccoli notwithstanding) I guarantee it will keep you in a better mood.

—SANDI PATTY (*Falling Forward*)

HE TAKES NO NOTICE

Honor God by accepting each other, as Christ has accepted you.
—Romans 15:7 CEV

The Christian life is full of challenges. For example, following God's command to accept others as he has freely accepted us is a great goal toward which to strive, but if the truth were known, not one of us is able to fully comply. Most of us even have trouble accepting ourselves. We know too much. We see others and ourselves in the light of reality, and sometimes we tend to step back from that reality. It isn't always to our liking; it isn't always a pretty picture.

That's why God's love for us is difficult to grasp. He knows what we know. In fact, he knows even more. Yet there it is: his unconditional love. It's interesting he does not circle around us to keep from encountering our weaknesses and imperfections. Why? Because once they are confessed and forgiven he takes no notice of them. Scripture says he does not even remember them.

Can you imagine greater freedom for our guilt-prone souls than to fully realize he does not remember our sins? And, in turn, can you imagine the gift we give others when we extend that kind of unconditional, fully accepting love to them—despite their flaws?

—MARILYN MEBERG & LUCI SWINDOLL (*Free Inside and Out*)

THE BLESSED RAINBOW

*God said: "I set My rainbow in the cloud . . . and I will
remember My covenant which is between Me and you and
every living creature of all flesh; the waters shall never again
become a flood to destroy all flesh.*

—*Genesis 9:13, 15*

Doesn't seeing a rainbow flood you with rest, awe, and amazement? While some people understand the scientific reason behind rainbows, I've always found those explanations real yawners. I like to think of rainbows as a signal that God is present and cares. They're symbols of rest for the weary, broken, and disheartened.

A few months ago, as I was driving home from the airport after a tiring trip, I glanced out the window and saw a double rainbow. It was vividly colored, almost neon, and so close. For a minute I thought about rushing over for those pots of gold. But then I remembered that rainbows *are* pots of gold, shining with God's love. And that's priceless.

But my amazement must have been small compared to what Noah must have felt when he saw the first rainbow. After all that work corralling the animals, feeding them, and cleaning up their mess, Noah was probably moaning, "I can't take it anymore, Lord." Then the skies cleared, and he knew that finally he and his family could disembark and let the animals loose. Ah, what a relief, especially when he looked up and saw the symbol of God's enduring promise of rest—the rainbow!

—PATSY CLAIRMONT (*All Cracked Up*)

THREE KINDS OF PRAYER

Pray in the Spirit on all occasions with all kinds of prayers and requests. With this in mind, be alert and always keep on praying for all the saints.
—*Ephesians 6:18* NIV

If the muddy path you've traveled has kept you from praying as much as you'd like (or at all), I want to encourage you to start talking to God again. Even just a few words a day. It gets easier, I promise.

I read once that there are three kinds of prayer we can practice, based on the example of Jesus when he walked this earth. First, there's praying without ceasing, which is our ongoing silent conversation with God throughout our days. Next, there's our "set aside" time each day for focused prayer, when we do nothing but converse with God, whether or not we choose to use words. Finally, there are the longer periods of prayer and meditation—a day or more maybe once a year—when we get away from family and responsibilities to spend extended time with God.

Now, my purpose in telling you this is not to give you more rules to follow or to persuade you to be legalistic about prayer! I simply find it helpful to conceptualize prayer in these three ways because it gives us options and allows for our varying personalities, schedules, and seasons of life. Whatever works best for you—start there. Personally, I tend to pray continually throughout my day, because I am always singing to God!

—SANDI PATTY (*Falling Forward*)

WHEN THE CHIPS ARE DOWN

When times are good, be happy; but when times are bad,
consider: God has made the one as well as the other.
—*Ecclesiastes 7:14 NIV*

How do you react to life's unpleasant circumstances? Do you look for ways to find happiness and joy or do you just give in . . . give up, and join the ranks of the "if-anything-bad-can-happen-it-will-happen-to-me" people? Granted, every dilemma doesn't have a humorous side, but I believe more do than we realize.

Here are a few principles that have helped me thrive through disappointments, turning around a difficult circumstance. Remember these when the chips are down:

- ✦ Realize most problems are inconveniences, not catastrophes.
- ✦ Don't take yourself too seriously, and stop being so literal.
- ✦ Count your blessings instead of your blunders.
- ✦ Take everything as a compliment.
- ✦ Enjoy your freedom because Christ has set you free.
- ✦ Look for the funny side of everything even if it's teensy-weensy.
- ✦ Don't sweat the small stuff.
- ✦ Do something fun just for yourself that makes you laugh.

—LUCI SWINDOLL (*Life! Celebrate It*)

GOD'S MYSTERIOUS WAYS

"My thoughts are not your thoughts, neither are your ways my ways," declares the LORD.
—Isaiah 55:8 NIV

At every conference I hear someone say, "I am so grateful that you share your experience with depression. It gives me hope. The fact that you still take your little blue pill makes me feel that I'm not alone, and that I don't have to be ashamed."

I don't always understand why God works as he does, why he heals one and not another, why he delivers one and not another, but I do believe that he is good all the time. Our faith is tested in many ways. Sometimes we are immersed in a situation that seems hopeless, and we wonder, *God, are you there?* Sometimes he delivers us from a situation in such a miraculous way that we know it had to be God; sometimes he calls us to walk with a limp, following the one who was wounded for us.

I don't know what you have walked through or what pain you have known. I don't know where you find yourself at this moment, but I encourage you to invite Christ into the midst of your struggles and heartache. Offer your scars to the one who is scarred for you. The very wounds that seemed that they might break you will be used by God to strengthen you and to give strength to others.

—SHEILA WALSH (*Extraordinary Faith*)

WISHING IT AWAY

There is an appointed time for everything. And there is a time for every event under heaven.

—Ecclesiastes 3:1 NASB

I remember often hearing as a college student, "These are the best years of your life." I always rolled my eyes and thought, *If these are the best, I'd hate to see the worst.* The pressure of studying, dating, roommates, and homesickness was not my idea of the best years. If I'd been a Smart Girl in that season, I would have studied harder, learned more, relaxed about the future, and soaked up the college experience. But I had no idea that it was a season to embrace. In fact, I took a couple of correspondence courses so I could qualify to graduate early. Why was I rushing like that?

As I look back over other seasons of my life, I feel as if I have wished most of them away. I spent so many years thinking about what it would be like when I got married, had children, and had an empty nest. Now I know the answers, but only in the past few years have I learned we have only today. That's it. We have the joy of yesterday's memories and the delight of future anticipation, but we have no tangible reality except today. This day is yours. This is your time to fulfill your reason for living.

I encourage you to take some time to think about your time. What are you doing now? What season are you living in? Do you need to let go of worries about the future and leave it to God?

—JAN SILVIOUS (*Smart Girls Think Twice*)

229

BELIEF AND FAITH

*May your unfailing love rest upon us, O LORD, even as we put
our hope in you.*

—Psalm 33:22 NIV

I can't impress on you enough how important it is to have an accurate understanding of God. When great difficulties beset us—when a child dies, a job is lost, a marriage fails, or some other calamity occurs—we long for reassurance that his love for us will not fail as well. We want assurance that God is actively working for good in our lives.

But when we have faulty thinking (a misunderstanding of who God is) we think we need a tangible, visible sign that his promises are true. And when there's no visible, emotional, or tangible evidence of his working things out in our lives, answering our prayers the way we want him to and within the time frame we want him to—we may sink into the dirt of discouragement.

To get past this pit of faulty thinking, we need to understand the difference between *belief* and *faith*. Though similar, the two have an important difference. The dictionary defines *belief* as "mental acceptance of or conviction in the truth or actuality of something." In contrast, faith goes beyond mental acceptance. *Faith* is believing what we can't see, what is not tangible, and in some cases, does not make sense.

Do you have faulty thinking? Move from belief to faith in God's enduring love.

—MARILYN MEBERG (*God at Your Wits' End*)

WHEN GOD LAUGHS

If we please God, he will make us wise, understanding, and happy.
—*Ecclesiastes 2:26* CEV

When we know God personally and have invited his Son, Jesus Christ, into our hearts as our Savior, we learn we can laugh in God's presence and he laughs with us. It may not be recorded in Scripture with clear definition, but I know full well that God has created us to be happy and full of joy.

When I think of laughing with God, I refer to those ways he communicates with us where we're comfortable settling into his presence. When we do things to please him, bring honor to him, share his grace with others, and exercise the gifts he's given us, I picture God laughing. I believe when we reflect who he is, he laughs. He's happy.

Here's an illustration of what I mean. When I was growing up, my family talked a lot about the Bible. We memorized scriptures, asked each other what we thought different verses meant, and kept little books and/or cards with different scriptures on them that we were trying to learn by heart and use in our lives. So tell me, when we learn of him and talk about what he likes and who he is and why he cares, are we not bringing him joy? Is it not conceivable that he is laughing in delight? I think so!

—LUCI SWINDOLL (*Life! Celebrate It*)

QUIETLY PERSEVERING

You must hold on, so you can do what God wants and receive what he has promised.
—Hebrews 10:36 NCV

The Bible provides us with good examples of folks who patiently persevered, working in the background until they were called center stage to strut their stuff. Why, Moses was so far offstage, it took a burning bush to get him to move in the right direction. Joseph was thrown in prison. He used that time to prepare for God's call. David was out in the field watching the sheep and learning how to take on lions, tigers, and bears when Samuel came calling to anoint David king.

Gideon was threshing wheat on his farm when an angel popped in for a little visit and an assignment to lead the Israelite army. James and John were fishing when Jesus called them to fish for men.

Moses, David, Gideon, James, and John all remind us that we should go about the business God has appointed for us today—whether that's tossing out our chipped china saucers, puzzling over a long-lost process (like remembering how to cook), or tending the garden.

The Lord is perfectly capable of finding us wherever we are and calling us forward for his service. It's his choice; ours is to persevere—preferably quietly—and to make sure we're fit to serve the King.

—PATSY CLAIRMONT (*All Cracked Up*)

OTHER SIDES OF THE DIAMOND

My flesh and my heart may fail, but God is the strength of my
heart and my portion forever.
—Psalm 73:26 NIV

Have you experienced a shift in your faith since there was a trauma, failure, or crisis in your life? That's not uncommon—life crisis can precipitate faith crisis. God hasn't changed. The Bible hasn't changed. But your faith in God and the way you read Scripture may have changed.

Think of God as a multisided diamond. Perhaps before you stumbled and fell, you saw only one or two sides of the diamond of who God is. Maybe you felt you were able to be a pretty good girl, spiritually speaking, and you were keen on the justice of God, on obedience. Maybe you loved the black-and-white, practical qualities of the epistles of Paul.

But in your broken state, perhaps you, like legions before you, found your comfort smack in the middle of the book of Psalms, or even that tragic book of Job, where all manner of emotions are aired and soothed. At this point, God is probably balancing you out, and you'll find yourself hungry to look at the other sides of God's diamond: mercy, grace, and compassion are now all-compelling.

Don't be overly alarmed if your faith feels a bit shaken up. You've probably not lost your faith at all! You are just searching for the other sides of the diamond that is God.

—SANDI PATTY (*Falling Forward*)

233

GOD IS LISTENING

When you call upon me and come and pray to me, I will hear you.
—*Jeremiah 29:12* NRSV

Perhaps you're thinking, prayer has never been easy for me. I stink at it! You feel like what you say to God is insincere, unsure. Or you question whether he even really cares to hear from you. Or you're so overwhelmed you don't even want to talk to him.

It isn't. He does. He still wants you to.

God hears all our prayers, the good and the bad. He is big enough to handle our honest questions and our doubts and even our anger.

God receives our prayers—the thankful ones and the not-so-thankful ones, the eloquent ones and the less-than-perfect ones. He accepts not only our joyful prayers and self-confident prayers, but the prayers we offer when we're not certain of things—or when we're not sure we really want the answer. He accepts our anguished questioning when we experience trauma or loss. He even accepts the prayers that beg him to rain down disaster on someone who has wounded us (although he may not answer them). He accepts all our prayers because they acknowledge we believe he is in control. When we're happy, when we're angry, when we're hurting to the point that words are lost and all we can offer is a cry for help—he is still there.

God is listening.

—SHEILA WALSH (*Get Off Your Knees and Pray*)

A SAFE HAVEN

"Store your treasures in heaven, where they will never become moth-eaten or rusty and where they will be safe from thieves."
—*Matthew 6:20* NLT

I lost all of the money I made on *The Facts of Life* even though my business manager invested my money in all the tried-and-true places: real estate, stocks, a retirement account, and so forth.

At the height of the show's popularity, I felt the Lord impress upon me to liquidate my assets, live on a fraction of what I was making, and give the rest of the money away to children in Third World countries. I had every intention of obeying God, but eventually "common sense" won out, and I was convinced that giving away my money would be foolish.

Long story short, within a few years a banking crisis, a real estate collapse, tax law changes, and more all lined up like the perfect storm to wipe all that money away.

Where is the only place you can invest on earth that will also be in heaven? People! God isn't asking us to give to a building but to the community of believers. When we invest in people, we are sending our money on ahead to heaven, where it is safe and pays dividends. I realized that the Lord hadn't told me to give away all my money because he wanted it. He was telling me to invest it in the only place it would be safe.

—LISA WHELCHEL (*Taking Care of the Me in Mommy*)

235

THIS WHOLE NOTION OF FORGIVENESS

Be gentle and ready to forgive; never hold grudges. Remember,
the Lord forgave you, so you must forgive others.
—*Colossians 3:13* TLB

Asking forgiveness or finding within ourselves the capacity to forgive others is a real cheer squelcher. As a Christian, the only way
you could have missed hearing that we have to forgive is if you
were somehow mistakenly left on a rock in Eden eating custard-
filled chocolate eclairs by a fern-shrouded waterfall. To make the
subject even more unpalatable, we have to forgive people who
don't deserve it.

Sometimes the subject of forgiveness seems just plain dumb.
Why forgive when someone has lied to us, cheated us, maligned
us, abused us, or deceived us? Forgiveness for those persons
simply goes against our emotional and logical sense of justice.
Our more civilized selves know not to put sharp tacks on their
driveway or send birthday cakes laced with arsenic. Though we
might experience short-term pleasure in imagining such retribu-
tion, most of us refrain from taking overt retaliatory action.
Perhaps we even congratulate ourselves for such restraint and
smugly think that such control in itself is virtuous.

The part that is *not* dumb about forgiving people who have
wounded us is that forgiving those who have wronged us restores
our sense of balance and allows us to "be of good cheer."

—MARILYN MEBERG (*I'd Rather Be Laughing*)

THE LAST LAUGH ON EARTH

May the righteous be glad and rejoice before God; may they be happy and joyful.

—Psalm 68:3 NIV

Perhaps it's the nature of what I do, but people often ask me if I think God laughs. They also sometimes ask, "Is God funny?" or, "Is there anything about God that's funny?" My answer is always "Yes." There are a lot of things that make me think God has a sense of humor. Maybe it's my quirky sense of humor, but when I think of some of the animals he's made (been to a zoo lately?) I know he laughs. Or situations that are so weird, nobody could put all the parts together but God. Even answers to prayer are hilarious sometimes. I think he laughs often.

Personally, I think the last laugh on earth will come from God. It will sound "like the laughter of the universe," as Dante said in his allegory *The Divine Comedy.* When the Easter story is completed, the risen Christ will come to earth again and take us with him to heaven. Scripture says, "We'll be walking on air!" (1 Thessalonians 4:18 MSG).

And God himself will have the last laugh. The entire universe will be proclaiming the love of God in Christ Jesus—and then we'll all laugh together, celebrating our risen and reigning Lord.

—LUCI SWINDOLL (*Life! Celebrate It*)

WINGED VICTORY

Thanks be to God, who gives us the victory through our Lord Jesus Christ.

—1 Corinthians 15:57

My favorite statue is a marble sculpture of a Greek goddess, discovered in 1863. It's best known as Winged Victory or Nike. What draws me to this figure is her name, Victory, and her elegant grace in spite of significant damage. The sculpture has lost her head—literally. Draped in marble, the folds of her garments fall like rare silk. Her outstretched wings appear luminous and ready for flight.

Victory originally was designed for the bow of a ship, proclaiming its triumphant fleet. She is believed to have had outstretched arms with an extended trumpet that she used to blow a victory song. Victory is just over ten feet of marble splendor. Her broken beauty is simultaneously strong and fragile. Her remains are a picture of defiance against the odds and of beauty, not only in spite of hardship, but also because of it.

What I love most about this statue is its ability to inspire. When I'm functioning "headless," Victory reminds me that my heart can carry me through. When I'm feeling helpless to assist others, as if my hands were encased, I'm reminded that I can rely on God's supernatural work. It's okay if I'm damaged by life's adversities; I can still stand strong because the Lord makes his strength known in our weakness.

—PATSY CLAIRMONT (*All Cracked Up*)

REVIVE YOUR FAITH

Those who are right with God will live by faith.
—Habakkuk 2:4 NIrV

You've experienced a crisis in your life—one of your own making. We all do from time to time. Now you are desperate to revive your faith. Here are some things to remember:

> → *Experience the freedom that comes with understanding that forgiveness is about God's grace, not about your mess.* Focus on that, and you'll make great strides.
> → *Cultivate the habit of the Trust Fall (letting go and letting yourself fall into God's arms) whenever a crisis comes, large or small.*
> → *Remember there is a time to deal with your crisis.* This involves the cultivation of old-fashioned courage.
> → *Be grateful to God, in any and all circumstances.* Realize that you can be thankful for the lessons gleaned from loss, even though you cannot thank God for the bad things that happen.
> → *Strike up a conversation with God again.* That can be daunting, especially after guilt or hurt, so go slowly. Your first prayer may be, "Hello, up there. It's me again." It's a start!

Stay proactive in your spiritual journey. The rewards are simply out of this world.

—SANDI PATTY (*Falling Forward*)

NOW THAT I'M FIFTY!

Though our outward man is perishing, yet the inward man is being renewed day by day.

—2 Corinthians 4:16

Now that I'm fifty, change in every arena of life has become an ongoing reality.

My eyesight has deteriorated to the shifting terrain of bifocals. At my last eye test, when the optometrist covered my left eye, I could only read the first two lines on the chart. When he covered my right eye, I couldn't see the wall!

I am definitely getting shorter. To remedy this, I have two clear choices: wear higher heels or have all my pants altered.

I need my roots retouched every three weeks now instead of every six. When I suggested going back to my natural color, my hair stylist said I no longer have one.

But in the midst of all these unsettling changes, I am discovering profound and simple gifts. I've learned I have good friends—friends I can count on. We laugh at all the petty indignities of aging and cry together when life takes one of us through a dark night.

I am changing in my understanding of my spiritual life too. I am more inclined to listen for God's voice than to present to him a list of requests. I have a quiet confidence that no matter what seems to be true, God is always in control.

—SHEILA WALSH (*Get Off Your Knees and Pray*)

IN HIS HANDS

But as for me, I trust in You, O LORD; I say, "You are my God." My times are in Your hand.

—Psalm 31:14–15 NKJV

A big stressor for women seems to be the inability to rest in the fact that God is in control and that he knows the times and seasons of our lives. Smart Girls, however, think twice when they are tempted to worry or to force life to move at their pace. They realize that God moves according to his sovereignty, not according to our timetable, and they have learned to trust his timing in every area of life. When you grasp the truth that God is in control and that when God moves it will be according to God's perfect plan, it makes a huge difference in your life.

When you waste time worrying about what door is going to open next, you aren't trusting that God is in control. When you do trust him, those questions may still trip through your head, but you surrender them to God, knowing he is the one who started your heart beating and he is the one who will stop it. There is no need to be anxious about when God is going to answer your prayer or move on your behalf. You can relax in the certainty that God's ways and God's timing are perfect. Keep in mind there is a "time for everything," and the last chapter hasn't yet been written!

—JAN SILVIOUS (*Smart Girls Think Twice*)

TWO DIFFERENT MATTERS

Wisdom is a tree of life to those who embrace her; happy are those who hold her tightly.

—Proverbs 3:18 NLT

Forgiveness is often a tough topic—even tougher because we sometimes harbor certain misconceptions. We need God's wisdom as we strive to embrace it.

Misconception Number One: If you forgive someone, you have to "get back together" with that person? Not true! That very thought could send us racing to the airport for a one-way ticket to Antarctica. We need to mentally separate the act of forgiveness and the act of reuniting. They are not the same. We can forgive our offender and still plan never to see that person again. Forgiving the offender does not change the offender . . . it changes you.

Misconception Number Two: Forgiving someone's offense against you excuses that person's behavior. Forgiving does not excuse or condone . . . it simply forgives. The behavior remains the same: unacceptable, immoral, or even life-threatening.

Misconception Number Three: Forgiving means forgetting the pain that individual inflicted on you. The concept of "forgive and forget" is something only God can do. We can't come anywhere near forgetting.

Don't let these misconceptions deprive you of the healing effects of forgiving those who have wounded you. It's the first step to reclaiming your laugh, your smile, and your merry heart.

—MARILYN MEBERG (*I'd Rather Be Laughing*)

LOVING THROUGH THE PAIN

Love covers over all wrongs.
—*Proverbs 10:12 NIV*

I don't believe unforgiveness and love can live in the same heart at the same time. And I also don't believe love comes to the person who has been offended until he or she forgives the offender. It might take weeks, months, even years. And it may never happen. The hurt is too deep, too hard to overcome, and too raw to find common ground. I've been there, so I know. What did it take for me to learn to love through the pain?

Let me try to list some principles I've learned.

→ *Work out in your own mind exactly what's wrong.*
Identify the problem; call it what it is and take it apart piece by piece. Admit where you were wrong and where the other person was wrong.
→ *Start talking to God about it.* Be very, very honest about what hurts and why. Stay at this task until you feel God's direction on how to change things.
→ *Be brave and courageous.* Contact the offender in your calmest manner and trust God to help you find creative ways to make things right.
→ *Don't back down from your commitment to get rid of the feelings of hurt and pain.* Love with all your heart, and never stop loving.

—LUCI SWINDOLL (*Life! Celebrate It*)

LET IT RAIN

> *The rain fell, the floods came, and the winds blew and beat on that house, but it did not fall, because it had been founded on rock.*
>
> —Matthew 7:25 NRSV

Texas isn't the only place that knows how to throw a storm. From sea to shining sea, tempests are to be expected in our weather patterns and in our lives. Try as you might, you can't find a picture-perfect weather spot in the world.

But do we want to? No clouds and no rain translate to no green terrain. Why, our gardens would be stubble, our trees stumps, flowers dried-up seeds, and our wells dust. Makes one want to sing, "Let it rain, let it rain, let it rain."

Clouds are typecast according to how far off the ground they are—high level, midlevel, and low level. Depending on their height, they are composed of water droplets, ice crystals, ice particles, or snow. The moisture content in the clouds, when touched by the light of the evening sun, creates the magnificent array of colors in a sunset.

That's true of our lives as well. Clouds will blow through our neighborhoods, whether we live in Texas or Michigan. Some will be fair-weather friends, while others will pummel us with the hail of hardships and swirls of sorrow. While we may have to step through the cleanup, we know the Son will once again fill our skies with color.

—PATSY CLAIRMONT (*All Cracked Up*)

I SURRENDER ALL

There's an opportune time to do things, a right time for
everything on the earth: . . . A right time to hold on and
another to let go.

—Ecclesiastes 3:1, 6 MSG

It is interesting how often surrendering to God is precipitated by hitting a wall in our attempts to orchestrate our own lives. Surrender is sincerely saying to God, "Lord, I'm out of energy. Have your way in this area of my life. I am choosing to let go of my expectations about how it turns out. I need to stop striving and I need to rest! I am giving this to you—please take over."

Though the hymn says, "I surrender *all*"—it is nearly impossible to surrender every part of yourself and your life at one time. It's more like a lifelong journey of small surrenders as circumstances present themselves. I've found that when I practice the small surrenders, the bigger ones come quicker, with less hanging on. The more I let go of my cherished delusions of having control over my life, the easier it is for me to surrender. The good news is that peace enters when the struggle for control is over. Freedom arrives when the last bit of self-sufficiency departs.

In order to turn the corner to freedom, I had to learn this lesson the excruciatingly hard way. I had to relinquish my right to everything, my expectation of anything. I had to say, "Whatever, Lord," and really mean it.

—SANDI PATTY (*Falling Forward*)

245

STOP AND LISTEN

Jesus said, "My sheep listen to my voice; I know them, and they follow me."
—John 10:27 NIV

You say you have questions? That's okay. My plea to you even in the midst of the questions is simple: talk to God and take time to listen. No matter how "vertically challenged" we may believe ourselves to be, God is listening and talking to us all the time. We only need to learn to stop and listen.

We are living in difficult times. War and terrorism are no longer a million miles away from home. Cancer and heart disease are waging an unprecedented battle against younger and younger people. The financial "golden days" of the 1980s are long gone. People worry if they will have enough savings to help their children through college or if they themselves will have enough to retire on. The bottom line is, life is hard.

God knows all about it. And more than that, right in the center of the tornado of our lives, he offers a quiet place, a shelter where he waits with open arms and an open heart to embrace any of us who will come. Whether you are young or old, full of hope or full of fear, angry or excited, bitter or grateful, this remains my conviction: God is listening.

—SHEILA WALSH (*Get Off Your Knees and Pray*)

JESUS LOVES THE LITTLE CHILDREN

How great is the love the Father has lavished on us, that we
should be called children of God! And that is what we are!
—1 John 3:1 NIV

As I watched a children's choir in church, I began to notice all the different personalities represented on the stage. A little girl in the front row was showing—well, pushing—all the other little girls to the spots where they were supposed to be standing. A small boy was crying and scanning the crowd for his mother. My favorite was the little boy who thought he was the only child worth watching. He was bowing and mugging to attract all the attention. Thankfully, he was so distracting that few noticed the boy behind him who was dying because he didn't know the words.

Each was adorable. I doubt even one person watched the bossy little girl and thought, *She's too controlling.* I doubt anyone considered the teary boy a wimp because he wanted to find his mother. Everyone was laughing at the little show-off rather than judging him as an egomaniac. And every person in the crowd could relate to the boy who looked lost.

The next time you wonder how God feels about you, consider how you feel when you watch little children act like little children. Or, if you find it difficult to think of God as a parent, imagine God as your grandfather. There were an awful lot of grandparents in the audience, and they had the broadest smiles of all.

—LISA WHELCHEL (*Speaking Mom-ese*)

247

LOVING ARMS OF THE FATHER

> *[The Lord] will feed his flock like a shepherd. He will carry*
> *the lambs in his arms, holding them close to his heart. He will*
> *gently lead the mother sheep with their young.*
> —Isaiah 40:11 NLT

What is your need right now? Let's suppose it is to overcome a difficult situation such as making it through the pain and anxiety of divorce. You need to be convinced that God is for you and not against you. Perhaps you need the strength and wisdom to deal with your kids, who have turned their backs on God and on the family. You must be certain that God cares even more for your children than you do. If your need has to do with the devastation that comes from a cancer diagnosis or some other debilitating disease, you have to know that God's love for you will never leave you as you begin to walk a path you never expected to make your way down. His love guarantees you won't walk it alone.

God is gently, lovingly, calling your name and inviting you to venture toward him, inviting you not to be afraid. Crawl into the loving arms of your Father, and let him rock you until you find quietness and peace. With the renewed confidence that you are loved, you will be able to find ways to deal with your circumstances and find reasons to have a heart full of cheer.

—MARILYN MEBERG (*I'd Rather Be Laughing*)

THANKS FOR THE LESSONS

*We also glory in tribulations, knowing that tribulation
produces perseverance; and perseverance, character; and
character, hope.*

—Romans 5:3–4

How do you handle crazy-making dilemmas like these? You're
treated unfairly by "the system." Somebody gets a promotion,
and you don't. Somebody gets selected for a team, and you don't.
What do you do then?

For me . . . I talk to myself first. I tell myself it's not fair and I
don't like it. (I'm a big fan of "fair." But, if I'm honest, I have to
admit that life itself isn't fair; and as long as I'm in this life, it ain't
ever gonna be fair. *So face that first, Lucille, and move on.*) I do my
best to get beyond it. And getting beyond something takes commitment. I think it also takes wanting to be an adult. Wanting
maturity. God's going to do his best to bring us all to maturity,
but we can help a bit by shutting up and getting out of his way.

I've come to realize that those disappointments, those situations in life that we feel aren't fair can be great teachers. There's
no amount of money that could pay for the lessons learned while
I was struggling, and there's no amount I would take in place of
the learning. They've taught me to be careful and prayerful and
to thank God for his lessons every day.

—LUCI SWINDOLL (*Life! Celebrate It*)

CREATING A MASTERPIECE

This is what the Sovereign LORD says, "I will give them an undivided heart and put a new spirit in them; I will remove from them their heart of stone and give them a heart of flesh."
—*Ezekiel 11:19* NIV

Imagine you have invested a great deal of time and creativity into a piece of art. You think it's coming along nicely, and then you concentrate on a feature of the face or on the arm. As you set mallet to hammer, you pound into a flaw—and the whole upper corner of the marble crumbles onto the floor. That's what happened to Michelangelo as he worked on his masterpiece *Madonna and Child.* Since Michelangelo had hand-cut the marble block himself, he must have felt like pounding the mallet into his own head.

Sometimes it feels like someone is swinging a mallet our way! But then we turn around and see that it's our loving Lord at work. He carefully selects his material and sets to work, chiseling and shaping us into his image.

Yet, like Michelangelo, God is dealing with flawed stone. Sometimes we crack and drop off chunks under the hands of the Artist. So what does he do? Toss out our rocklike souls? No, he works around our hard heads and stony hearts to make us into something remarkable. Like Michelangelo, God knows how to make the best of the material at hand and manages to create something out of so little.

—PATSY CLAIRMONT (*All Cracked Up*)

EXTRAORDINARY LOVE

We saw it, we heard it, and now we're telling you so you can experience it along with us, this experience of communion with the Father and his Son, Jesus Christ.

—1 John 1:3 MSG

What a wonderfully amazing gift God has given us: freedom that comes from knowing and loving our authentic self, freedom that takes us beyond our past hurts and still-bleeding wounds, and freedom from the fear of what lies in the future. Such a gift of extraordinary love is really too good to keep solely for our exclusive use, don't you think?

As believers, we know we're loved by a compassionate God, and we're taught by his Word to love ourselves as Christ loves us, unconditionally. We may have behaviors that require determined work in order to be changed, but we are to love ourselves despite our shortcomings because that's how Christ loves us.

Once we accept and understand the extraordinary love Jesus has poured out on us through the gift of salvation, we're ready to take the next step: sharing that same unconditional love with others. Are you ready to open your heart and your lips and tell others what he has done for you?

—MARILYN MEBERG & LUCI SWINDOLL (*Free Inside and Out*)

A CLEAN HEART

Create in me a clean heart, O God, and put a new and right
spirit within me.

—*Psalm 51:10* NRSV

What exactly is a "clean heart"?

As women, our hormones lead us on a lively dance for most of our lives. So what do we do on those days when we don't feel very holy or sometimes even sane? Does God hear our prayers when our emotions are taking us on a roller coaster ride? What if we want to have a clean heart, but we're having trouble with it? What if we believe we have a clean heart, but there is some little seed of unforgiveness buried deep inside us we've forgotten about? Are we only responsible for the sins we remember or for every little offense we've committed in our lifetime?

When it is our earnest desire to be clean, God sees that— whether we can remember every detail of our lives or not. Yes, he wants us to come before him with a pure heart, but he also tells us that he hears our honest petitions.

We can't keep worrying about how clean the corners of our soul are. If we get caught up in that whirlpool of self-loathing and doubt, we're only headed down. But if we come before the God who makes all things new, believing in faith that he knows our true hearts, we are certain to be uplifted.

—SHEILA WALSH (*Get Off Your Knees and Pray*)

CAN YOU WAIT?

*What man is there among you who, if his son asks for bread,
will give him a stone? . . . If you then, being evil, know how
to give good gifts to your children, how much more will your
Father who is in heaven give good things to those who ask Him!*
—Matthew 7:9–11 NKJV

Keeping a healthy perspective on what we don't have can be just as challenging as properly handling what we do have. In a consumer culture, it's hard to teach kids the joys of delayed gratification. But trust me, when they become adults, you both will be glad you made the effort.

Children who fail to learn the lessons of delayed gratification grow into adults with a dangerous sense of entitlement. Patricia is such an adult. Her parents didn't have a lot of money, and what they did have wasn't handled well. So Patricia arrived at adulthood convinced that she had missed out on a lot of things, and she saw no reason to wait until she had the money to buy them. Her faulty logic landed her in a pit of financial trouble.

Delayed gratification is a matter of trust. Can you trust God to hold something for you until he provides the money to buy it? If God knows it is truly in your best interest, he will give it to you. And if he knows it is not in your best interest, do you still want it?

—JAN SILVIOUS (*Smart Girls Think Twice*)

253

CAN YOU IMAGINE!

"Cheer up, don't be afraid. For the Lord your God has arrived to live among you. He is a mighty Savior. He will give you victory. He will rejoice over you in great gladness; he will love you and not accuse you." Is that a joyous choir I hear? No, it is the Lord himself exulting over you in happy song.

—*Zephaniah 3:16–18* TLB

Can you imagine that God's delight in us is so genuine, so spontaneous, so spirited that he exults over us by singing happy songs? Can you imagine that he not only lives among us (within us) and promises to give us victory, but also that he rejoices over us in great gladness? Who in your lifetime—past, present, or future—has ever been or will ever be so utterly in love with you?

Only God! Plain, simple, profound. That realization is enough to cause me to look up, up, up, and topple over with cheer-inducing, heartfelt gratitude. It's wonderful to know that no matter what or whom I meet on the road, I can be of good cheer. How? Why? It is because Jesus lives within me, and he is an overcomer. And because of his indwelling presence, so too am I.

So come on! Grab your robe and join the joyous choir. There's a lot more living, loving, and laughing to do. Sure, there's plenty of stuff in this world to steal your joy. But remember, you have Jesus. You have a choice. You can choose cheer over fear. And after all is said and done, wouldn't you rather be laughing?

—MARILYN MEBERG (*I'd Rather Be Laughing*)

THE SECRETS OF FRIENDSHIP

Those who love a pure heart and are gracious in speech will have the king as a friend.

—*Proverbs 22:11* NRSV

I'm often asked if I have a formula for maintaining rich, meaningful relationships.

Honestly, there's no formula because every relationship is different. But for me there are two major qualifiers for having friends and being a good friend to somebody else.

First, hold people loosely in your heart. I used to be very hurt when people didn't do things my way or when they chose to be with somebody else. I pouted. I was rude to the one who hurt me. But when I got sick enough of acting that way, I brought God into the problem and asked him to help me grow up. He taught me to release my will and my grip on those who really meant something to me. There's nothing like being free, and that's one of the main ingredients in a meaningful friendship—to be free and let the other person be free.

Second, a rich relationship has to have an investment from both persons. Friendships don't grow rich unless you make deposits: you spend time together, you connect with each other, and you change things around to give balance where it's needed. You constantly have to study the input of that account to see what it needs. I promise you, if you take care of the relationship, it will grow.

—LUCI SWINDOLL (*Life! Celebrate It*)

DIRECTIONALLY MUDDLED

I will instruct you and teach you in the way you should go; I will guide you with My eye.
—Psalm 32:8

I've spent a lifetime directionally muddled. But logistically challenged or not, we are all travelers. Life forces us to hit the road in search of doctors, banks, dry cleaners, groceries, and many other things. My husband, Les, and I divide our time between Texas and Michigan, which means for me, a non-mapper, that I seldom know where I am, much less where the bank is in relationship to our home. So sweet Les, in an attempt to simplify my perpetual lostness, chose the bank directly across the street from our subdivision. No missing piece there—out the driveway, into the bank. Now, if only life were that simple!

Thank heavens for Jesus, who offers to walk with us wherever we are. He promises to guide our steps and light our path. Jesus is there for us if, like Zacchaeus, we are out on a limb. He's there for us if, like Eve, we've taken the wrong path. He's there for us if we are wandering aimlessly or high-stepping with certainty.

Jesus never loses sight of us, even when we're feeling hopelessly lost. He holds all our puzzle pieces. What looks broken to us is whole to him, because he is the beginning and the end of all things.

—PATSY CLAIRMONT (*All Cracked Up*)

BELOVED PILGRIM

When pride comes, then comes disgrace; but wisdom is with the humble.

—*Proverbs 11:2* NRSV

You might be amazed at how freeing it is to lose your reputation. Devastating, yes. I have to admit, it has been one of the most painful experiences of my life. But I'll tell you what—it has freed me from worrying that I might lose my reputation! Been there, lost that, and I'm still breathing. When you survive what you once thought would be an insurmountable loss, you realize that you and God can face just about anything together. I have found that being real, being yourself, is a lot more attractive to others than trying to impress them anyway.

It has forced me to rely not on my own reputation but on God's. It's been made painfully clear that I am not perfect—but *he* is. I can't atone for my sins—but *he* did. God is the only credential we need, and that frees us from worrying about our own lack of certifications, diplomas, and degrees.

To find ultimate freedom, you begin to let who you really are inside shine to the outside world. The world becomes a sort of "come as you are" party—where you are happy to show up just as plain old you: a beloved pilgrim, very much in progress.

—SANDI PATTY (*Falling Forward*)

BETTER BOYS AND GIRLS

The LORD has heard my supplication; the LORD accepts my prayer.
—Psalm 6:9 NRSV

Both of my grandfathers died before I was born. But my mom tells a story about her father that I think is hilarious.

From what I understand, my grandfather was a hardworking man with a simple faith. At mealtimes, his standard grace was: "For what we are about to receive, may the Lord make us truly thankful." But on one particular occasion when they were having guests for lunch after church, my nana asked him to embellish the usual blessing a bit.

He must have forgotten her request, because he started out as he always did: "For what we are about to receive, may the Lord make us truly thankful."

There was a noticeable pause before he added, "And make me a good boy, amen!"

Now, at this point my granddad must have been in his sixties— but I guess that's the only other prayer he could remember from his childhood. I am so sorry I wasn't there. I would have fallen off my chair in hysterics, high-fiving my granddad on the way down!

My nana wanted my granddad to come up with a few more impressive words, but I am convinced that the words we use are of less interest to God than the intent of our hearts. God hears our heart no matter the words we use. Just by being in God's presence, we become "better" boys and girls.

—SHEILA WALSH (*Get Off Your Knees and Pray*)

ITCHY EARS

The time will come when men will not put up with sound doctrine. Instead, to suit their own desires, they will gather around them a great number of teachers to say what their itching ears want to hear. They will turn their ears away from the truth and turn aside to myths.

—2 Timothy 4:3–4 NIV

I was at a meeting when a prayer request was made for a deaf baby scheduled to receive a cochlear implant. The baby's parents asked for prayers that the surgery would go well so the baby would be able to hear and speak. They also requested prayers that the baby's recovery would not be too traumatic—the doctors had warned them that their child, upon hearing sounds for the first time, would probably scream and cry for days.

Immediately, I was struck by the similarities between that little baby and the rest of us. Think about the irony of the baby's situation. Her mother's sweet voice, her brother's laughter, even the sound of her daddy singing a lullaby would initially make this baby cry. And yet, how many of us react the same way when we hear the words *sin, obedience,* or *sacrifice*? Our heavenly Father knows that these are words of love that will bring redemption, blessings, and meaning to our lives, but like that tiny baby, we would rather block out his voice and retreat to our comfortable world.

How about you? Is there something you need to hear, even if it's hard to accept?

—LISA WHELCHEL (*Speaking Mom-ese*)

259

FOUND WORTHY

Come now, let us argue it out, says the LORD: though your sins are like scarlet, they shall be like snow; though they are red like crimson, they shall become like wool.

—Isaiah 1:18 NRSV

God's heart is always tuned to the needs of his creation. Our cries for help are always heard. In addition to that good news, there's no sin he cannot or will not forgive. There are no good deeds we must first perform in order to be good enough for salvation. The thief who hung next to Jesus on the cross brought nothing to him but his splattered record of sin. And yet, the second he asked, he was granted forgiveness. He was immediately deemed worthy to join Jesus in paradise.

What motivates Jesus' selection of those who are imperfect? What motivates Jesus to put aside his own agony and focus on the request of a man who was scum before he met Jesus on the cross? The answer reverberates and fills the entire universe; it is the love of God for those whom he created to receive that love.

If we persist in thinking there's just something about us that God does not cotton to, we would have to rewrite the Bible to prove it! There is instead just something about us he is crazy about! To think otherwise is faulty thinking. To think otherwise is to have no faith in the Word of God, which tells us just how strong his love is for us.

—MARILYN MEBERG (*God at Your Wits' End*)

AN ATTITUDE OF JOY

I will greatly rejoice in the LORD, my soul shall be joyful in my God.
—Isaiah 61:10

My life is not full of joy every minute, but it's true that joy is my most natural posture. I had a happy childhood, and that no doubt makes a big difference in the way I am today. In addition, I've trained myself to look for the bright side of things. I'm rarely around negative people, and if I am, I don't make camp there.

Joy is not only a marvelous gift from God, it's a command (Philippians 4:4 says, "Rejoice!"). Joy is also a learned behavior. If you're generous with other people, they will be generous with you, and that alone will bring you unspeakable joy. Joy starts inside yourself. You can't expect to get it from somebody else first.

Although I experience abundant joy in life, laugh heartily and often, and appreciate humor at every turn, my temperament poses certain challenges: when I tire, I get cranky. When things are out of order, I can be stubbornly controlling. When I find myself at the mercy of another's plans or schedule, I can be very frustrated. In that sense, joy does not always come naturally to me . . . it's an attitude I choose and try very hard to maintain.

—LUCI SWINDOLL (*Life! Celebrate It*)

THE RISEN SAVIOR

> *They said to one another, "Did not our heart burn within us while He talked with us on the road, and while He opened the Scriptures to us?"*
>
> —Luke 24:32

Long ago and far away, two men traveled by foot on a dusty road. As they walked, they were deep in conversation about someone they knew, a teacher. They had heard of him in the conversations of others in the villages, and as time went on, more and more stories of him were exchanged among the townspeople. Finally, these men were drawn into his company and followed his teachings.

But this day, the men spoke of his shocking crucifixion. He had left behind a handful of stories, promises, and unanswered questions. Their expectations were dashed. Great mystery surrounded this teacher as they spoke of his intentions and his resulting death. It was said he died of a broken heart—a heart broken for humankind.

They wondered aloud about him. They had many stories—and what stories they were! What did it all mean?

A thousand thoughts whirled through their minds as they chattered on. In fact, they were so caught up in their questions that they hardly noticed that the Answer had joined them on their journey. Until he spoke . . . and their hearts burned within them. What man is this? They took a second look. Then their eyes were opened. It was Jesus, the risen Savior.

—PATSY CLAIRMONT (*All Cracked Up*)

TESTING GOD

Fear not, for I am with you.

—Isaiah 43:5

During a particularly tough time in my life, I asked myself a difficult, life-changing question. Is the God I have been following since I was eleven years old big enough to handle my questions, fear, and anger? I needed to know.

So I tested him. I questioned his will. And every time I expressed to him my fear and weakness, he was there with me. At first I didn't want to acknowledge his presence, as if by doing so I was saying I accepted what was going on. In some strange way it was almost as if I thought my protests would keep the pain away.

But even though I continued to struggle, I was deeply aware of God's comfort and understanding. And in time, I opened my heart to what he was speaking to me. And slowly but surely, as the weeks passed, I found a strength I hadn't had before. It was nothing to do with me. I didn't see myself as any stronger than I was before. In fact, quite the opposite. I became aware that God was right beside me and that when I fell down, he would pick me up. He imparted his own strength to me.

—SHEILA WALSH (*Get Off Your Knees and Pray*)

NO REGRETS

We all make many mistakes. If people never said anything wrong,
they would be perfect and able to control their entire selves, too.

—James 3:2 NCV

I was in California speaking at a conference, and my mother was in an Alabama hospital. She'd been sick for a few days but was quite content. She liked her room, her nurses, and even the food.

She had been fragile for several years. After she broke a hip and it failed to heal, she was left a virtual invalid. Her world became small, but her capacity to communicate remained large. She checked e-mail regularly and kept a cell phone near her bed. We talked twice a day, and being her only child, I visited in person often.

When I called her from California, she told me she wasn't feeling as well. I called several more times, and with each call I could tell she was feeling worse. I closed each conversation with "I love you," and she said, "I love you too."

Those were the last words we spoke to one another. She died before I could get to her bedside.

But it was all right in my spirit. We closed that last chapter of our lives together with "I love you," and although I miss her more than I ever knew I would, there are no regrets.

Are there any words you need to say to someone today? We never know when a conversation may be our last encounter, leaving one of us to hold in our heart either thankfulness or regret for the words spoken—or left unsaid.

—JAN SILVIOUS (*Smart Girls Think Twice*)

FAITH IS NOT BLIND

Jesus said, "So, you believe because you've seen with your own eyes. Even better blessings are in store for those who believe without seeing."
—John 20:29 MSG

Many people seem inclined to consider faith a more or less blind system of belief while others just can't quite fall for it. It seems too hard to do, blindly believing without any evidence. The Danish philosopher Kierkegaard referred to the need for a "leap of faith" to enter into a realm of spirituality.

But thinking that faith is a hard, complicated concept that must be blindly accepted is faulty thinking, because viewing faith as "blind" totally misses the scriptural teaching of what faith is. When the Bible describes blindness, it is an image representing people who have chosen sin as a way of living. They walk in darkness. The plan of God is to call people out of the darkness. Faith cannot be blind, because faith is authored by he who leads us to the light.

The word *faith* means "trust." To trust God is not an act of blind, unreasonable belief, because God proves himself to be utterly trustworthy at all times. Christianity is not based on myths or made-up stories. It is based on the testimony of those who witnessed jaw-dropping evidence that God sent his Son, Jesus, to this earth. Our faith is not blind. It is based on facts we can trust, facts that inspire faith.

—MARILYN MEBERG (*God at Your Wits' End*)

265

DOUBTS AND FEARS

Let us hold fast the confession of our hope without wavering,
for He who promised is faithful.
—Hebrews 10:23

By nature, I'm not prone to doubt and fear. I really, really, really try to believe what God says and trust him to come through with the goods. When he says I don't have to be afraid, I try hard to believe that and go on. When he says he will always be with me, I know he will. When he promises to provide for my needs, I look to him to do that. In short . . . when I take God at his word, I don't have many doubts or fears.

The key to all this is learning to trust God in every little nook and cranny of your day. Life works when we trust, and the love comes because we feel blessed in that trust. We love the one who keeps his word.

Commit your way to the Lord, and see where he takes you. When you hit a bump in the road, ask yourself, "What could God be teaching me in this?" Remember, even when you are struggling, he is not making a mistake with your life. You don't have to live with doubt and fear. Let God help you turn your fear to fearlessness and your doubt to miracle-working faith!

—LUCI SWINDOLL (*Life! Celebrate It*)

SO SAY THE JOYOLOGISTS

When the righteous see God in action they'll laugh, they'll sing, they'll laugh and sing for joy.

—Psalm 68:3 MSG

According to some joyologists (uh-huh, *joyologists*—those given to the promotion of joy), you can lose weight if you guffaw daily. So does this mean we can titter till our tummies tuck? Or better yet, chortle till the cellulite runs smooth? I'm afraid I'd have to be permanently hysterical to accomplish that task.

Can't you see it now? A world emphasis on belly laughing, with people lining up single file around the block, waiting to slip into a joy booth so they can laugh off lunch. Or employers offering health incentives for workers who snicker heartily. Have you ever wondered why God designed us with the ability to laugh and cry? I guess he knew we would need to do both as a way to pour off emotional excess; otherwise, we might blow a gasket.

I've heard it said that hearty laughter sends fresh shipments of oxygen to the brain, which causes it to loosen up. Hmm, if it can loosen up my brain, then maybe, just maybe, the joyologists are right, and it could loosen up my jeans. That would be great. Then I wouldn't have to unsnap them to eat, sit, travel, and breathe. I'd much rather chuckle myself fit than deny myself indulgences, but I have this nagging feeling I may need to do both.

—PATSY CLAIRMONT (*All Cracked Up*)

UNPACK THOSE BAGS

Praise be to the LORD, to God our Savior, who daily bears our burdens.

—Psalm 68:19 NIV

I wonder how many of us are weighed down by the stuff we drag around, day after day. Baggage is inevitable; who among us can walk through life without picking up some shame or fears or insecurities, right? The question is, why do we persist in hanging on to these things, jealously guarding our junk as though it's worth keeping?

Scripture reminds us to cast our cares on our Father, but even though we have God's open invitation to unpack our heavy bags, we seem to find that very hard to do.

I have asked people why they don't just surrender their burdens to God in prayer. Here are a few of their answers:

+ I don't have time to pray.
+ I'm too tired to pray.
+ I start all right, but then I get distracted.
+ To be honest, I'm not sure God is listening.

I empathize with those concerns, yet I am convinced it would revolutionize our lives if we were better able to understand that prayer is a gift, rather than a chore. Something to look forward to, rather than something we're graded on. It's not about how well we pray, but about who is listening to our prayers.

—SHEILA WALSH (*Get Off Your Knees and Pray*)

SEND IN THE CLONES

*"I am the LORD, who made all things, who alone stretched
out the heavens, who spread out the earth by myself ... Woe
to him who strives with him who formed him, a pot among
earthen pots! Does the clay say to him who forms it, 'What are
you making?'"*
—Isaiah 44:24, 45:9 ESV

I remember a photo I had taken while on *The Facts of Life.* I was
so worried on the day of the photo session because I woke up
with a huge zit. I tried everything to cover it up and, of course,
made it worse. I was so naïve. When I arrived at the studio, the
photographer acted like I was a country bumpkin for worrying.
He not only airbrushed my pimple away, but he also shaved off a
few pounds by "contouring" my chin and cheeks. Now, that is my
kind of diet!

Maybe that is why everyone starts looking alike in
Hollywood—they must all use the same software. How boring.
If God's other works of art are any indication, he likes variety.
Consider flowers, fish, and animals. They come in all shapes and
sizes. Look at trees. Are they all pines? No, as a matter of fact,
many of the most beautiful trees are the largest and oldest.

Are you content looking the way God created you? I really
wrestle with that. I'll probably always struggle with a few extra
pounds, but I'm learning to be comfortable in my own skin.

—LISA WHELCHEL (*Taking Care of the Me in Mommy*)

SATISFYING THE MIND

This is my prayer: that your love may abound more and more in knowledge and depth of insight, so that you may be able to discern what is best and may be pure and blameless until the day of Christ.

—Philippians 1:9–10 NIV

Faith is not a mindless leap into the unknown that's too hard for us to fathom. Faith enables reason to go beyond its human limitations. But faith is not a simple result of reason; it is reason submitting to the truth of Scripture, which is saturated with and enlivened by the Holy Spirit of God. There are mysteries of faith that lie beyond my human understanding, but I believe them because they are rooted in the strength of God's Word. I don't pretend to understand the mystery of his ways, but Scripture describes God in ways that satisfy my mind.

Reason is a gift of God. It speaks to that God-placed center within us all that recognizes truth. We choose to believe that truth. We choose to embrace that truth. And we choose to live by faith, which is trustworthy.

I am not advocating an academic or sterile approach to our faith, but I am thrilled that it can stand up to scrutiny. Faith produces in us responses that go far beyond our scrutiny once our scrutiny is satisfied.

—MARILYN MEBERG (*God at Your Wits' End*)

THE DINNER PARTY

*God, who gets invited to dinner at your place? How do we get
on your guest list?*

—Psalm 15:1 MSG

We all want to sit at God's dining table. We long to have fellowship and fun with him. We want to see how he sets the table and who else is there and find out what will be the topics of conversation. And here's the great part—in Psalm 15, he tells us what it takes to get on that list. He says, "Walk straight, act right, tell the truth. Don't hurt your friend, don't blame your neighbor; despise the despicable. Keep your word even when it costs you, make an honest living, never take a bribe" (vv. 2–5).

That list is perfect because there's not one thing about how the person has to be dressed or what she must weigh, or whether she has money or is educated or famous. There's nothing about looks or beauty or ability. It's all—*all!*—about character. It's about the inside of the person. And who doesn't want to be with people like that? This is what we want in a dinner guest. It's what God requires in order to be on his guest list. And you can bet your bottom dollar if you value these attributes as well, you'll be right at the top of everybody's list.

—LUCI SWINDOLL (*Life! Celebrate It*)

THE FINE ART OF SPINNING

*Be constantly renewed in the spirit of your mind [having a
fresh mental and spiritual attitude].*
—Ephesians 4:23 AMP

Did you know that you can tell if an egg is raw or hard-cooked by
spinning it? If the egg spins like a top, it's hard-cooked, but if it
wobbles like a Weeble, it's raw. Try it.

Spinning people is far riskier. If they're raw, well, who knows
what they might do? They could break open and slobber all over
you. I hate when that happens. And if they're hard-cooked, all I
can say is watch out when they run out of spin.

I personally am a conundrum—both hard and delicate
(sounds better than "raw"). Perhaps that's true of most of us. We
have our ornery times and our fragile moments. I become very
Weeble-like when my nerves are frayed and my coping mecha-
nisms are stretched rubber-band thin. Whereas, if I'm full of my
agenda and pressed for time when you twirl into my space and
set me in a spin, I can be hard-boiled. My shell thickens, and the
color of my yolk fades.

A yolk's color depends on the hen's diet. Similarly, I find that
if I've had a regular diet from the Scriptures, I'm not only brighter
but I also handle an unexpected spin with greater finesse.

Lesson? Don't let your Weeble wobble. When life throws
you into a spin, enjoy the ride!

—PATSY CLAIRMONT (*All Cracked Up*)

TOO TIRED TO PRAY

Jesus came to the disciples and found them sleeping, and said to Peter, "What? Could you not watch with Me one hour?"
—Matthew 26:36–41

In the Garden of Gethsemane, as Jesus agonized over his coming crucifixion, he found Peter sleeping. Peter loved Jesus and was devoted to him, but he was clothed in human flesh like you and me. I'm sure he agonized when Jesus woke him that night. Imagine how Peter felt when he saw Jesus' tear-stained face and realized he had fallen asleep instead of obediently watching and praying.

Scripture explains that there is a war between our spirit and our flesh, between wanting to do more and wanting to take five before doing it. Of course, we often bring it upon ourselves by doing too much. The apostle Paul describes this battle between spirit and flesh in Romans 7. He writes, "Why don't I do the thing I want to do but instead do the thing I don't want to do?" (verse 15, my paraphrase). I'm sure Paul knew that when we relegate prayer to the bottom of our priority list, we won't have enough energy left to do more than mutter a few familiar phrases before we call it a day.

So we have to consciously work toward increasing our strength for prayer. I encourage you to fight the "I'm too tired to pray" blahs.

—SHEILA WALSH (*Get Off Your Knees and Pray*)

WORDS CAN BLESS

May God, who gives this patience and encouragement, help you live in complete harmony with each other, as is fitting for followers of Christ Jesus. Then all of you can join together with one voice, giving praise and glory to God, the Father of our Lord Jesus Christ.

—Romans 15:5–6 NLT

On a recent family vacation, my husband and I took our five grandchildren to the hotel breakfast. We seated them at a table, found out what they wanted, and then began gathering their food. The children quietly talked among themselves while they waited for us.

When I set their food in front of them and turned to fill a plate for myself, a woman sitting several feet away said, "Are those your grandchildren?" When I said yes, she lavished this grandmother's soul with words of life. "They are so well behaved," she said. "You don't see much of that these days."

I grinned from ear to ear and thanked her profusely. Then I told my grandchildren—and later my children—what had been said and how proud I was of them. One comment from a stranger sent words of life washing over the whole Silvious clan. In the same way, your words of life can bless others in ways you may never imagine.

—JAN SILVIOUS (*Smart Girls Think Twice*)

WHO IS YOUR FAITH CENTER?

*Let us run with perseverance the race that is set before us,
looking to Jesus the pioneer and perfecter of our faith.*
—Hebrews 12:1–2 NRSV

My mom was the faith person in our family. Both my father and I would seek out the encouragement of her gentle but unwavering faith. Early in life my thought about faith was that some have it and some don't, and I believed I fell into the "don't have it" category. For that reason I wanted always to be near my mom's faith center.

Do you recognize the faulty thinking in that? Somehow I felt I had to find a "faith person" to help me with my challenges because I wasn't sufficiently faith-endowed. There is nowhere in Scripture that says God has a faith camp where some of his children "have it" and some don't—that thinking is totally unscriptural. But I'll have to admit this thinking still seeps into my soul from time to time and says, *You need to find someone to believe for you, Marilyn. . . . Your faith is shaky. It's too small.*

We must remind ourselves of a very basic truth. Our faith source is Jesus. He is the author of my faith. He is the giver of my faith. I am not. My mother was not. Any other person is not. Jesus gave me faith when I received him into my heart and life. That faith is totally, personally my Jesus-given faith.

—MARILYN MEBERG (*God at Your Wits' End*)

275

LOVING YOURSELF

We love because he first loved us.
—1 John 4:19 NIV

God's desire is for you to love yourself and accept yourself just as you are. He doesn't want you to go through life trying to fake it because you wish you were somebody else. He puts stock in character rather than playing charades. But the apostle Paul was right when he said that which we don't want to do we find ourselves doing and that which we want to do, we so often don't (see Romans 7:19). That's why being yourself is "the hardest battle that any human being can fight and never stop fighting." But it's a battle you can win, just like so many others already have.

Let me suggest ten areas I work on when I get bogged down and forget to love myself as God commanded me to:

+ Be content with what you have.
+ Stop comparing.
+ Count your blessings.
+ Quit personalizing every comment.
+ Maintain a servant spirit.
+ Do the unexpected for a loved one.
+ Keep a heart of gratitude.
+ Don't be negative.
+ Respect yourself.
+ Take God at his word.

—LUCI SWINDOLL (*Life! Celebrate It*)

TRUE VIEW

Let me live whole and holy, soul and body so I can always walk with my head held high.

—Psalm 119:80 MSG

Do you ever wonder where your self-esteem resides? Which body part houses it? Does it bunk in your heart? Or lease a room in your mind? Perhaps it's a vagabond or a multi-tasker and divvies up its locales. Or perhaps it's sharing a room with emotions.

I have no idea where my self-esteem lives, but I do know it's alive. Some days, it lags behind what I know to be true; while other days, it inspires me to do cartwheels.

I guess what we should ask ourselves is whether we need to replace the mirror on our self-worth so we can capture a true view of who we are. While I believe we can spend too much time on myopic examinations, I also think we can spend too little effort embracing our value. Before we realize it, that delicate balance slips a notch, which leaves us off kilter. That puts us in as much trouble as viewing ourselves through a fractured mirror, which suggests we are irreparable.

Life comes with distortions—proof the enemy has a strategy, which includes diminishing our view of ourselves so we don't live fully or joyously. Christ has come to heal the network of cracks in our self-esteem, that we might view him more clearly and therefore see our own worth.

—PATSY CLAIRMONT (*All Cracked Up*)

ALONE WITH GOD

Devote yourselves to prayer, being watchful and thankful.

—*Colossians 4:2* NIV

It's easy to get so caught up in the physical challenges of our days that we forget the very real spiritual battle that rages on around us. We have an enemy who would love to keep us so distracted and busy that we forget to focus on what really matters: our relationship with our Father.

Jesus knew this and he purposely pulled away, not only from the crowds, but even from his friends, to be able to be alone with his Father. He obviously craved that time to restore himself.

Of course, not all of us are refreshed by being alone the way Jesus was. Each of us has a unique, God-given personality that affects how easily we're distracted and by what, what helps us refocus and what doesn't. What matters is finding a place where you know you can block out other distractions and enjoy being with the Father, who longs to spend time with you.

Even more important is making the commitment to fight our human tendency toward distraction. Sometimes I will take a notebook and write down twenty things that I love about being God's daughter. I can only imagine that our specific declarations of love to God are precious to him.

—SHEILA WALSH (*Get Off Your Knees and Pray*)

CREATIVE IN HIS IMAGE

All things were created through him and for him.
—Colossians 1:16 ESV

When I was a little girl, my mom sewed almost all of my clothes. Once I had kids, the DNA took over and I was overcome with the desire to sew like the wind. One of the things I loved best about our little house when my children were small was the fact that I could place my sewing table next to the sliding-glass door and watch my children play in the backyard. Now that I have teenagers, I can't even safely pick out my children's clothes, much less sew them. So I've transferred my obsession to scrapbooking.

I once received an e-mail asking, "Are hobbies necessary?" Well, I don't know that I would deem them necessary, but they have helped preserve my sanity. I think I could go so far as to say that hobbies are downright godly! God's very first action in the Bible was to create. He is called our Creator. "Everyone who is called by My name, whom I have created for My glory; I have formed him, yes, I have made him" (Isaiah 43:7 NKJV). I believe it is the spirit of God within us that yearns to create and is refreshed when we do.

From Beth Moore's studies, I have learned that to glorify God means to reflect his nature. What a great way to bring glory to God! The next time you feel a twinge of guilt for spending time on yourself with a hobby, remind yourself that even God likes to do a little something for himself by exercising his creativity.

—LISA WHELCHEL (*Taking Care of the Me in Mommy*)

CHOOSING TO BELIEVE

Without faith it is impossible to please God, because anyone who comes to him must believe that he exists and that he rewards those who earnestly seek him.

—Hebrews 11:6 NIV

What about faith? What does it require? Faith requires choosing: choosing to believe. For example, I choose to believe the evidence I see of God in his creation. I can't deny that creative power came from somewhere. In addition, I believe Jesus, God's Son, was with him in the beginning and created everything there is.

I also choose to believe the Word of God, and when I am at my wits' end I crawl into its pages so my spirit can be enlivened, strengthened, and enabled to believe beyond what I see. The Bible is my faith object. It is crucial to my spiritual balance and my understanding of the degree to which God loves me. It teaches me about faith.

Faith is not as complicated as I have sometimes made it. It is not hard. Quite simply, faith is a gift, and this gift is mine for the taking. It is not a gift I work to be worthy of or can work to achieve. As is true of any gift, I reach out for it. I accept it from the hand of God my Father. My part in all this is to believe in the giver of the gift and then in the gift itself. I trust. I believe. I receive Jesus as Savior. Faith initiates that process.

—MARILYN MEBERG (*God at Your Wits' End*)

DOORS OF POTENTIAL

Jesus said, "I came so they can have real and eternal life, more and better life than they ever dreamed of."
—*John 10:10* MSG

The year I turned seventy, it didn't seem possible. Where did all those years go? The reflection in the mirror answers the question to the whereabouts of some of them, but only my heart can tell me whether or not I have lived well. And it's very important to me to live well. God wants us all to live fully . . . and well. It is part of his dream for us.

We have no idea what lies ahead or how God will open doors of potentiality when we consciously choose to get out of the ruts we're in and start moving down new paths about which we can be excited—even passionate. Some think being adventuresome means taking a trip around the world, bungee jumping, or walking into a lion's cage at the zoo. Not at all. It's an attitude, not a behavior. It's daring to be curious about the unknown, to dream big dreams, to live outside prescribed boxes, to take risks, and above all, daring to investigate the way we live until we discover the deepest treasured purpose of why we are here.

—LUCI SWINDOLL (*I Married Adventure*)

GOD'S AMAZING ARTWORK

[Christ] is the image of the invisible God, the firstborn over all creation. For by Him all things were created that are in heaven and that are on earth, visible and invisible . . . All things were created through Him and for Him.

—Colossians 1:15–16

We live in a broken world in which many things are askew; so it's no wonder we forget all the lovely things God has written his signature on, starting with the heavens and the earth.

Perhaps because children live so close to the earth, they often are the messengers that remind us of a frog's throaty croak or a cricket's high-pitched chirp or a katydid's tattletale song. Kids are the ones who affirm the dandelion's beauty, a stick's usefulness, and a pebble's colors.

When was the last time you stared into the dazzling pattern of the stars? Or gathered a fistful of lilies of the valley or crammed a jar full of hydrangeas or arranged a vase of peonies? When did you sit at the water's edge and lean in to hear its song? Has it been too long since you sifted sand through your toes or traced the lines on a beautiful shell that you discovered? Who was the last child you introduced to a tadpole? Or helped to catch a turtle?

Creation is bursting with discoveries. A billowing cloud, a sun pattern on a patch of pumpkins, or a bulging garden all comfort us. I guess the Lord knew we would need these undeniable reminders of his presence on earth.

—PATSY CLAIRMONT (*All Cracked Up*)

THE DISCIPLINE OF PRAYER

Never stop praying.
—*1 Thessalonians 5:17* CEV

Sometimes we find it difficult to pray because we're not sure God is listening to us. That's what a man—he looked to be in his forties, successful, married with children—once said to me. When I asked him why he thought God might not be listening, he said he could see no evidence of God having heard him. He told me he has been in the church most of his life but recently has found himself wondering if anything he believed was actually true. To be honest, he's not alone. I hear similar concerns in many e-mails and letters I receive.

I think one of our greatest challenges in prayer is feeling God's presence. We live in a sensory age where we are bombarded by ads for quick fixes and miracle drugs. The discipline of prayer offers no easy solutions for the wounds and worries of life, and it often goes without physical sensation. It's therefore tempting to believe prayer isn't worth the time.

But prayer isn't supposed to offer a simple solution. It's meant to be a place to take our concerns and lay them at Jesus' feet. When we approach our petitions in that way, they become not just a time to test God's response but an opportunity to release the cares of our lives.

—SHEILA WALSH (*Get Off Your Knees and Pray*)

THE GARDENER KNOWS BEST

"I am the true vine, and My Father is the vinedresser. Every branch in Me that does not bear fruit, He takes away; and every branch that bears fruit, He prunes it so that it may bear more fruit."
—*John 15:1-2* NASB

When God is working on a certain area of your life, it seems like everywhere you turn he is repeating something he's already told you a hundred times. By letting his voice echo in my mind, the Lord has taught me a bunch of great lessons. For example, he has to tell me again and again to focus on prioritizing my time well.

Often, his lessons surprise me. One particular time, I distinctly felt him telling me not to wake up so early to spend time with him. After getting up before dawn, I was wiped out early in the evening. Jesus caught me off guard when he pointed out that my "window times" with the kids—our special time for those heart-to-heart chats—were getting shorter and shorter when I put them to bed at night. Meanwhile, the kids needed to talk to me more than ever, and I needed to get up later to make that possible.

The lessons the Lord has taught me are precious. In fact, I'm learning to love his pruning shears. I don't always understand why he cuts away certain branches, but I do know that by staying connected with him, I will bear fruit that lasts. What is he trying to trim in your life?

—LISA WHELCHEL (*Speaking Mom-ese*)

MORE GOOD NEWS ABOUT FAITH

*"If your faith were only the size of a mustard seed," Jesus
answered, "it would be large enough to uproot that mulberry
tree over there and send it hurtling into the sea! Your
command would bring immediate results!"*

—Luke 17:6 *TLB*

Want some good news about faith? If you feed it, it grows! We don't
need to continue thinking we are feeble and weak in our faith. Jesus
talked about the mustard plant, an annual plant with very small
seeds. It grows to a considerable size in Palestine.

When his disciples told Jesus they needed more faith and
asked how they could get it, Jesus said, "Believe." Then he walked
away.

With all due respect, I don't find that a very satisfying answer.

I would like it if Jesus spelled out how to get more faith in an
easy formula that I could slip into my purse. When I am feeling
feeble, I could pull out the list . . . mutter over it . . . find the
problem . . . and then fix it. But the whole thing about our spiritual walk is that it is not defined by formulas.

My job is to remember I can choose to believe because it was
God who authored my faith—enabled my faith in the first place.
"I believe, Lord; help my unbelief." In other words, "Help me
grow." And just look what can happen if my faith is no bigger than
a mustard seed!

—MARILYN MEBERG (*God at Your Wits' End*)

THE ADVENTURESOME SPIRIT

The way you tell me to live is always right; help me understand it so I can live to the fullest.

—Psalm 119:144 MSG

It seems like there is something electrifying about individuals with adventuresome spirits. They see life through a different lens. They don't wait on the sidelines. They don't keep saying, "If only . . ." or "Why me?" They don't battle against unusual circumstances or departures from the norm. It's as if they operate from a whole different voltage or current. They almost emit electricity because nothing about them is dull or uninteresting or unplugged.

A life of adventure is ours for the taking, whether we're seven or seventy—whether we throw a paper route, take care of an aging parent, study for a degree, work around the clock, stay at home to raise our children, or circle the globe in the service of our Creator. I'm convinced that the whole world is better when we, as individuals, capture and savor each moment as the gift that it is, embrace the challenge or joy of it, marry it (if you will), and thereby transform it with the magic of creative possibility. Life, for the most part, is what we make it. We have been given a responsibility to live it fully, joyfully, completely, and richly, in whatever span of time God grants us on this earth.

—LUCI SWINDOLL (*I Married Adventure*)

FLOOD DAMAGE

"I will restore health to you and heal you of your wounds," says the LORD.

—*Jeremiah 30:17*

After Hurricane Katrina blasted the Gulf Coast, officials warned that it would take a lot of time, money, and cooperation to restore people's lives to anything resembling normal. New Orleans experienced not only damage caused by rain and wind but also from cracks in the levies, which caused severe flooding.

At one time, my life was awash with emotional whirlpools, I felt hopeless. I didn't want to pray. . . . I felt like my power lines were down and fear rampaged its windy way through my life, leaving a swath of instability. I could feel my life cracking apart—my emotions were erratic, my relationships were troubling, I was flooded with regret, and my future was dim.

That is, until I committed to rolling up my sleeves and doing the hard work of recovery. That meant I had to begin hauling away the debris of anger and fear, repairing the wind-damaged roof of my mind, and become willing to receive outside assistance from wise counselors.

Waiting for all the broken pieces of a life to be reworked is neither fast nor easy, but the end result is transformation. Nothing is more satisfying than to see God's light peering through. It changes everything.

—PATSY CLAIRMONT (*All Cracked Up*)

A DOOR IN THE WALL

Cast all your anxiety on him because he cares for you.
—*1 Peter 5:7 NIV*

Yes, it is hard to pray. It's much easier to spend our free time flopping down and turning on the television than following the example of Christ and pulling away from the noise and distractions for alone time with our Father. Every believer has experienced the difficulties of an intentional prayer life. But when we persist in seeing prayer as a challenge—as a wall between us and God—and walk away in defeat, we walk away carrying the same burdens we arrived with.

Instead of walking away unsatisfied, see if you can imagine that there's a door in that wall, like the wonderful wardrobe that took Lucy into Narnia in C. S. Lewis's *The Lion, the Witch and the Wardrobe*. Prayer is our escape from this world. Prayer is not a chore or something we'll be tested on at the end of each week. It's our time to crawl into our Father's embrace and lay our cares upon him. It's only when we are able to quiet the noises outside and within that we remember all his amazing promises to us. Prayer is not something that belongs on our to-do list, but rather on our to-live list.

—SHEILA WALSH (*Get Off Your Knees and Pray*)

FOOT IN MOUTH

We use our tongues to praise our Lord and Father, but then we curse people, whom God made like himself. Praises and curses come from the same mouth!

—James 3:9–10 NCV

One day I was chatting with a man as we waited in line. We began talking about words, which led him to describe a recent incident in his own life. He'd been chatting casually with two women when they started bitterly denouncing the war in Iraq. Having been the commander of a military police unit in Iraq, he didn't enjoy hearing their harsh words on a topic they knew so little about. He hoped they would soon change the subject.

Finally it became obvious they weren't going to stop. He then reached down to his knees with both hands and tucked his trouser cuffs into the top of what obviously were prostheses. He had lost both legs in Iraq. He said he looked up at the women but said nothing. They gulped and fell silent.

One of the most practical ways to avoid awkward situations in which we find ourselves wishing we could snatch back our words is first to filter them through the grid of *Is it true? Is it kind? Is it necessary?* As you interact with friends and family today, take a moment to think twice before speaking, knowing that words can pack a powerful punch.

—JAN SILVIOUS (*Smart Girls Think Twice*)

HELP, GOD

Faith comes by hearing, and hearing by the word of God.
—Romans 10:17

The apostle Paul said that faith comes from hearing the Word of God. The Bible is our faith object. Our faith grows as we study it.

Scripture reassures us, "No one who trusts God like this—heart and soul—will ever regret it. Everyone who calls, 'Help, God!' gets help." I am blown away by the fantastic encouragement these words from Scripture provide. Forgive me, but I'm going to throw out a formula I see in Romans, chapter 10:

+ You say the words "Help, God."
+ You trust him to help you.
+ You remember you're not doing anything, just calling out to God and trusting him to do it for you.

Does this sound too easy? Too passive? Too laid back in my hammock and munching Milk Duds while God works? It is not passive at all, in that God not only invites our participation as he builds our faith lives, he requires it. You try lying back in your hammock, and he'll tip you out of it. You are in a loving partnership, but he's in charge. You first say the words, then you trust him with your growth, and he takes over. But he takes you with him.

—MARILYN MEBERG (*God at Your Wits' End*)

BRINGING THE WORLD DOWN TO SIZE

Jesus said, "Anything is possible if a person believes."
—Mark 9:23 NLT

One of my most treasured possessions is a big, elaborate world globe. Sometimes I just twirl it and think about the cultures spinning across my mind's eye. When something earth shattering happens on the other side of the world, and I read about it in the newspaper or see it happen on TV, I go over to the globe and find that very spot. If I'm reading a book about a particular place in the ocean or on a mountain peak, I check it out on my globe. I like knowing what country borders on another, where the oceans meet, what's on the equator. I'm a nut for all that stuff.

Even though the world is huge, there's something personal and intimate about it when it's right in front of me, in a round ball, with all the countries and oceans delineated. Everything seems accessible, within reach. No borders or boundaries or impasses. I love that. Anything is possible.

This outlook gives us the capacity to dream big, dare to try new things, and believe we can overcome detours and obstacles that get in our way or hold us back. If the world isn't such an ominous, scary place, then we are more inclined to reach out to others and give our hearts to them.

—LUCI SWINDOLL (*I Married Adventure*)

JIGGLE WITH JOY

You have let me experience the joys of life and the exquisite
pleasures of your own eternal presence.
—Psalm 16:11 TLB

On my birthday last year, a friend sent me a duck. Yep, a duck. He's short and squat, which seemed a tad too personal, but my perception changed when I squeezed his wing. He began to sing and dance, and I began to laugh aloud. He was the cutest bundle of yellow, wrapped up in a song. His toe tapped, his wings flapped, and his shoulders (do ducks have shoulders?) gyrated to the song "Singin' in the Rain." He was touting a yellow slicker hat atop his fuzzy head and a green-and-white striped bow around his chubby neck. I'm crazy about this perky bundle of fun because he never fails to make me jiggle with joy.

Ever notice how a good giggle renews your energy and refreshes your attitude? I think that's why comical folks are so popular. Humor makes everyone's life a little easier.

My friend Marilyn, when feeling unheard in a group, will walk to the nearest wall and begin talking to it. It cracks me up every time. I've taken to imitating Marilyn. I just release my verbal offering on a nearby door, empty chair, or painting on the wall. Even if no one in my group notices, it makes me chuckle. Of course, be prepared to receive odd stares from passersby.

—PATSY CLAIRMONT (*All Cracked Up*)

OUR FATHER

Jesus said, "You should pray like this: Our Father in heaven, help us to honor your name."

—Matthew 6:9 CEV

If you ask me, one of the reasons it is important for us to talk to God is that prayer implies trust. It's our way of saying to God:

+ I believe you are in control.
+ I believe you love me.
+ I believe you make everything work out for good no matter how things may appear.

The first words of the prayer Jesus taught his followers were, "Our Father." The picture is a very intimate one—an invitation to come as a child and curl up on your father's lap and tell him all about it.

I've heard Donald Miller speak of the way believers often approach God as if he were their boss, apologizing for being late or not quite "on task." He reminded us of Christ's welcome to pray to "Our Father" and asked, "When was the last time you curled up in your boss's arms and shared your heart?"

Avoiding the obvious bad jokes, Miller's point is clear. We are invited into a relationship of absolute trust and draw close to our Father's heart. The more time we spend in God's presence, the more our trust grows even when things don't go as we planned.

—SHEILA WALSH (*Get Off Your Knees and Pray*)

EMBRACE THE JOURNEY

Do not neglect to do good and to share what you have, for such sacrifices are pleasing to God.
—Hebrews 13.16 NRSV

God has put the world on my heart—he's put it on all our hearts. His desire is that we would go into it—in whatever way we can. He has a gift for the entire world and it is in us, his people.

Every person is a combination of many factors woven together from the joys and sorrows of life. We're also the product of our choices. We're the result of what was or was not done for or to us by our parents, siblings, associates, and friends. The journey we're on is planned and watched over by a loving God who wants us to treasure the gift of being alive and who sets us free to participate in our own destiny. Embracing that journey— whatever it is for each of us, wherever it takes us—is imperative to capturing the spirit of adventure.

When we realize our lives are to be given away, everything about our outlook changes and grows. God takes our youth and gives us in exchange his truth. We see and do things differently as a result. We think beyond our own borders. The world becomes accessible through the power of God's Spirit and love. We capture each moment, embrace the journey, and go forward.

—LUCI SWINDOLL (*I Married Adventure*)

STAYING AFLOAT

> *Be of good courage, and God shall strengthen your heart, all ye that hope in the LORD.*
>
> —Psalm 31:24 *KJV*

Hope can float a boat. And that's great news for those of us who have been at the helms of our lives for more than a half century. Wind in our faces, hands on the wheel, eyes on the horizon, we've learned to appreciate any gusts that fill our sails and keep us seaborne.

Mom's life had spanned many years, and I knew her time to leave was near. But no matter how securely we batten down our emotional hatches, no matter how storm-savvy we might be, no matter how many warnings we receive, nothing prepares us for the tsunami of the death of a parent. The vacancy it leaves in our lives howls like straight-line winds.

Yet I found solace in the life preserver of hope, that irrepressible buoy that keeps us afloat. I had hope that this generational waterspout within me would lose intensity, hope that my churning emotions would eventually even out, and hope that Mom's charted course to her "home in Glory" lay ahead for me as well. Until I step onto that shore, I choose to lift anchor and reenter the thrill of the open seas, to risk the exploration of uncharted waters (even if it means getting in over my head), knowing that the final destination will be worth the sometimes-upending voyage.

—PATSY CLAIRMONT (*All Cracked Up*)

WHAT'S LOVE GOT TO DO WITH IT?

I love those who love me, and those who seek me diligently will find me.
—Proverbs 8:17

When I was twenty-five years old, British pop star Cliff Richard produced an album for me using his band members. One of Cliff's guitar players was a shy, sweet man named Terry Britton. Terry was also a songwriter, and one day he played a little bit of a song he had just written. I'm sure Terry had no way of knowing when he sat down with his trusty guitar that this song—"What's Love Got to Do with It?"—would be recorded by Tina Turner and go straight to number one on the Billboard charts.

As I think about the title of that song and our question on the relevancy of prayer, it would seem clear to me that love has everything to do with it. Prayer is a way for us to experience love—and not just us showing our love for God, but receiving love from God!

God longs to share his heart with us. He is not looking for perfect little robots to follow directions but people who will share his love. I think it's very difficult for us to embrace the love of God because we have never been loved that way before. That's because all human love—even the best—is conditional and impacted by our behavior or changing circumstances. But God's love is not.

—SHEILA WALSH (*Get Off Your Knees and Pray*)

THE BEST MEDICINE

You will show me the path of life; in Your presence is fullness of joy; at Your right hand are pleasures forevermore.
—*Psalm 16:11* NKJV

When I left show business to concentrate on being a full-time wife and mother, I was thrilled. But even as I enjoyed it, there were times I felt isolated. One day, I invited a couple of friends over for lunch. They brought their kids, and we put them all down for naps. Then we ate lunch and played games for two hours. We laughed like we hadn't laughed in years.

Psalms 16:11 says God's presence is fullness of joy. God receives our joy as a form of worship. He created us with the capacity for joy and laughter and fun. I believe he loves to see us enjoying ourselves and the gift of life he's given us.

Of course, we must use wisdom. Proverbs 21:17a says, "He who loves pleasure will be a poor man" (NKJV). Something tells me that most women reading this book aren't struggling with having too much fun. Our dilemma is trying to find time for a bit of refreshing laughter.

If we make fun a part of our lives, we will create an atmosphere that is lighthearted and full of healthy laughter in our homes or workplaces. Let's all make an effort today to be quicker to laugh over spilled milk than to cry.

—LISA WHELCHEL (*Taking Care of the Me in Mommy*)

QUESTIONS FOR GOD

Grace and peace be multiplied unto you through the knowledge of God, and of Jesus our Lord.

—2 Peter 1:2 KJV

Max Lucado refers to the AIDS epidemic in Africa as the worst global disaster since the days of Noah. One wonders about God in such a disaster. We read accounts of the Holocaust, the Killing Fields of Cambodia, and the torture chambers in the Middle East. We see television coverage of hurricanes, floods, and earthquakes where thousands lose their lives, and we wonder about God.

As C. S. Lewis watched his wife suffer during her terminal illness, he said, "Not that I am in danger of ceasing to believe in God. The real danger is of coming to believe such dreadful things about him. The conclusion I dread is not 'So, there's no God after all'; but 'So this is what God's really like.'"

Feeling abandoned by God is soul shattering. It raises the question of whether or not God truly is involved with his creation. Is that involvement motivated by the overwhelming love and compassion we were led to believe characterize his attitude toward us? Why do our experiences sometimes not coincide with that image? Why does he allow suffering?

Sooner or later in life our circumstances will force us to ask these questions. Admittedly, much about God will remain a mystery, but we can seek knowledge where it may be found.

—MARILYN MEBERG (*God at Your Wits' End*)

FULLY ALIVE

Your life is a journey that you must travel with a deep
consciousness of God.
—1 Peter 1:18 MSG

Moments come and go so fast, but they are what make up the whole of life. Little bitty moments here and there. They turn into hours and days and weeks—ultimately an entire lifetime. When I consciously think about that, it makes me want to slow down. Sometimes I can't slow down. I don't have the time to go slowly. But I can capture a moment in a postcard or photograph. Then, years later it all comes back to me as a sweet gift to myself.

Life is short and everything is irrevocable. No matter what we do to lengthen the moment, we can't. No matter how eager we are to shorten uncomfortable events, that can't be done either. If we don't learn to live fully in the present, much of life passes us by, lost in the cobwebs of time forever. The passage of time can't be retrieved except in our memory banks. That's why we must be all there at any given moment. Even during the times that are frightening or difficult.

Everything has a purpose, and if we don't want to miss that purpose and the adventure along the way, then we must be conscious, alert, curious, open-hearted. When we capture the moment we're in, we're fully alive.

—LUCI SWINDOLL (*I Married Adventure*)

THE COLORS OF HOPE

It came to pass in the process of time that Hannah conceived and bore a son, and called his name Samuel, saying, "Because I have asked for him from the LORD."

—1 Samuel 1:20

Hope is a type of kaleidoscope. Through its lens, we can believe the impossible and *see* what might be. Hope's hues are rainbow in promise, bringing rays of light into once dark corners. When I think of the colors of hope, I think of Hannah . . .

Hannah was heartsick because she couldn't have a baby. She stopped eating and cried continually. Yet she never gave up hope. She continued to pray. A priest named Eli observed Hannah at the altar and spoke to her. When she explained her anguish, Eli blessed her and sent her on her way.

After that encounter, something shifted inside Hannah. Someone spun the wheel of her heart, for we are told color returned to her cheeks, she ate, and her face was no longer sad. We don't know how long it was before Hannah gave birth. Over the years, Hannah must have found the waiting cruel. But after her prayers and her breakthrough moment with Eli, it appears that she was liberated and at peace.

Eventually, Hannah gave birth to the prophet Samuel and a house full of others. She marveled at what God had done. It was as if she were looking through a kaleidoscope. All the things that had seemed so splintered now refracted dazzling light.

—PATSY CLAIRMONT (*All Cracked Up*)

JESUS KNEW . . .

Jesus said, "Father, if it is Your will, take this cup away from Me; nevertheless not My will, but Yours, be done."
—Luke 22:42

Jesus, our Savior was fully man, and he suffered during his crucifixion just as a man would (although without sinning). Jesus knew that he was about to walk into the greatest inferno ever faced by one in human flesh and that this was the plan from the beginning of time to redeem fallen humanity. He knew that his Father would allow him to drink from the cup of his wrath and not deliver him.

Jesus prayed but he *knew* his Father would say no. He also knew that even when God was telling him no, he was still with him. His prayer is left as a gift for us, a light in the darkest night.

Why does God sometimes say no to our prayers? As I'm sure you realize, I don't have the answer to that question. No one does. But what we do have is the knowledge that when we keep praying—when we move beyond "Why?" to "Be with me, Lord"—we begin to learn more about our faith and our strength in our Father. Confronting God with our why becomes being with God in our need. He is there when we need him—always. He might not answer our prayers as we would like, but he will be there to hold us through the trials.

—SHEILA WALSH (*Get Off Your Knees and Pray*)

GIVING UP WORRY

For anyone who enters God's rest also rests from his own work, just as God did from his.

—Hebrews 4:10 NIV

During one of my morning quiet times, I was reading Hebrews chapters 3 and 4, which talk about entering into God's rest. I'd just experienced a night of unrest, so my interest was especially piqued. My anxiety was nothing serious, just the normal things: worried about my children's attitudes, overwhelmed by writing a Bible study, concerned about spending money on a new washer and dryer, and distressed over the busyness of our lives. These weren't Third World–sized problems, but they were huge in my little universe, and I just didn't know how I would be able to give up worrying about them. I told the Lord that I trusted him—but I knew that if I really believed he was in control, I would be able to lay my concerns at his feet and then rest easy. The Bible said it was possible.

God began to guide me. As I reread the chapters in Hebrews, I started to put together my own little recipe for rest: **Remember** God's character (Hebrews 3:10b). **Recount** God's faithfulness (3:8b–9). **Recite** this reminder (13:8). **Reexamine** your motives (4:13a). **Recruit** a prayer partner (3:13). **Receive** God's promises (4:12). **Request** your heart's desires (Philippians 4:6–7). **Resolve** to believe (Hebrews 4:11). **Respect** God's authority (3:4). **Release** it to God (4:10). **Rest** in God (4:3a)!

—LISA WHELCHEL (*Speaking Mom-ese*)

SAVORING EACH MOMENT

God deals out joy in the present, the now.
—Ecclesiastes 5:20 MSG

Perhaps you remember the *New Yorker* cartoon in which two monks in robes and shaved heads are sitting side by side, cross-legged on the floor. The younger one, with a quizzical look on his face, is facing the older who is saying: "Nothing happens next. This is it."

That's exactly what it means to live in the here and now. We aren't waiting for something else to occur, we aren't distracted by anything around us, and we aren't trying to escape mentally to another time. We are "mindfully awake." Paying attention. Savoring the moment for all it's worth. We are fully alive!

I feel this when I'm engaged in rich, meaningful conversation with an interesting person. Questions are enticing, listening is acute, and eye contact is direct. I also experience this feeling when I'm alone . . . in an art museum or lost in a good book. When I'm all there—or rather, all here!—I never want the moment to end. It's as though I can actually hear my heart beat—my very own heart, which sustains the life I'm living. I'm breathing. I'm feeling myself breathe . . . in and out, in and out. It's wonderful. It's this moment. It's the "it" to which the wise old monk referred.

—LUCI SWINDOLL (*I Married Adventure*)

CELEBRATING THE GIGGLE PHRASE

If one has the gift of encouraging others, he should encourage.
—Romans 12:8 NCV

A friend gave me a magnet for my refrigerator that reads, "There's only one more shopping day until tomorrow."

That made me giggle aloud. I love giggle gifts because a dose of laughter is a gift in and of itself. The magnet business seems to be soaring these days, and I think it's because the makers have discovered the marketability of a good giggle-phrase.

What day couldn't use a hearty chuckle? If I can laugh aloud, I don't even mind that my eyes narrow to slits, leaving me discombobulated.

Have you ever wanted to make your own magnets? I have. Here are the possibilities:

Menopause: a target for heat-seeking devices

Need a facelift? Try smiling!

Hormones: emotional chiggers

Trifocals: triple ripple

Well, you can sure tell my age. But since I can't change the modifications or the complications that come with maturing, let me toss back my head and chortle.

How long has it been since you laughed yourself sane? Today, go in search of a giggle—you won't be sorry, no matter your age. And remember to give some giggles to others along the way.

—PATSY CLAIRMONT (*All Cracked Up*)

GO TELL PETER

Jesus said to them, "Do not be afraid. Go and tell My brethren to go to Galilee, and there they will see Me."
—Matthew 28:10

God's Word is full of stories of those who messed up and were forgiven by God and restored to a place of far greater joy and purpose. I think especially of the apostle Peter. This rough and tough fisherman who was devoted to Christ took quite a fall when he heard the words, "I don't know this man!" tumble from his own lips. I am sure he beat himself up over the next few brutal hours and days as Jesus was crucified and placed in a tomb.

On that glorious Easter morning, the women encountered an angel guarding an empty tomb. The angel told them to go tell Jesus' disciples—and Peter—that they would see him in Galilee. There was to be no doubt that Peter should know that he was welcomed.

Have you messed up? Perhaps you are ashamed to even face what you have done. It may have been something that caused harm not just to you but to others. If so, have the faith to remember that with God all things can be made new. Your past is just that. But your future in him is limitless. All God looks for is a desire to begin moving in the right direction, and he will be there to embrace you.

—SHEILA WALSH (*Get Off Your Knees and Pray*)

MY FAVORITE BAD FEELING

Each time he said, "My grace is all you need. My power
works best in weakness." So now I am glad to boast about my
weaknesses, so that the power of Christ can work through me.
—2 Corinthians 12:9 NLT

I have two daughters-in-law who are a delight to my soul. One mild spring day the three of us were standing around my van making plans for lunch while my grandchildren played inside the vehicle. When we'd finalized our choice, my daughter-in-law Heather opened the door to the van and *Boom!* her daughter Rachel fell out. She'd been leaning against the door, and the sound of her impact on the driveway was horrific.

Shocked and worried, each of us women immediately went to our favorite bad feelings. Heather began to cry. I got angry and made rules. Sandi tried to make everyone happy. Rachel was fine, but we learned that day about our "favorite bad feelings."

A friend introduced me to this phrase several years ago. She explained that a favorite bad feeling is the place to which we revert when things don't go our way. Some people yell. Some release a torrent of words. Others clam up. Others slam doors, clean house, drive fast, or seek chocolate.

How do you react to stress? Does this reaction help or make things worse? Whatever your response, know that God can work through you, helping you to handle whatever challenges you face, including the "favorite bad feelings" that accompany them.

—JAN SILVIOUS (*Smart Girls Think Twice*)

BANDING TOGETHER IN PRAYER

Where two or three have gathered together in My name, I am there in their midst.

—Matthew 18:20 NASB

I want to say how vital, even crucial, I believe it to be for us to band together with other believers in prayer. We are his children. We unite our hearts as a faith family, bringing our heart cries to him. Jesus modeled for us the role of group prayer support as he implored the disciples to help bear his burden and pray for him as he entered the Garden of Gethsemane.

The early church met regularly to pray together and to experience the growth of each person's faith in the company of one another. For us to bear one another's burdens requires sharing, requesting prayer support, and allowing ourselves to be vulnerable in each other's presence. In these ways we build one another up and further the work of the church. There's power in corporate prayer.

Paul reminds us in Ephesians 6:18 (MSG), "Pray hard and long. Pray for your brothers and sisters. Keep your eyes open. Keep each other's spirits up so that no one falls behind or drops out." There is no doubt we need to pray together, and by the same token, there is no doubt that when we are alone, we need to believe God hears us as clearly as he hears the giants of the faith.

—MARILYN MEBERG (*God at Your Wits' End*)

SNAP THE WHIP

> *Discipline isn't much fun. It always feels like it's going against the grain. Later, of course, it pays off handsomely, for it's the well-trained who find themselves mature in their relationship with God.*
>
> —Hebrews 12:11 MSG

One of my favorite paintings is a lineup of boys playing a game called Snap the Whip outside a one-room, red schoolhouse. Using vivid colors, artist Homer Winslow beautifully captured the bare-foot boys, and the lush summer day. But I also like that the painting is filled with contrasts and relationships. You feel the tension as two lads have fallen, while the others remain upright. The boys are playing, yet you are aware their schoolwork awaits them.

My pleasure in the painting isn't because I like the game. That's for sure. My mom knew how to play Snap the Whip too. Did I say, "play"? Mom was a no-nonsense lady. On occasion, she would send me out to bring her a switch, which she applied to my lower legs. And talk about snapping the whip!

Then there are times that God "snaps the whip."

God's loving design is to guide us onto a higher path. It's always for our good. I like that a lot. Guidance that's dispensed for our betterment gives us a sense of security. It helps me not to resist what God is doing in my life, and it reassures me that my difficulties have not launched me outside of his care, even when I feel I've fallen headlong into my muddled circumstances.

—PATSY CLAIRMONT (*All Cracked Up*)

THROUGH THE STORM

Be merciful to me, O God, be merciful to me, for in you my soul takes refuge; in the shadow of your wings I will take refuge, until the destroying storms pass by.
—Psalm 57:1 NRSV

As I was driving home from the studio one day, a storm began to build. The sky became a strange shade of deep red I had never seen before. Thunder rumbled overhead, and lightning slashed across the sky as if someone had taken a blade to rip the heavens to shreds. Rain battered my car and traffic slowed to a crawl.

Finally, I pulled over and stopped my car. I felt so abandoned. The storm seemed to me a physical representation of my spiritual turmoil: nothing made sense to me anymore. I even wondered if I had caused the storm because somehow God was angry with me. I felt as if I had lost my way—or as if God had lost me.

That afternoon I called my mom, and told her what was going on with me. She encouraged me to take a long look back down this road I have traveled with God. "Has he ever left you before?" she asked.

I knew that he never had. But this time it felt different.

"Sheila," she said, "no matter where you are or what is happening with you, God has promised that he will never leave you. And he can't lie."

Is there a storm in your heart? Let my mom's wise words see you through!

—SHEILA WALSH (*Get Off Your Knees and Pray*)

CREATED FOR GOOD WORKS

For we are God's workmanship, created in Christ Jesus to do
good works, which God prepared in advance for us to do.
—Ephesians 2:10 NIV

I had about ninety minutes before I was to go onstage at a speaking event, and I was attempting to prepare both my heart and my face. First, my daughter walked into the room and asked to borrow my hairbrush. Soon she was standing in front of the mirror, singing into the "microphone."

Then the phone rang. "Hon," my husband said, "will you order some room service for me? When it's there, call me and I'll come eat with you." He was setting up the room where I would be speaking, but I wanted to tell him, "Order it yourself!" Instead, I ordered a club sandwich.

I had just gotten back to praying when my phone rang. For the next fifteen minutes I bounced between feelings of frustration (over so many interruptions), guilt (over feeling frustrated), and fear (because I needed to prepare).

As I fretted, God reminded me of Ephesians 2:10. I didn't feel prepared, but God was. Any good works that God had planned for me to do would most certainly be taken care of by him. So I changed course. I finished my makeup, said a quick prayer, and had dinner with my husband, thankful that after so many years, he still wants to be with me.

—LISA WHELCHEL (*Speaking Mom-ese*)

GOD'S SOVEREIGN HAND

The Sovereign LORD has given me an instructed tongue, to know the word that sustains the weary.

—Isaiah 50:4 NIV

God is sovereign, and he has a sovereign design for each of our lives. But knowing, believing, and having faith in God's sovereign design does not necessarily mean we like the design. We may actually hate the design.

Do we dare tell God we aren't crazy about his plan? Of course. He already knows our feelings anyway. He knew what we would be feeling long before we had the experience that produced those feelings. He knows the beginning from the end, including our emotions. So go ahead and boldly tell him what he already knows. And don't worry, he will receive your emotions.

How do I know? The Bible tells me he knows that humans "are as frail as breath" (Isaiah 2:22). It also tells me, "All humanity finds shelter in the shadow of your wings" (Psalm 36:7).

A part of experiencing his shelter is trusting the one who provides that shelter. We can settle into the comfort of that sheltering promise. We can trust him and have faith in his character of love that a higher good is in the making and that one day, we will look back and say, "Ah, yes . . . God's hand was in that."

—MARILYN MEBERG (*God at Your Wits' End*)

GOD'S SOUL-TRANSFORMING LESSONS

Whoever catches a glimpse of the revealed counsel of God—
the free life!—even out of the corner of his eye, and sticks with
it, is no distracted scatterbrain but a man or woman of action.
—James 1:25 MSG

The soul in each of us is imprisoned until it is set free by Jesus
Christ. We all have shells around us, protecting us from being
eaten alive by the pain of life. And when those shells break, we
believe we are at grave risk of being hurt, depressed, or even
dying on the spot. To prevent this pain and loss, we guard ourselves by retreating deeper and deeper into the shell, being
available only to what is pleasant, predictable, and safe.

But every person I've ever known who really had something
to give has been burst open by the explosive force of God's soul-
transforming lessons. They have each been willing to be
vulnerable to the truth about themselves, to admit selfishness
and behavior patterns that are maddening to other people and
destructive to their own souls.

If we aspire to pay complete attention to the present, then we
must stay connected to our individual centers, and at the same
time get out of our own ways. Living fully in the present starts
deep inside as we allow the self-protective shell to break open so
the liberating grace of God can flow in to heal and renew and
establish genuine meaning in our lives.

—LUCI SWINDOLL (*I Married Adventure*)

ALWAYS WITH ME

I am not alone because the Father is with me.
—*John 16:32* NRSV

I saw a drama play out on a National Geographic special. A father bird ushering his son to the edge of a broken cliff for his first flight, which just happened to be a thousand-foot drop to the ocean below. The father stayed at his baby's side as he teetered to the edge; and when the baby toppled forth into the air, his dad went with him.

The father stayed close for the plummeting ride down until they both sliced into the water, safely bobbing to and fro on the churning sea. It was amazing. I wondered if that little bird knew his father had been with him all the way down, ready to swoop under him if he spun out of control. The baby was always safe; but his descending perspective was probably very different as he frantically beat his little wings.

Ever feel that way? I have. But as my history with the Lord has accumulated into a growing faith, I realize he is with me, ever so close, even as I thrash about in my littleness and my frailty. I'm learning that I can trust his presence, and that realization buoys my spirit, whether I'm on the edge of the ledge, floundering in problems as vast as the sky, or in my splashdown to the valley below.

—PATSY CLAIRMONT (*All Cracked Up*)

LETTING GO

> *Whenever you stand praying, forgive, if you have anything against anyone, so that your Father who is in heaven may also forgive you your transgressions.*
>
> —Mark 11:25 *NASB*

In my life, one of the greatest rocks to climb over has been when I am unwilling to forgive. I'm sure I'm not alone in that burden. It's hard to admit we've done wrong and say we're sorry. But often it's even harder to forgive. We sometimes thrive on self-righteousness—knowing we've been wronged and wanting to hold that hurt against another indefinitely instead of letting it go.

To my mind the most amazing declaration from the cross is when Jesus cried out, "Father, forgive them, for they do not know what they are doing" (Luke 23:34). Jesus asked God to forgive his torturers while he was still in physical and spiritual agony, not after he had risen from the dead. He prayed that prayer of forgiveness in the midst of the storm, not when the sun began to remind the earth there are better days ahead. Can you imagine how difficult that must have been?

Forgiveness is hard. It is even more difficult when the person who wronged us is not sorry in the least. But when I listen to Christ's words recorded in Matthew's gospel, it's clear to me that if I want to live freely and lightly, then I need to study how Jesus lived.

—SHEILA WALSH (*Get Off Your Knees and Pray*)

GREAT EXPECTATIONS

*A rich man had a fertile farm that produced fine crops. He
said to himself, "What should I do? I don't have room for all
my crops." Then he said, "I know! I'll tear down my barns and
build bigger ones. Then I'll have room enough to store all my
wheat and other goods."... But God said to him, "You fool!
You will die this very night. Then who will get everything you
worked for?"*
—Luke 12:16–20 NLT

We tend to enter adulthood with great expectations. Young girls
do a lot of dreaming about what their lives will be like when they
grow up: how many children they will have, what their homes will
be like, and how Prince Charming will behave after the wedding.
Of course, dreams and reality don't always run on parallel tracks.

I wonder how different your family life is today from what you
wanted it to be. Are you making the best of relating to the child you
expected to be cuddly but who has turned out defiant? Are you
holding the household together while your husband travels constantly? Are you living single in a family of married siblings? Are
you caring for an ailing parent who can't remember you?

We can dream, yet in the end we'll have to deal with the reality of what is, rather than what could have been. If we remain set
on our dreams, we'll miss God's delights. Remember, today is all
we are promised. Yesterday is gone, and tomorrow is not yet here,
so accept God's invitation to live in the moment.

—JAN SILVIOUS (*Smart Girls Think Twice*)

315

THERE IS NO GREATER POWER

With God's power working in us, God can do much, much
more than anything we can ask or imagine.
—Ephesians 3:20 NCV

Have you ever wondered what hand God has in the calamities in your life? I did and yet, it seemed blasphemous to ever think of God that way. My assumption was that calamities originated with Satan's efforts to overthrow my soul's peace, joy, and equilibrium. And of course that is Satan's resolve, but now I know God fits in there in ways I had refused to think about.

The God I know and love came to earth to heal and restore. He was compassionate and wept over death, and he ultimately conquered it by dying on the cross. How could anyone possibly assume God would choose suffering for us? The truth I've come to embrace is that God is indeed compassionate, loving, and kind. And yet I need to recognize another dimension of God; he is the sovereign initiator. There is no greater power.

Knowing this frees me to simply say, "Lord, let me rest in this experience even though I may not want it, like it, or understand it. You know what you intend to accomplish; you have the big picture, and I don't. Thank you that I don't have to figure out, *Where did this come from and why?* It came from you in one way or another, and I choose to trust you in it."

—MARILYN MEBERG (*God at Your Wits' End*)

CAPTURING EACH MOMENT

The Spirit of God has made me, and the breath of the Almighty gives me life.
—Job 33:4

Are you the kind of person who is curious about life, saying "yes!" to its strange and unusual possibilities? God gave us life and vitality and a sense of wonder, and an enormous capacity to flourish emotionally, personally, and spiritually.

The most interesting people I know drink in life and savor every drop—the sweet and the sour. The good and the bad. The planned and the unplanned. And isn't that what God intends? When Jesus modeled humanity for you and me to see, he was out there—everywhere! He took risks. He embraced life and responded to everyone and everything, the tender and the tumultuous. His capacity for life was without measure. And, we are designed like him. I don't want to miss anything he has in store for me, even if the path he takes me on winds through some pretty rough terrain. Right in the midst of what seems to me to be a detour from the map, I'm often gifted with something precious and unforgettable.

Capturing the moment is a choice, a way of life. It requires us to wake up, live life, and be present—here, there, and everywhere. Sometimes that's scary; sometimes it's exhilarating. Always, it's an adventure I keep learning to welcome with a full and grateful heart.

—LUCI SWINDOLL (*I Married Adventure*)

LESSONS LEARNED IN THE LOWLAND

> *Blessed are those whose strength is in you ... As they pass*
> *through the Valley of Baca, they make it a place of springs; the*
> *autumn rains also cover it with pools. They go from strength to*
> *strength, till each appears before God in Zion.*

—Psalm 84:5–7 NIV

Do you remember when the disciples left the valley and joined Jesus on the Mount of Transfiguration? They experienced such a rush of joy that they wanted to stay there. Who wouldn't! But Jesus let them know they had to go back down, down, down to the people and the problems—because that's where our faith is forged. The valleys are littered with lessons; the wise lean in and learn.

The sights are spectacular from the rocky pinnacles, and we get a great overview of the orchards, but I also want to hold the pear in my hand and taste its sweet offering. That happens in the lowlands. From the peaks, we see the lakes; but in the valley, we can explore the water's refreshing depths. From the crest, we see the canopy of trees; but in the valley, we can sit in the cool shade and listen as the wind sings through the branches.

We live the majority of our lives in the lowland; yet, if we look close enough, we'll find fruit, catch breezes, and hear music as we learn lessons along the way. For me, that makes the jolts of valley life more bearable and, at times, downright joyful.

—PATSY CLAIRMONT (*All Cracked Up*)

HE IS WITH YOU

[God] is not far from each one of us.
—*Acts 17:27* NRSV

As I have told my son countless times, forgiveness is God's gift to help us live in a world that is not fair. More important, though, is the lesson: the more we allow our anger to fade, the more we center ourselves on forgiveness and God, the more opportunity we have to feel his presence and response to our petition. The boulder of bitterness and resentment rolls from our path, and once again we're in communion with God and his will.

There's no doubt this is a difficult topic. The reasons for God's seeming distance from us are many, and we've all felt that separation at one time or another. But no matter what, we need to remember this: God is sovereign.

One of the greatest lessons I took from a dark moment in my life is that God is always there, no matter how we feel. There will be times in our lives that illness or depression, insecurity or doubt, the enemy of our souls or the enemy that we can be to ourselves will make us doubt God is listening. Our feelings, however, do not change the facts and do not alter the character of God. He is with you! Hold on to that truth!

—SHEILA WALSH (*Get Off Your Knees and Pray*)

GOTTA HAVE GIRLFRIENDS

Two people can accomplish more than twice as much as one;
they get a better return for their labor. If one person falls, the
other can reach out and help. But people who are alone when
they fall are in real trouble.

—*Ecclesiastes 4:9–10* NLT

One of my first orders of business when we moved to Texas was to start another MomTime group in my home—a chance for moms to visit, play games, eat, and develop deep friendships. I knew one other person in the area, so I asked her if she would like to come over for lunch and bring some friends. A few days later, I was at the mailbox when our neighbor across the street was getting her mail, so I asked if she would like to join us. I invited the student pastor's wife. Now, I have friends in their twenties who are popping out babies, friends in their fifties who are dropping off babies at college, and friends in-between who feel like "popping and dropping" their teenagers somewhere.

In this day and age, it is difficult to cultivate friendships. We have to write them on our calendars and take deliberate steps to grow them. But they are worth it! I am so grateful for the friends God has given me. I beg you to make an effort to develop new friendships and nurture the ones you have. You never know when you will need their support.

—LISA WHELCHEL (*Taking Care of the Me in Mommy*)

FINISHED AT THE CROSS

Yes, I have loved you with an everlasting love.
—*Jeremiah 31:3*

When I'm hurting, I don't want someone explaining the *why* to me. I want to know God truly loves me. Is his heart truly one of love and compassion in spite of how it appears? Paul described Jesus as "the image of the invisible God" (Colossians 1:15 NIV). The writer of Hebrews referred to Jesus as the "exact representation" of God's being (1:3 NIV). When Jesus wept at the tomb of Lazarus . . . so did God. When Jesus invited the children to come to him . . . that was God. The touch of Jesus restored sight, healed bodies, and renewed physical life . . . and that was also the touch of God.

Our faith is encouraged by knowing that the compassionate acts of Jesus were the compassionate acts of God. He sits with us in our pain and refuses to leave us. He turns his ear toward our cries and listens until we're spent. Jesus hung on a cross for our sins and said, "It is finished!" (John 19:30). What started in the Garden was finished at the cross. The price was paid, the death sentence lifted.

What motivates such intense attention? Love. The love of God. The love of God demonstrated through the earthly ministrations of Jesus, God's Son.

—MARILYN MEBERG (*God at Your Wits' End*)

CAPTURING THE LIGHT

How precious is Your lovingkindness, O God! . . . with You is
the fountain of life; in Your light we see light.
—Psalm 36:7, 9

Living in the light is one of the most difficult tasks we have. It means getting out of the way so there is no shadow blocking the source. When we read or write or engage in hobbies or reach out to others, why do we do that? What do we hope to gain? I think it's to be illuminated . . . enlightened . . . or we hope to give off illumination of some kind. That's what light is: illumination—whether emotional, financial, mental, physical, or spiritual. To capture the light available to us is one more aspect of divining the spirit of adventure. The more light we live in, the more we grow and change.

God reminds us to quit holding things too tightly—whether an event, a viewpoint, a desire, a particular time in life, or a person we thoroughly enjoy. He urges us to stop struggling, resisting, coercing, or manipulating for what we want. When we simply do what he asks, no matter how hard it seems, and we keep our focus on the Light of the world, an amazing brightness comes, all within the embrace of his love.

—LUCI SWINDOLL (*I Married Adventure*)

EXPECT DELAYS

My soul waits for the Lord more than those who watch for the morning—yes, more than those who watch for the morning.
—*Psalm 130:6*

When the gentleman put up his hand to stop me from going through security at the airport, I complied. I already had stripped off my shoes, jacket, and purse to be scanned. Finally, the man waved me through and then immediately began wanding me. The wand sounded like a loaded Geiger counter. The woman on the scanner then pointed out that my purse and carry-on needed to be searched.

I bet the Israelites never anticipated that it would take forty years to reach the promised land. Talk about delays. Enemies, rebellion, war, sickness . . . there was always something slowing them down and delaying their arrival.

What looked like sheer inconvenience and man-made barriers actually had been orchestrated by the hand of God. He knew the exact moment they would reach their destination. Delays were as much in his plan as manna and quails.

I remind myself of that when a flight is canceled, a mistake is made, an order is lost, a doctor's report is delayed, or a request is misunderstood. We don't know, but God might be protecting us with these delays. They may be God's way of helping us realize our need for trust, patience, adaptability, and relinquishment.

—PATSY CLAIRMONT (*All Cracked Up*)

323

WHO'S THE BOSS?

Let the favor of the Lord our God be upon us, and prosper for
us the work of our hands—O prosper the work of our hands!
—Psalm 90:17 NRSV

Can you imagine what an impact it would have on the world if everyone who follows Christ would wake up each morning and thank God for the gifts he or she has been given and ask for opportunities that day to use them for his glory?

I'm not saying this is always easy. The trouble is that some gifts receive immediate praise and recognition, and others don't. We must keep in mind who we're working for. If we're dependent on the approval of others, life will be very discouraging. But if we wait only on the Lord, his love will uplift us no matter what. To God, there are no small jobs or menial tasks. He sees all the late-night laundry and lunches packed. He sees the extra work your boss never credits you for. He sees it all.

As far as I am concerned, I work for God. He is my boss, and he is my King. So whether I am writing a book, recording a CD, speaking to thousands of women, or sitting in the carpool lane waiting to pick up my child, it doesn't matter. No one thing that I am called to do is more important than another; all that matters is my heart.

—SHEILA WALSH (*Get Off Your Knees and Pray*)

ACTIONS SPEAK LOUDER

If I could speak all the languages of earth and of angels, but didn't love others, I would only be a noisy gong or a clanging cymbal.

—1 Corinthians 13:1 NLT

The men in my family are not what I would call sensitive communicators. They have never been given to affectionate outbursts. If I depended solely on their words to tell me that I am loved and appreciated, I could be starved for affection.

Their actions, however, lavish me with love. My husband knows I love Perrier, so he keeps the refrigerator stocked. My sons take care of my two aquariums, care for our dog and cat when we go out of town, keep my computer working, and update my Web site. Mushy, they are not! Dependable and kind? Absolutely.

The differences between male and female brain structure has been one of the premier scientific findings of the past years. I only wish I had known this early in my marriage! I agonized for years about my husband's supposed emotional deficits. Why did he not feel the way I did? Why did he not want to talk everything through? Now I know. It was *his brain*. I needed to accept the way he was wired and respond accordingly.

If you're feeling slighted because the men around you are not great communicators, take heart. If their behavior is good, let it speak for them. Watch for the nonverbal ways they express their love; then let them know you appreciate their efforts.

—JAN SILVIOUS (*Smart Girls Think Twice*)

CHOOSE LIFE

> *To choose life is to love the LORD your God, obey him, and stay close to him. He is your life.*
> —Deuteronomy 30:20 NCV

From the beginning of recorded time God has committed himself to loving his people. He will continue loving his people until we all gather in that place called "eternity" where all tears will be wiped away, all pain will be eliminated, and all anguishing memories will be forgotten.

In the meantime, how do we cope with the problems pain presents to our faith? How do we maintain faith when suffering wrenches it from our feeble grasp? I go back to one of the freedoms given to me at creation: I choose.

I can choose to turn away from God in bitterness, despair, and disbelief, or I can choose life. What does it mean to choose life? It means to believe God's love for me is a dependable fact and in that love to find sustaining encouragement. It means I choose to live in the mystery of what I may not understand but feel buoyed by faith in the midst of that mystery. It means taking God's promises and believing they were written for me.

In choosing life, I choose to believe the enormous implications of those promises when I'm at my wits' end. What will you choose? Will you believe and depend on God's love for you?

—MARILYN MEBERG (*God at Your Wits' End*)

WHAT TURNS YOUR CRANK?

We all have different gifts, each of which came because of the grace God gave us.

—Romans 12:6 NCV

In the formative years of my childhood, my parents were the human factors that provided the nourishment I needed to begin growing. They put me on a playing field where the game of life began. With their teachings as a springboard, I started making decisions that caused me to be the person I am today, for good or bad.

As I branched out and began seeing patterns form, traveling revealed an adventuresome side of my temperament. I went here, did this, saw that, and felt thus and so. My friend Mary says, "People do what makes sense to them," and it's true. We all have to determine what makes sense to us and do it, whether or not it seems logical to anyone else. We don't live fully until we do this for ourselves. Some of the things that make sense to me are art, music, photography, literature, and theater. These are the considerations in life that turn my crank, make me think, and fill my heart with appreciation and wonder. They are vehicles that transport me into the light that illuminates and enriches my journey.

What are the things that transport you into the light? What makes sense to you? If you don't yet know, it may be time to look around you and discover what turns your crank!

—LUCI SWINDOLL (*I Married Adventure*)

EMBRACING THE GOOD

> *Endure hardship as a good soldier of Jesus Christ. Consider what*
> *I say, and may the Lord give you understanding in all things.*
> —2 Timothy 2:3, 7

It isn't natural to look for good in bad. It's far more human, when bad rears its ugly head, to gaze upon it stymied. But when we believe that God designs and redesigns all things for our good, even when the intent of others is for our demise, it allows us to let them off the hook and look up. Our task is to detect and embrace the good, which means we will have to be alert and discerning if we are to benefit from the windbreaker of gratitude.

I'm not thankful when my heart is broken, yet I'm grateful that through internal ruptures comes a deeper compassion for others who grieve. I had no idea how unaware and indifferent I was toward the agony of others until I suffered through a season of intense winds and came out of that time with enhanced sensitivity. It wasn't that I hadn't cared about others; I just didn't have a clue what their struggles were costing them until hardships exacted a high price from me.

Someone once said, "We can only know joy to the degree we have known pain." Hardships have the potential of carving out greater space for God's grace within us. And grace helps us to live with life's inequities without the disabling residuals of anger, bitterness, and disillusionment.

—PATSY CLAIRMONT (*All Cracked Up*)

CELEBRATING CHRIST IN OTHERS

It is God who is at work in you, enabling you both to will and to work for his good pleasure.

—*Philippians 2:13* NRSV

If the whole point of our lives is to become more like Christ and be a conduit for the love of God, then we will each be given different paths to take—which may or may not correlate to our prayers. Some paths seem more attractive than others, but no one really knows the burdens another carries. What I am convinced of is that God loves his children. I don't know why he answers one person's prayers one way and another person's differently, only that he has a reason for it.

One of the ways we can measure whether we are at peace in the love of God is by asking ourselves whether we are able to celebrate Christ shining through another's life—whether we can recognize God's wisdom as he lovingly hand-packs each life himself. Because only when we can do that—when we can accept his hand working differently in your life as opposed to mine, answering each prayer in his own time and understanding—can we truly be at peace with God. Believing that God is not listening to us dampens our relationship with him. But taking joy in living out his plan for us—that's freeing!

—SHEILA WALSH (*Get Off Your Knees and Pray*)

WITHOUT REGRET

> *When the Woman saw that the tree looked like good eating and realized what she would get out of it—she'd know everything!—she took and ate the fruit and then gave some to her husband, and he ate.*
>
> —Genesis 3:6 MSG

Choices inevitably bring consequences; it was quite a lesson for the first girl in history to learn. God had given Eve a simple, easy-to-follow command with clear and established consequences for disobedience. Unfortunately, Eve moved on impulse rather than thinking twice.

Sometimes it's easy to look at Eve and think that *we* would not have fallen for the manipulations of the enemy. Yet when it comes to our own choices, we find that thinking twice is not as easy as it may seem.

Our cravings and our pride make good choices difficult, especially if we haven't decided ahead of time what principles will guide our decision-making process. It's hard to choose against eating that piece of cake or buying that darling outfit that's out of our price range. And it's hard to say no to a great job offer even when we know it would take us away during a time when our family needs us. That's why the second thought, that deeper consideration of potential consequences, is so crucial to making the best choices possible. As the master seamstress reminds her student, "Measure twice, cut once!"

—JAN SILVIOUS (*Smart Girls Think Twice*)

A LITTLE LESS IMPERFECT

The God of all grace, who hath called us unto his eternal glory by Christ Jesus, after that ye have suffered a while, make you perfect, stablish, strengthen, settle you.

—1 Peter 5:10 KJV

Have you ever thought life might be easier if you could be someone else altogether? Here's one woman's fantasy for her own identity change: she'd like to be a bear. Her reasons?

- If you are a bear you get to hibernate; you do nothing but sleep for six months.
- Before you hibernate, you must eat huge amounts of food—the more calories the better.
- The children (cubs) are born while you are sleeping and are the size of walnuts.
- As a mama bear, you swat anyone who bothers your cubs. Swatting is socially acceptable behavior.
- Your mate expects you to wake up growling and have hairy legs and excess body fat.

Life is not perfect. We know that, but the longing for perfection has always been with us. Why? We were created for perfection. We live hoping for what we've never known, somehow knowing one day it will be ours. The good news is, perfection is on its way. One day all evil will be banished, taking with it all that is not perfect.

—MARILYN MEBERG (*God at Your Wits' End*)

GOD'S TRUTH

We should no longer be children, tossed to and fro and carried about with every wind of doctrine, by the trickery of men, in the cunning craftiness of deceitful plotting, but, speaking the truth in love, may grow up in all things into Him who is the Head—Christ.
—*Ephesians 4:14–15*

I don't know about you, but I don't always get God's truth exactly right, and sometimes I'm way off, but I do believe a great part of my adventure in living is nourished at the well of having built my foundation on solid doctrinal truth.

In his letter to the Ephesians, Paul says that being grounded in the truth makes us strong adults who know the ropes. We can't be pushed around. Because we know that Christ is our leader, we don't ever have to waver in our beliefs. We are secure in him.

In my lifetime, I've seen thousands of fads come and go, philosophies of life change like the weather, political systems overturned in revolutions. Nothing stays steady. Except God! The essence of his being is always the same: yesterday, today, and forever. We can trust him and his Word.

Is your life anchored in the truth? If not, it's never too late to build a foundation for your life based on God's Word. Ask the Holy Spirit to teach you, and make yourself a student of the Bible. When you bank your life on God's truth and "grow up into him who is the Head," you will be stable, secure, and immovable in your faith.

—LUCI SWINDOLL (*I Married Adventure*)

THE BEGINNING OF THE CONVERSATION

Jesus said, "My sheep listen to my voice; I know them, and they follow me."
—John 10:27 NCV

In my twenties and thirties, I was surrounded by people who seemed to hear from God on a remarkably frequent level. Almost every week, people reported that God was showing up and giving them specific directions. But those kinds of experiences never happened to me. I worried that somehow I was missing God—that everyone else had a better listening ear than I did. Perhaps I was destined to hear from God secondhand.

What about you? What do you rely on when you want to hear from God on a specific issue or a general direction? Do you sit and wait, hoping you'll find direction in a book or through someone else? Or do you take time to pray and meditate on God's Word?

Yes, that's right. I'm saying that prayer is sometimes just the beginning of the conversation. Sometimes we need more. It takes an intentional choice to carve out time in our overfull schedules to listen to the voice of God. Perhaps we have lived such busy lives for so long that we have forgotten how, or perhaps we have never learned to listen for God in that way. But Jesus assured us that when we look past all the books and speakers and seek to commune with him, we will know his voice.

—SHEILA WALSH (*Get Off Your Knees and Pray*)

333

CATCH THAT THIEF

Submit . . . to God. Resist the devil and he will flee from you.
—James 4:7 NASB

Our neighborhood was having a Christmas lights contest, and my husband had signed up to be one of the judges. I was excited about the opportunity to create a wonderful family memory. In my mind, the whole family would pile into the minivan; I would pop in my favorite Christmas CD, we would eat Jack in the Box (a tradition), and then we would drive through the neighborhood, enjoying and rating the lights. Later, I would scrapbook about it.

We made it as far as Jack in the Box. Then the kids started bickering. I started yelling at them to stop yelling. Steve clammed up and wouldn't say a word. I pouted and said, "Take me home!" We all went to our rooms while Steve went out alone to judge the lights.

The devil had crept in and stolen from our family, and we had just let him! We all repented, kissed, and made up the next morning, but by that time Satan had already won the battle.

The next day, I berated myself, thinking, *When will I learn that every time I lose my self-control, we all end up losing?* We don't have to stand by and watch Satan destroy our families. The Lord tells us exactly what to do in such circumstances: we're to resist and rebuke the devil. So the next time you wake up and realize your family is under attack, stand firm and remember Jesus' promise to you: "Behold, I give you the authority to trample on serpents and scorpions, and over all the power of the enemy" (Luke 10:19 NKJV).

—LISA WHELCHEL (*Speaking Mom-ese*)

FINDING OUR HOME IN GOD

Jesus answered him, "Those who love me will keep my word, and my Father will love them, and we will come to them and make our home with them."

—John 14:23 NRSV

There is a homelessness of the self we impose upon ourselves when we don't realize it is God who is our home. We know believers anticipate a mansion in heaven, but here on earth God is also our home.

It is he who provides the comforts of home. These comforts are the security of being adored—nurtured and comforted, approved of and cherished—as he walks our human path with us. I believe many of us are afraid to cry out because we think to do so would alienate us from God. The result of that faulty thinking is that we don't go home, where honesty is rewarded and faith is increased. We stay in a homeless state, perhaps toughing it out on a park bench somewhere. What we need to do is cry out in the comfort of home.

Home is that interior place in our spirits where God speaks words of encouragement to us. It's where he soothes our tattered souls and promises comfort. Home is that place where I can be real . . . where I can be honest . . . where I dare to say what I feel. Come home, dear friend, you will find him there.

—MARILYN MEBERG (*God at Your Wits' End*)

COMPLETE IN HIM

*May the God of peace... make you complete in everything
good so that you may do his will, working that which is
pleasing in his sight, through Jesus Christ.*
—*Hebrews 13:20, 21 NRSV*

It's not so easy to balance between your head and your heart?
Have you noticed? I sure have! How *do* we establish ourselves
firmly in the unshakable foundation of truth and at the same
time feel things deeply? The integration of what we think with
how we feel affords a rich, authentic spiritual life and ensures
meaningful connections with others. But where do we find the
formula? Is there one?

As simplistic as it sounds, we find it in relationship to God.
He created us—will, intellect, and emotions. Scripture says we
are complete in him. By nature, I'm more cerebral than emotional. I have friends who are just the opposite. And I've known
folks with wills like steel, but they don't necessarily think straight
or care. But none of us can create within ourselves that harmoni-
ous blend that echoes the essential ground of our being in Christ.
Only our Maker can synthesize us and make us whole.

When we find our center, when our identity is in him, when
the core of our being revolves around him, we're not just academic (as I tend to be) or emotional (like Eeyore in
Winnie-the-Pooh) or willful (like a two-year-old I once knew).
We're whole, because he's made us so.

—LUCI SWINDOLL (*I Married Adventure*)

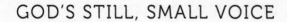

GOD'S STILL, SMALL VOICE

I will instruct you (says the Lord) and guide you along the best pathway for your life; I will advise you and watch your progress.

—*Psalm 32:8* TLB

You only have to watch the news or read a newspaper to be aware of the evil that is rampant in our world. We hear stories of those who are called to be servants to God's people and then are arrested for misappropriating funds or embezzlement. Perhaps you are discouraged by the times you live in and wonder how you can hear God's voice in the midst of all the evil in this world. God looks for those who still have hearts open to him and gives them ears to hear his voice.

Do you recognize moments when God has been speaking in your life? Perhaps you have felt a prompting to do something, go somewhere, stop for coffee somewhere you wouldn't normally go, speak to a stranger and only in retrospect can you see the hand of God. There might have been someone there who just needed a word of encouragement or you might have seen a book that answers something you've been asking God about. You may be surprised to realize how often these things occur in your life. We have a Father who loves to talk with his children, so listen for his still, small voice.

—SHEILA WALSH (*Get Off Your Knees and Pray*)

337

BREAKING WITH TRADITION

"And don't be concerned about what to eat and what to drink. Don't worry about such things. These things dominate the thoughts of unbelievers all over the world, but your Father already knows your needs. Seek the Kingdom of God above all else, and he will give you everything you need."

—Luke 12:29–31 NLT

I well remember when it hit me that clinging to a tradition could bring sadness instead of comfort. Our first baby and I were living with my parents while my husband was in Vietnam. Usually we had a great Christmas with a tree, presents, a wonderful meal, and family gathered around. This year my dad was in bed with a terrible flu, my young husband was fighting a war halfway around the world, and Mother and I were left to "do Christmas" with a one-year-old. I remember dressing in the kimono my husband had sent, standing beside the flowers he had ordered for my December 23 birthday, and taking pictures so he could see how happy we were. In reality it was pretty bleak.

That's when I realized that holidays are not about observing one particular day or having all the family together. They're about being grateful that we have a family, even if we're separated. A Smart Girl is willing to rethink her view of what will work and to try things a different way. Good times, relaxed interactions, and stress-free memories are easier to come by when we let go of "but we've always done it this way."

—JAN SILVIOUS (*Smart Girls Think Twice*)

DOUBTING YOUR DOUBTS

Lord, when doubts fill my mind, when my heart is in turmoil, quiet me and give me renewed hope and cheer.

—Psalm 94:19 *TLB*

Doubt may be a difficult topic for you. I'd like to make a few suggestions that may contribute to your "renewed hope and cheer."

→ Be assured that you do not lose your heavenly citizenship when you doubt.

→ Make a conscious decision about your doubt: do you will to believe? If so, you will need the Author of your belief to help you.

→ Read the Gospel of John over and over and over again. (It has the greatest number of Jesus quotes.)

→ Get involved in a Bible study where you will not receive gasps and groans when you honestly share your doubts.

→ Keep a prayer journal. Write your prayers to God. Then read your prayers out loud to him.

→ Go to church. Jesus went to church, and I can't imagine how he kept from being bored. After all, he knew more than anyone there! But he went to worship.

Our challenge is to love him for what we do see and trust him for what we cannot see. Our doubts may occasionally persist, but they do not have to dictate our behavior.

—MARILYN MEBERG (*God at Your Wits' End*)

OUR ADVOCATE

Humble yourselves under the mighty hand of God, that He
may exalt you in due time, casting all your care upon Him, for
He cares for you.
—I Peter 5:6–7

There is no escaping the undeniable fact that we need an advocate to go before us as well as run with us. Someone who will fight our battles and cheer us on. Someone who will renew us and strengthen us for the next task. This person is the Savior, Jesus Christ, God and man in one person forever. This hypostatic unity of undiminished deity and true humanity enables him to know my need, receive my burden, heal my wound, and send me on my way with his blessing and power. Not only that, but it enables me to experience his love, forgiveness, and solace because he knows my longing heart so intimately.

At the moment we cast our anxiety on our heavenly Father, believing he'll listen, understand, care, and act on our behalf, our burden is lifted. Believing he truly cares is worth a fortune in hope, victory, and spiritual rest. And knowing he is able to respond to our need is a comfort beyond all measure. I know he can do anything, and I feel safe and carefully tended, knowing he will accomplish what concerns me. These precious truths are in my head, and they've become priceless treasures buried deeply in my heart.

—LUCI SWINDOLL (*I Married Adventure*)

USING WISDOM

I am continually with You; You hold me by my right hand. You will guide me with Your counsel.

Psalm 73:23–24

We don't live in the days of Samuel or Moses—the days when God spoke only through prophets or kings. We live in a time when God speaks to each of his children through his Word and through the Holy Spirit and through wise counsel. Whenever I have found myself in a place of wanting to hear God's voice before I move in one direction or another, I ask myself several questions:

* Does anything in this situation go against the revealed Word of God?
* Do I feel a great urgency and stress to do something right away? When I feel a compulsion to move quickly, I wait. God is a God of order and peace.
* Do those whom I respect and trust sense God's presence in this situation too? There will be times when God will ask us to step outside of what others understand, but it has been my experience that those situations are rare.

If we can follow these three guidelines, our lives will be much simpler and more fulfilled. God loves to talk to his children, so ask for ears to hear and a heart to know his voice.

—SHEILA WALSH (*Get Off Your Knees and Pray*)

SEARCHING FOR CLUES

You who seek God, your hearts shall live.
—Psalm 69:32

The "searching for clues" mentality undoubtedly characterizes many of us as we puzzle through Scripture in an effort to find God's truth, especially when we're spending wits'-end time with our backs against the wall.

For example, we tend to think there's no possible place for humor as we cry out to God and wait for him to deliver us. But that's faulty thinking. In fact, humor can be a great source of strength and encouragement during our wits'-end wall-waiting time. It helped me see how our search for God's sovereign will and his purpose in our trip to the wall can be a benefit in itself, inspiring us to find hidden rewards in the experiences we've been called to endure. Those rewards—or that deliverance—may be different from the way we imagined them. And one of those hidden treasures we find during our search might be the gift of humor God may have left for us in unexpected places . . . even places like that wits'-end wall.

The Bible frequently speaks of searching and of the reward to those who seek spiritual truth found only in God. Let me encourage you to begin looking for hidden treasure.

—MARILYN MEBERG (*God at Your Wits' End*)

GIVING FREELY

*Remember this: Whoever sows sparingly will also reap
sparingly, and whoever sows generously will also reap
generously.*

—2 Corinthians 9:6 NIV

One of the greatest adventures available to us as God's children
is trusting our Father with respect to our finances, our time, and
our energy. Giving from our wealth—no matter how small or
large—is not even a gamble, although we're dealing with the great
unknown because of our own limited vision. But God has promised to meet our needs, and he won't go back on his promise.

Giving freely of the resources he has given me has become
downright enjoyable. I figure if he can turn water into wine, he
can provide riches out of nowhere. He's got the goods to do it! I
could recount story after story of his surprises to me in terms of
replenishing my well of money, time, and energy.

I also find in the matter of giving that the greater the trust,
the wider the blessing. And the wider the blessing, the sweeter
the joy. I couldn't have made those statements forty years ago, or
maybe even twenty, when I wasn't as free in my spirit as I am
now. But I've learned from personal experience that God keeps
his word and continually gives out of a well that never runs dry.

—LUCI SWINDOLL (*I Married Adventure*)

EMBRACING GOD'S WILL

I cry to God Most High, to God who fulfills his purpose for me.
—Psalm 57:2 NRSV

I celebrate the fact that God accepts us in all of our humanity. We are allowed to ask questions, to be sad when we don't get the answers we long for, to grieve over losses no matter how insignificant they may seem to others. Yet, as I think about the requests I myself have made to God through the years and the stories I have heard from others, I see one big problem: when we take what we want and try to twist God's arm to answer us, we shift from worshippers to spoiled children. That is not the heart Jesus displayed while he walked in human flesh. When Jesus prayed in the Garden of Gethsemane, the pattern he modeled in agony and tears was this:

- → Total honesty and vulnerability.
- → Total surrender to God's plan.

Jesus lived every moment of his life with an awareness of what mattered. He knew that the purpose of this life we are gifted with is to bring honor and glory to God, not to make life easy or comfortable for us. He knows how hard it is at times to embrace God's will, but he urges us to reach out and grasp hold of whatever will bring glory to his Father.

I want to live like that!

—SHEILA WALSH (*Get Off Your Knees and Pray*)

GOD'S DELIVERANCE

They cry to the LORD in their trouble, and He brings them out of their distresses.

—Psalm 107:28

Scripture tells us when we "cry out" to God, he delivers us from our "distresses." What we do not know is how or when he delivers. We assume, as well as hope, his deliverance means a change in our circumstances. We want to see that deliverance!

As much as we would like to see a change of circumstances as evidence that God is delivering us from our distresses, often our circumstances do not change. Then how can God promise he will deliver us from our distresses? Is there a little clause somewhere that we missed? Is it written in invisible ink?

I believe God always delivers us from our distresses just as he promised, but sometimes that deliverance is within our hearts, where the pain of our circumstances has shredded our interior being. God meets us at the shredding place. His deliverance may be simply to give us comfort in that place. His deliverance may be a lifting of our heads . . . of our spirits . . . and an assurance that he is there with us. His deliverance may be giving us the knowledge that we will have his strength to endure even though our circumstances may not change.

—MARILYN MEBERG (*God at Your Wits' End*)

YOUR SINS ARE FORGIVEN

I write to you, little children, because your sins are forgiven you
for His name's sake.
—1 John 2:12

One of the most liberating truths we find in Scripture is that bad things happening to us are not God's punishment for sin. Isaiah 13:11—"I will punish the world for its evil, and the wicked for their iniquity"—was written for those who never sought forgiveness from the God who freely forgives and thoroughly cleanses us from the stain of our sins. He tenderly says to us, "My child, your sins are forgiven for my name's sake!"

We need always to keep in mind the distinction between the consequences of sin and punishment for sin. Punishment for sin, which is death, has already taken place. That occurred at the cross. But the consequences of our sins may go on for a lifetime. Those consequences may be felt in our daily lives. For example, drugs, alcohol, or sexual addictions leave their mark upon our bodies as well as upon our psyches. But the good news is, whatever was the sin that held us in its grip is forgiven. We can look at the consequences as reminders of God's grace and love for us. He is not holding that sin against us but is encouraging us to move on with our lives and enjoy the grace of his forgiveness.

—MARILYN MEBERG (*God at Your Wits' End*)

TURNING POINTS WE ALL FACE

Give yourselves completely to God. Stand against the devil,
and the devil will run from you. Come near to God, and God
will come near to you.

—James 4:7–8 NCV

When life doesn't make sense anymore, we can give up, or we can remember who Jesus really is and that, no matter how dark it gets, he is worth it all.

When low self-esteem and doubt paralyze us, we can give up and accept these clouded images of ourselves, or we can remember who we are in Christ.

When guilt occupies the secret places in our lives, we can let it cripple us, or we can open our hearts and allow God to set us free.

When the heat of problems and pain burns into our very souls, we can crawl away and hide when it gets too hot, or we can choose to be living sacrifices who stay on the altar for his sake.

Christian service is a poor substitute for Jesus himself. We must ask, "Do I want to run myself ragged doing things for God, or do I want the best part—being his friend and knowing him face-to-face?"

When this complex, plastic world tries to squeeze us into a designer mold, we can let pride take over, or we can shake free to live the simple truth of the gospel with humility.

—SHEILA WALSH (*Life Is Tough But God Is Faithful*)

347

MORE TURNING POINTS WE ALL FACE

Obey God because you are his children; don't slip back into your old ways.
—1 Peter 1:14 TLB

When God seems far away and our prayers bounce off the ceiling, we can give in to despair, or we can keep holding on to heaven in simple trust. Hold on, my friend, hold on!

When we feel weak and overcome, we can wallow in self-pity, or we can choose to reach out and help one another. You really aren't the only one going through a tough time.

When life is tough, we can give up, or we can come before the Lord with our problem—and wait patiently for his answer. It is always worth the wait.

When the needy cross our path, we can choose to show selfish indifference, or we can take our eyes off our own needs and follow the example Jesus set by loving the unlovely.

When our dreams seem to go sour or remain unfulfilled, hopelessness can dominate our lives—or we can hold on with open hands, knowing that we have hope because God is faithful.

When we face our choices, large or small, we can settle for lukewarm, diluted faith—or we can seek the real thing, because we know that one life does make a difference now and through all eternity.

—SHEILA WALSH (*Life Is Tough But God Is Faithful*)

GOD'S PURPOSES

The human mind plans the way, but the LORD directs the steps.
—*Proverbs 16:9 NRSV*

I want a reason to get up in the morning. When I ask God for a sense of personal destiny, and then listen carefully, I get a sense of direction. Not always, and not always immediately, but I rely on God's promise to consistently guide me toward fulfilling the purpose for which he created me.

I know that nothing any of us experiences is pointless or useless. The good, the bad, the ugly, even the things we think will kill us—God uses it all, and he devises our destiny out of the stuff in our trash. He sifts it out, shows us the value, and then uses us to help others because of it.

When we look at the desires of our hearts in light of reality, we know none of them is achievable all the time. They're changeable, like the weather. Some days we're content; others we're not. There are places in the world we feel completely at home, others less so. There are even days when we wonder if we have a purpose at all, and the uncertainty lingers for a while. But our desires give shape and substance to our unique essences. And when we pray out of the depth of those desires, our faith is strengthened and our fellowship with the Lord is sweeter.

—LUCI SWINDOLL (*I Married Adventure*)

IT WORKS EVERY TIME

You never saw him, yet you love him. You still don't see him,
yet you trust him—with laughter and singing.

—1 Peter 1:8 MSG

I've been to the wall of adversity. I've wondered about God's promise to deliver, and I've tried to seek out answers to the dilemmas I've faced. In the wall-waiting, searching time, I've learned something very valuable about how to do that waiting. It's a method that joins forces with my will to believe God is working on my behalf and affirms the fact that God is sharing the wall with me. (Remember, he is wherever we are. If we're at the wall, he is too.) The method? Humor. It works every time.

Laughter serves a greater purpose than just distracting us from our misery as we do our time at the wall. It's good medicine. We now know laughter releases the brain's natural painkillers, endorphins, which can be fifty times more powerful than morphine. Laughter not only reduces pain, it lowers blood pressure and relaxes the skeletal frame. A good laugh may drive us to our knees simply because the skeletal frame can no longer hold us up.

Many of my experiences have taught me the value of using humor during wits'-end times. In fact, laughter often precedes trust. When I laugh, I am in essence saying to God, "I trust you, even though I'm not sure what you're doing."

—MARILYN MEBERG (*God at Your Wits' End*)

ASKING THE RIGHT QUESTIONS

Teach me to do your will, for you are my God. Let your good spirit lead me on a level path.
—Psalm 143:10 NRSV

If you can, imagine for a moment that before Jesus left this earth he commissioned you to represent him (which he did!). So, when you come to the Father with your prayer requests you are representing the person of Jesus, coming in his authority. I believe that if we carried that awareness with us, it would impact how we pray and what we ask for.

That notwithstanding, can we ask God for anything if our faith is strong enough? Well, yes. But is that really the right question? It's not so much about our level of faith as what we put our faith in. Are we asking for the right things? Are we seeking God's will in the situation? And are we comfortable with his response if things don't end up the way we wanted?

I hope so. It's not always easy. But we have a guide. When you meditate on the life of Christ you see how often he pulled away from the crowd to be alone with his Father. He lived every moment of his time on earth as a representative of the heart of God. Looking at that and longing to be like Jesus are changing the way I pray—as I hope it will change yours.

—SHEILA WALSH (*Get Off Your Knees and Pray*)

351

THE SEEDS OF POSSIBILITY

Jesus replied, "I tell you the truth, if you have faith as small as a mustard seed, you can say to this mountain, 'Move from here to there' and it will move. Nothing will be impossible for you."
—*Matthew 17:20* NIV

It has been said that sixty-five thousand thoughts float through our minds each day. Every one of those thoughts has the seed of possibility in it. We choose with our will what we'll do with that thought. Will we stay stuck in "If only . . ." or "Why me?"—or will we open our minds to "What if?" and "Why not?"

Asking the right questions keeps us open-minded and open-hearted to what was and is and might be in the years to come. They send us on our way into all sorts of journeys in search of adventure.

Being a spiritual sojourner, now seems like a good time to pause and look back. I want to assess where I've come from and where I'm going—I want to ask myself what things I'd do the same, might do differently, or regret I never did at all.

Want to come with me? I invite you to make your own list as we go along. We'll both see how the possibilities never end. We can do all things through Christ. His is the hand that launches us; his Spirit propels us. The voyage doesn't get any better than that.

—LUCI SWINDOLL (*I Married Adventure*)

PART OF THE SALVATION PACKAGE

Think of yourself with sober judgment, in accordance with the measure of faith God has given you.

—Romans 12:3 NIV

Another crucial clue for understanding our lives with God is to realize that faith is his gift to us. We can't scrunch it into existence. We received that gift when we received him into our hearts and lives for salvation. With salvation came faith to believe. Without faith, we would not have it in our hearts to receive Jesus in the first place. In our natural selves, we would be indifferent to the spiritual light, which is Jesus. Why? The sinner prefers darkness. So no one who knows Christ can say, "I have no faith." Faith is part of the salvation package.

Do you fear that your faith is too poor or weak? Remember this, all faith, no matter how poor or weak, serves as our conduit . . . our contact to the source of our faith, who is Christ Jesus, who is not small or feeble.

Our faith depends on our choices. We can will in our spirits to grow, develop, and mature in that God-given faith by eating the "food" found in Scripture. Everything we need for healthy faith-growth is in the Bible. We may eat all we can hold and not gain weight. If you supplement with chocolate . . . that's your choice.

—MARILYN MEBERG (*God at Your Wits' End*)

GOD IS SOVEREIGN

To You, O Lord, I lift up my soul. O my God, in You I trust.
—*Psalm 25:1–2* NASB

As I look at my life today, I believe God is sovereign all the time, not just some of the time. Nothing—absolutely nothing—that comes into your life or my life is a surprise to him. Everything has to pass through his merciful hands. Now, much of the time we don't see it coming, so it knocks us over. But even in that prone place, as we are reeling from what just happened, we can say thank you.

I am not suggesting we just up and move into a place of denial, as if nothing happened. Not at all! What I am saying is that even in some of life's most painful moments deep in my spirit, I thank God. I thank him because he knew it was coming and has provided everything I need to get through it. The saying goes that we're either victims in this world or we are not. If Christ had not come and taken all the sin and hatred on himself, we would be without hope. But he did come and he did die and he did rise from the dead, so we are not victims! We are beloved children of God Almighty, the Sovereign King of heaven and earth.

—SHEILA WALSH (*Get Off Your Knees and Pray*)

REGRETS ARE REVERSIBLE

The desires of the diligent are fully satisfied.
—Proverbs 13:4 NIV

A few years ago I was enjoying casual conversation with friends and asked if they could identify their greatest regret in life. After thinking a long while, one friend said, "I wish I would have taken a really good writing class." The rest of us looked at her for a few seconds then roared with laughter. After the initial shock, she joined us. It struck us all so funny because it certainly wasn't too late for her to take that really good writing class. If that is her greatest regret in life, she is one child of fortune.

The truth is that many of life's regrets are reversible. Sometimes what we wish we'd done when we were younger or in different circumstances, we can still pursue. And even mistakes that loom in our history like savage beasts don't have to define us or devour us.

When we start believing anything's possible, regrets turn into challenges, defeats into lessons learned, and heartache into magnanimity. It's all in our outlook—the lens through which we choose to view life. Besides, if we had it all to do over, how do we know we wouldn't do it the same way again? Better to live fully in today and place our hope in the future God has planned for us.

—LUCI SWINDOLL (*I Married Adventure*)

GOD RULES

This is what the Sovereign LORD, the Holy One of Israel, says: "In repentance and rest is your salvation, in quietness and trust is your strength."

—Isaiah 30:15 NIV

God is sovereign—not just a little bit sovereign, but utterly and completely sovereign. He controls everything. Not just some things . . . *everything*. Plain and simple: he rules.

There is a settled peace deep within my soul as I realize I am not in charge of my life. I'm responsible to that life, but I don't have the power to orchestrate the events in my life any more than I have the power to make the moon appear twice every month instead of once. What I can do is enter into a partnership with God about my life.

In that partnership, I know I'm to daily seek his guidance and wisdom. I also know I'm to conscientiously live my days according to the practical principles he has laid out for me in Scripture.

God's sovereignty will always hold levels of mystery for me, but that mystery actually feeds my peace. Why? Because I have faith in him. He has a good track record. I like it that he knows more than I do. I also like his style. He's creative, has a flair, and does the unexpected. But coupled with that drama and flair are his tender love and regard for me.

—MARILYN MEBERG (*God at Your Wits' End*)

JOURNALING YOUR GRATITUDE

Let them thank the LORD for his steadfast love, for his
wonderful works to humankind. And let them offer
thanksgiving sacrifices, and tell of his deeds with songs of joy.
—Psalm 107:21–22 NRSV

I don't know what your life is like today, whether you would say you are in the best days or the most difficult days—or perhaps, like me, a mixture of both. I want to suggest that you start keeping a gratitude journal. This is not a prayer journal, which is obviously a great thing to do and something that can greatly enrich your prayer life. Rather, this is just to write down all the things you are grateful for. Our prayer journals reflect our requests, but our gratitude journals can contain how God has answered our prayers or simply be a gateway to wonder and worship. I find it very helpful to use my gratitude journal in prayer. It gives me a written account of the faithfulness and goodness of God.

You might think if you add one more thing to your to-do list, it will push you over the edge and you'll be calling me for the number to the wee place with locks on the windows! Relax, this is not a major undertaking. Just keep any kind of journal by the bed, and each night jot down three things you are grateful for. It's just a way to refocus away from all the stuff that isn't working and thank God for what is.

—SHEILA WALSH (*Get Off Your Knees and Pray*)

THE BEST ADVENTURE OF ALL

Your ears shall hear a word behind you, saying, "This is the way, walk in it," whenever you turn to the right hand or whenever you turn to the left.

—Isaiah 30:21

I can say with confidence that the Lord has led me every step of the way into a life of adventures worth remembering and celebrating. Through the years he's opened door after door of possibility. Some of those doors I've walked through, others I haven't. And, so many of my dreams have come true. I've followed the road map, and although I can't see very far ahead, I feel certain I'm going in the right direction.

The most important thing for each of us is to embrace and celebrate life for what it is. Being alive is a gift, and we will never exhaust all the adventures or possibilities that are ours because Jesus Christ has provided an inexhaustible legacy for us, established before the foundation of the world. Every day he opens new doors for us to walk through. He gives us a new way of looking at old problems. He challenges us to take him at his word as we consider how to resolve different dilemmas. He assures us of his constant presence. And here's the best adventure of all—he lives in us! We can go anywhere and do anything, because the one who leads us never fails.

—LUCI SWINDOLL (*I Married Adventure*)

FAITH THINKING

Jesus said to Thomas, "Reach your finger here, and look at My hands; and reach your hand here, and put it into My side. Do not be unbelieving, but believing."

—John 20:27

Remember Thomas? He's the most famous doubter on record—a disciple of Jesus who saw miracles only Jesus could do. But in spite of all he had seen that should have translated from belief to faith, after the crucifixion, Thomas lost his faith. Why? What he saw did not make sense. Jesus died on a cross. Thomas was doing some faulty thinking that eroded his faith.

We all need encouragement to raise the level of our faith from seeing to trusting. But we must remember that the author of our faith is Jesus. He meets us at our level of need, just as he did Thomas.

When you and I are at rock bottom, Jesus will meet us there. Faulty thinking would be to think our faith development is our job and we had better get on the ball! Faith thinking is trusting God to give us what we can't produce apart from him.

My prayer is that we all will avoid faulty thinking and shaky faith, that we will always choose to joyfully live out our days of prosperity and trust his sovereign design for our days of adversity.

—MARILYN MEBERG (*God at Your Wits' End*)

SIMPLE TRUST

Steadfast love surrounds those who trust in the LORD.
—*Psalm 32:10* NRSV

In my life, I have been challenged to take an honest look at how much I trust God.

We live in the visible world. Even though I believe the invisible world, the kingdom of God, is far more real, the visible world is what we see and deal with every day. When we are faced with bills we can't pay or a diagnosis we did not expect, it's hard to remember God is in control and can be trusted all the time. We live in a world where we are barraged with messages about how to take care of our health, our family, and our future. But although it is obviously wise to use common sense and responsibility, our lives ultimately rest in God's hands. Doctors can make well-educated guesses, but God is the one who has numbered the hairs on our head and knows how long our race is. Financial planners can offer good advice, but only God knows what tomorrow brings.

Isn't that great news? He has promised to lead us and guide us, and he is the one who invites us to come to him in simple trust. As I've heard Max Lucado say, "You have never lived an unloved moment in your life."

—SHEILA WALSH (*Get Off Your Knees and Pray*)

ACCEPTED: AS IS!

He made us accepted in the Beloved.

—Ephesians 1:6

I'm a girl who likes to go to the mall. Okay, I love to go to the mall. I go to the mall a lot. I love a good bargain, but I'm not typically the type who scours the sale racks trying to find the perfect buy. I don't have the patience for that. There are times, however, when the ideal item crosses my path. I instantly fall in love with it . . . but then I see there's something wrong with it—a missing button, a broken zipper, or a seam that's starting to come apart. But usually when I find those flaws, I'm happy, not sad, because that's an instant discount, one I'm all too happy to take advantage of. So I purchase the item, get my discount, and say, "Thank you very much." Often the salesperson writes on the tag, "Sold as is, no return."

That is how Jesus accepts us. AS IS. Broken, cracked, tattered, and in all of our ordinariness, he receives us with a no-return policy. He never gives up on us, and he will never give us back. He looks at me with my freckles, my large pores, and my even larger sins, and says, "You are wonderfully and beautifully made."

—NATALIE GRANT (*The Real Me*)

AMAZING GRACE

Being justified by faith, we have peace with God through our Lord Jesus Christ: By whom also we have access by faith into this grace wherein we stand, and rejoice in hope of the glory of God.

—Romans 5:1–2 KJV

As Christians, the grace of God is ours. The grace of God differs from the grace afforded by people simply because people *sometimes* come through and sometimes they don't. The giving of human grace may depend on temperament, circumstances, or level of personal generosity. God, however, is constant and totally committed to giving grace to his people. His grace is not dependent upon his temperament, circumstances, or level of personal generosity. The bestowing of grace is a part of God's divine intent and passionate love. Next to your salvation experience, grace is the most important facet of God's love.

Many Christians feel they need to do things for God as a way of earning his grace and love. Those people believe they need to be better and better Christians so God will be glad his Son died for them. But that is not how grace/love operates. *It's a gift.* Not a solitary thing we do (none of our "works") will make us good enough for his grace. Jesus already made us good enough. God's love (grace) declares us worthy even though we are not. Human grace may not find us worthy, but God's grace never wavers.

—MARILYN MEBERG (*Assurance for a Lifetime*)

December 28

WHY NOT?

God, make a fresh start in me, shape a Genesis week from the chaos of my life.
—Psalm 51:10 MSG

Crisis is often just the invitation we need to cross the threshold into a new adventure. Crisis can give you the courage to try things you've never tried before. Perhaps the pride that once held you back has been thoroughly sifted out of you. Postcrisis people, particularly those who are determined to let the crisis make them better instead of bitter, find themselves no longer protesting, "Oh, I could never do that." Instead, they greet invitations into adventure with a hearty "Why not?"

Here is a profound bit of wisdom. Allow your past, even your worst failures, into your present only as part of the experience that led up to the person you are today. But do not let one experience determine who you will be tomorrow.

It's been said that there is the life you learn from and then the life you live. Many of us can relate to this concept. Take whatever lessons you can possibly glean from your past—especially from your sorrows, your losses, and your failures. Scoop up this backpack of wisdom so you can peek into it now and then for its profound lessons. Finally you can begin hiking toward your new life and new mountaintops.

—SANDI PATTY (*Falling Forward*)

363

LIFE IS ALL CRACKED UP

The LORD is close to the brokenhearted and saves those who are crushed in spirit.

—*Psalm 34:18 NIV*

I don't know who spun the dial on my internal compass, but I'm not laughing. I just came from the mall, where I misplaced my car in the parking lot; and then, after finding it, I immediately got lost, detouring through three strip malls before careening (not purposely) onto the correct road headed for home. No, there are no strip malls on the way to my house. And no, the mall is not in another town. And yes, I had been there many times.

What I've learned thus far in life (besides never travel alone) is that my internal compass isn't the only thing broken. We also have obvious fissures of the heart, like fractured relationships, weakening moral fiber, and religious disillusionment. That's where our Redeemer comes in. We need someone who can fix broken hearts, adjust our perspective, and even give us a reason to laugh.

God sent Jesus as a Redeemer to do just that—to redeem the shards of our lives and create a stained-glass perspective. When we realize we're broken and acknowledge Jesus as our Redeemer, then the crushing blows of life do not destroy us. Instead we live with hope, we dance more often, we laugh more deeply, and we are not taken by surprise by the fact that life is all cracked up.

—PATSY CLAIRMONT (*All Cracked Up*)

COMPASSION IS LOVE AND GRACE

Never walk away from someone who deserves help; your hand is God's hand for that person.

—Proverbs 3:28 MSG

The ultimate meaning of compassion is love and grace. When we grasp what God's love and grace have done for us, we cannot help but show compassion to others.

I think it's important to remember that Jesus told the story of the Good Samaritan in answer to the lawyer's question, "Who is my neighbor?" This simple story, which almost every Christian knows by heart, surely shows that we may find ourselves in situations where we need compassion, but we might not always get it. Those whom we think will offer it do not, and when compassion does appear, it comes from unlikely neighbors, indeed.

We westernized Christians are in grave danger of staying within the comfortable confines of our own lives, failing to have compassion for others, and simply sitting at home to struggle with our own failures and temptations.

Fortunately, many have learned a vital secret to keeping on when life is tough. That secret is compassion. When you reach out to others in the name of Jesus, you have to take your eyes off yourself. It is then that you suddenly realize you don't have to hold on at all. Because you are so close to Jesus, he has you in the hollow of his hand.

—SHEILA WALSH (*Life Is Tough But God Is Faithful*)

OUR ULTIMATE TOMORROW

Jesus said, "In My Father's house are many mansions; if it were not so, I would have told you. I go to prepare a place for you. And if I go and prepare a place for you, I will come again and receive you to Myself; that where I am, you will be also."
—John 14:2–3

My daddy's favorite Bible verse was 1 Corinthians 2:9, "No eye has seen, no ear has heard, no mind has conceived what God has prepared for those who love him." He quoted it many times to me, wrote it in letters, and jotted it on gift cards. It makes me wonder if he, too, wondered what was in the distance, over life's horizon. Now he knows, of course, since he's been in the presence of the Lord many years. He knows, even as he is known.

Gratefully, my own ultimate tomorrow is a given as well. When I put my faith in Jesus Christ as my Savior, I sealed my destiny. The finished work of Christ and his promise about what is to come assures me I'll spend eternity with him. God has made it clear in his Word that someday he will come get me and take me to live with him forever.

Frankly, I love the fact that God has a plan for the future, for every tomorrow of my life on earth and beyond. Even though I can't figure it all out, he's got it wired. This reassures me that I'm loved and safe. God knows our course and he knows us. He loves us. He provides. He plans ahead.

—LUCI SWINDOLL (*I Married Adventure*)